S0-BLM-666

the Unofficial Guide™ to Buying a Home Online

Kathleen Sindell, Ph.D.

IDG Books Worldwide, Inc.

IDG Books Worldwide, Inc.
An International Data Group Company
919 E. Hillsdale Boulevard
Suite 400
Foster City, CA 94404

ISBN: 0-02-863751-8

Manufactured in the United States of America

10 9 8 7 6 5 4 3 2 1

First edition

In loving memory of my parents,
Warren Harding Mountain (1921 to 1999) and
Dorothy Jane Mountain (1914 to 1999)

Acknowledgments

My thanks to Jessica Faust and Brice Gosnell, IDG editors, for their thoughtful guidance. Thanks to Doris Michaels and all the folks at the Doris S. Michaels Literary Agency for their unwavering support. My appreciation to Kitty Jarrett for her dedication to high quality. Thanks also to Lynn Northrup for her fine editing. My appreciation to everyone who worked behind the scenes, especially all the people who are listed on the credits page. Thank you for making this book happen.

My gratitude to my husband, Ivan Sindell, for his advice and encouragement. A very special thank you and note of appreciation to my brother-in-law, Gerald Sindell, for his profound counsel on everything relating to the business of publishing.

And finally, my thanks to the folks who put real estate information online for the public. They have changed the real estate community forever.

The *Unofficial Guide* Reader's Bill of Rights xv

The *Unofficial Guide* Panel of Experts xxi

Introduction xxv

**I So You're Thinking About Buying
a Home 1**

1 Preparing to Buy a Home 3

Should you purchase a home? 4

Can you save big bucks by buying a home
online? 5

Getting connected and going online 7

What does buying a home online mean? 8
What you can do online 9
What you can't do online 10

Where should you start online? 11
Finding real estate Web sites 12
The process of buying a home online 16
Real estate supersites 20

Using the Internet to be prepared 21

Just the facts 23

2 Creating a Financial Game Plan 25

Getting your financial house in order 26

The personal financial planning process 27
Determining your net worth 28
How are you using your income? 30
Making a budget based on your goals 33
Creating your financial plan 34
Using personal finance software 35

How much can you afford? 36

Understanding the credit reporting system 39
What credit reports do and don't contain ...40

Contents

Credit bureaus..*41*
Checking out your own credit report..........*42*
FICO scores..*44*
Improving your FICO score.......................*46*
Correcting errors on your credit report........*49*
Deleting credit inquiries..........................*51*

Getting financial help 53
    Getting help with your credit problems *54*
    Avoiding getting into credit trouble..........*55*

Just the facts 56

3   Is Now the Right Time to Buy a Home?.....57

Financial profiles of homeowners 58

Where do you stand? 59
    Looking at your finances.........................*60*
    Looking at the market *60*
    Sorting your housing needs and wants.......*62*
    Housing options *63*

Rent or buy?..67
    Why rent?...*68*
    Why buy? *69*
    The math aspects of the rent vs. buy
      decision *70*

Setting a realistic price range 71

Avoiding the time crunch 74

Just the facts 76

II   Shopping for a Home Without Leaving Your Computer.................................77

4   Finding a Neighborhood Next Door or Across the Country 79

Nationwide and regional housing trends 80

Relocating to a different state 82

Finding the right city................................84
    Comparing the cost of living for
      different cities *85*
    Using online cost-of-living calculators........*87*

Finding the right neighborhood....................88
    Learning about a neighborhood firsthand...*89*
    Learning about a neighborhood online.......*89*

Analyzing and understanding a
   neighborhood report...........................90
Just the facts 96

5 Using a Real Estate Agent 97
How a real estate agent can help you 98
   Types of real estate professionals............101
   The responsibilities of real estate
      professionals 102
The awful truth about commissions 104
What to look for in an agent.....................106
Finding an agent 111
   Finding a buyer's agent.........................112
   Finding an out-of-state agent................114
Is your real estate agent doing the job? 117
Just the facts 118

6 Finding Your Dream Home Online............119
Organizing your search 120
   Using a scorecard to compare houses.......120
   Focusing your search 122
Determining whether to buy a new or an
established home......................................124
Purchasing a new home............................124
   The advantages of a new home 125
   The limitations of a new home 126
   Checking out the trends in new homes.....127
   Getting the right stuff in a new home......128
   Using the Internet to locate new homes...129
   Purchasing a model home......................130
Purchasing an established home 131
   The advantages of an existing home........131
   The limitations of an existing home 132
   Getting the right stuff in an existing
      home..133
   Purchasing a fixer-upper.......................134
Using the Internet to find the best homes
at the best prices 136
   Using the Internet to spot overpriced
      homes...139
   Pay less by using online comparable
      market analysis 140
Just the facts 142

III Getting Financing with the Help of the Internet 143

7 Online Mortgage Advice and Lending.......145

What is a mortgage? 146

Online home loan intermediaries—aggregators 147

What counts to mortgage lenders..............148

The mortgage process...............................149
    The paperwork you need to provide 151
    The fees you need to pay 152
    Finding the best interest rate.................155
    Getting the best deal by comparing
      mortgage loans..............................156

Types of mortgages..................................158
    Conventional loans 158
    HUD/FHA loans....................................160
    VA loans...161
    Choosing a program that's right for you ...162

Finding a mortgage online 162

Getting ahead of the game with prequalification or preapproval 166
    The online prequalification process..........167
    The online preapproval process 169
    Comparing online preapproval and
      loan application forms 170

Just the facts 171

8 Avoiding the Down Payment Cash Crunch 173

Coming up with a down payment 174
    How much should you put down?............176
    The lowdown on private mortgage
      insurance..177
    Buying a home with little or no
      money down 178

Government-sponsored no and low down payment plans.......................................180
    VA loans...180
    RHS loans...181
    FHA loans...181
    State and local government loan
      programs 182

Other no and low down payment
  programs 183
When none of the traditional options work:
creative financing................................184
  Assuming someone else's mortgage 184
  Doing a seller-take-back 185
  Renting with the option to buy...............187
  Using equity sharing..............................188
Special programs for first-time
homebuyers 189
Just the facts 192

IV Closing In on Your New Home 193

9 Online Help with Appraisals, Inspections,
   and Insurance 195
Getting a property appraisal......................196
  How property is appraised.......................200
  Online comparable sales reports..............201
Getting a home inspection 203
  Doing your own home inspection 204
  The benefits of professional home
    inspections 205
  How to select a home inspector..............206
  How to read a home inspection report 207
Finding homeowners insurance 209
  The basics of homeowners insurance
    policies 210
  Keeping your insurance costs low............213
Getting title insurance 214
Just the facts 216

10 Negotiating and Closing the Deal............217
Everything is negotiable 218
  Gathering information...........................218
  Being prepared 220
  Being realistic 221
  Using the Internet to be a better
    negotiator 221
Making an offer they can't refuse..............222
  Determining your offer price...................224
  The reality of "low-ball" offers 225
  How large a deposit?............................225

Adding contingencies to your offer 226
Adding optional contingencies 227
Online help with making an offer 228

Counteroffers 228
Negotiating tips 229
Typical seller counteroffers 230

Sold! 231

The final walk-through 232

Closing the deal 233
The closing meeting 233
After the closing 236
*Online resources to help you prepare
    for the closing* 236

Just the facts 238

**11 Costs and Tax Benefits Associated with
Buying a Home**...................................**239**

Understanding closing costs......................240
Documents related to closing costs 242
*Comparing actual closing costs
    with estimates* 245

The types of closing costs.........................246
Lender-based closing costs 248
Government-based closing costs 250
Other costs for establishing ownership 251

Reducing your closing costs 252

Using an escrow account 254

The tax implications of buying a home 255
What can you write off? 255
Online tax help 256

Just the facts 257

**V The Real Estate Road Less
Traveled** **259**

**12 The Internet and Do-It-Yourself
Real Estate**..**261**

Why go FSBO? 262
The benefits of FSBOs 264
The problems of FSBOs 264
Fair housing and FSBOs 265
FSBO financing options 265

Finding FSBO listings online......................266
  Nationwide online FSBO listings..............267
  Regional online FSBO listings 269
  FSBO notification services......................271

Closing the FSBO deal 272
  Potential FSBO negotiating difficulties 272
  Congratulations! You've struck a deal!......275

Just the facts 275

**13 Getting Online Help with Becoming an
Owner-Builder 277**

Deciding to build your own home 278
  Reading all about it 279
  *Getting smart with owner-builder seminars
   and classes* 280
  Contractor-assisted programs..................281
  Estimating the cost of a building project..283

Location, location, location 285
  *Determining how much to pay for
   your lot*...286
  *Using the Internet to find the perfect
   residential lot*....................................287
  *Using the Internet to find land for sale by
   owner* 288

Selecting your house plans 289
  Finding an architect online 289
  *Finding ready-made house plans on the
   Internet* 290
  *Selecting the right house plan for
   the lot* 292

Online help with selecting and evaluating
contractors 292

Finding owner-builder financing online.......294

Tips for staying on schedule and within
your budget...296

Working with building regulations..............297

Acquiring building hazard insurance 299

Just the facts 300

**VI Wrapping It Up, Moving In, and
Moving Out....................................301**

14 Getting Moving Help Online....................303

Developing a moving plan.........................304
　Establishing a timeline for moving 306
　Estimating the cost of moving................308

Deciding whether to move yourself or hire a
moving company 311
　Moving yourself 311
　Using a moving company......................314
　Using a corporate relocation service 315

Insuring the valuables you are moving........317

Other moving issues................................319
　Moving children 319
　Moving pets 319
　Moving automobiles.............................320

Using the Internet to change your address ..321

Packing for your move.............................322

Deducting moving expenses from your
income taxes 324

Just the facts 325

**15 Online Help for Making Your House
a Home..327**

Remodeling your new home......................328
　Planning what to do and how to do it.....329
　Dispelling myths about contractors..........330
　Defining your home improvement project
　　online 332

Finding expert home improvement help.......333
　Avoiding home improvement scams 336
　Getting it in writing.............................338

Do-it-yourself home improvements 340

Getting the most bang for your home
improvement buck 342
　Getting the most for your restoration
　　money..345
　Paying for your home improvements........346

Just the facts 348

**16 Marketing and Selling Your Home
Online 349**

Deciding when to sell..............................350

Using the Internet to set a price 352

Getting your house ready..........................354
Making your house look its best..............355
Getting your own inspection....................356
Marketing your home online and offline......357
Advertising...357
MLS...357
Holding open houses 359
Working with a listing agent 360
Selling your home without an agent...........363
The problems of FSBOs........................364
FSBO help from discounted real estate
brokerages 365
Just the facts 366

VII Appendixes.....................................367

A **Glossary...369**

B **Online Home Buying Resource Directory..381**

C **Home Buying Bibliography 413**

Index...419

The *Unofficial Guide* Reader's Bill of Rights

We Give You More Than the Official Line

Welcome to the *Unofficial Guide* series of Lifestyles titles—books that deliver critical, unbiased information that other books can't or won't reveal—*the inside scoop.* Our goal is to provide you with the *most accessible, useful* information and advice possible. The recommendations we offer in these pages are not influenced by the corporate line of any organization or industry; we give you the hard facts, whether those institutions like them or not. If something is ill advised or will cause a loss of time and/or money, we'll give you ample warning. And if it is a worthwhile option, we'll let you know that, too.

Armed and Ready

Our hand-picked authors confidently and critically report on a wide range of topics that matter to smart readers like you. Our authors are passionate about their subjects, but have distanced themselves enough from them to help you be armed and protected, and help you make educated decisions as you go through the process. It is our intent that, from having read this book, you will avoid the pitfalls everyone else falls into and get it right the first time.

Don't be fooled by cheap imitations; this is the genuine article *Unofficial Guide* series from IDG Books. You may be familiar with our proven track record of the travel *Unofficial Guides*, which have more than three million copies in print. Each year thousands of travelers—new and old— are armed with a brand new, fully updated edition of the flagship *Unofficial Guide to Walt Disney World*, by Bob Sehlinger. It is our intention here to provide you with the same level of objective authority that Mr. Sehlinger does in his brainchild.

The Unofficial Guide Panel of Experts

Every work in the Lifestyle *Unofficial Guides* is intensively inspected by a team of three top professionals in their fields. These experts review the manuscript for factual accuracy, comprehensiveness, and an insider's determination as to whether the manuscript fulfills the credo in this Reader's Bill of Rights. In other words, our Panel ensures that you are, in fact, getting "the inside scoop."

Our Pledge

The authors, the editorial staff, and the Unofficial Panel of Experts assembled for *Unofficial Guides* are determined to lay out the most valuable alternatives available for our readers. This dictum means that our writers must be explicit, prescriptive, and above all, direct. We strive to be thorough and complete, but our goal is not necessarily to have the "most" or "all" of the information on a topic; this is not, after all, an encyclopedia. Our objective is to help you narrow down your options to the best of what is available, unbiased by affiliation with any industry or organization.

In each *Unofficial Guide* we give you:

- Comprehensive coverage of necessary and vital information
- Authoritative, rigidly fact-checked data
- The most up-to-date insights into trends
- Savvy, sophisticated writing that's also readable
- Sensible, applicable facts and secrets that only an insider knows

Special features

Every book in our series offers the following six special sidebars in the margins that are devised to help you get things done cheaply, efficiently, and smartly:

1. **Timesaver**—Tips and shortcuts that save you time.

2. **Moneysaver**—Tips and shortcuts that save you money.

3. **Watch Out!**—More serious cautions and warnings.

4. **Bright Idea**—General tips and shortcuts to help you find an easier or smarter way to do something.

5. **Quote**—Statements from real people that are intended to be prescriptive and valuable to you.

6. **Unofficially...**—An insider's fact or anecdote.

We also recognize your need to have quick information at your fingertips, and have thus provided the following comprehensive sections at the back of the book:

1. **Glossary**—Definitions of complicated terminology and jargon

2. **Resource Directory**—Lists of relevant agencies, associations, institutions, Web sites, etc.

3. **Bibliography**—Suggested titles that can help you get more in-depth information on related topics

4. **Index**

Letters, Comments, and Questions from Readers

We strive to continually improve the *Unofficial Guide* series, and input from our readers is a valuable way for us to do that.

Many of those who have used the *Unofficial Guide* travel books write to the authors to ask questions, make comments, or share their own discoveries and lessons. For Lifestyle *Unofficial Guides*, we would also appreciate all such correspondence—both positive and critical—and we will make our best efforts to incorporate appropriate readers' feedback and comments in revised editions of this work.

How to write to us:

Unofficial Guides
Lifestyle Guides
IDG Books
1633 Broadway
New York, NY 10019

Attention: Reader's Comments

About the Author

Kathleen Sindell, Ph.D., has more than 20 years of experience in financial services and is the founder of a firm that provides management consulting to the financial services industry and authoritative publications about management, finance, and real estate in the e-commerce environment. She and her colleagues work with organizations to deliver effective business solutions for new ways of conducting business and managing finances in the emerging electronic environment. She is the former Associate Director of the Financial Management and Commercial Real Estate Programs for the University of Maryland, University College Graduate School of Management & Technology.

Dr. Sindell recently completed the third edition of *A Hands-On Guide to Mortgage Banking Internet Sites*, a directory published by *Mortgage Banking* magazine. She is the author of *Investing Online for Dummies*, 2nd Edition (IDG Books), and *The Handbook of Real Estate Lending* (McGraw-Hill Professional Publishing). She is also the editor of the book *Essentials of Financial Management Kit* (Dryden Press).

Dr. Sindell developed the Lending Solutions Decision Support Program to identify, assess, monitor, and mitigate the credit quality of real estate loans. This software application is based on her hands-on experience as a Real Estate Vice President for American Savings & Loan and as the Construction Lending Services Manager for Perpetual Federal Savings Bank.

She has taught more than 25 graduate-level courses in financial management; she lectures for the New York Institute of Finance; and she is a well-known speaker at regional and national conferences. Dr. Sindell is on the adjunct faculty of The Johns Hopkins University, School of Professional Studies and Education, where she teaches graduate-level financial management courses. She has provided seminars to senior bank examiners and real estate instructors from the Federal Reserve and various other regulatory agencies.

She received her B.A. in Business from Antioch University, an M.B.A. with a concentration in Finance from California State University at San Jose, and a Ph.D. in Administration and Management from Walden University, Institute for Advanced Studies.

Dr. Sindell lives and writes in Alexandria, Virginia. She is interested in your comments about this book and can be contacted at her Web site (www.kathleensindell.com) or send e-mail to ksindell@kathleensindell.com.

The *Unofficial Guide* Panel of Experts

T he *Unofficial Guide* editorial team recognizes that you've purchased this book with the expectation of getting the most authoritative, carefully inspected information currently available. Toward that end, on each and every title in this series, we have selected a minimum of two "official" experts comprising the Unofficial Panel who painstakingly review the manuscripts to ensure the following: factual accuracy of all data; inclusion of the most up-to-date and relevant information; and that, from an insider's perspective, the authors have armed you with all the necessary facts you need—but that the institutions don't want you to know.

For *The Unofficial Guide to Buying a Home Online*, we are proud to introduce the following panel of experts:

Tamara and Robert Gordon bought the condo where they currently live almost three years ago, when it was the right size for the two of them and their 3½-year-old son. The addition of a dog to the family has made the Gordons think that either the dog is too large or the condo too small, so they've decided to find another place, with enough room for the whole family and any little sisters or brothers who come along.

The Gordons are shopping for a home both on their own, using the Internet, and with the help of a real estate agent. They have found houses online and then visited in person to find truth in the old saying, "What you see is what you get." They haven't found the house of their dreams yet, but the Internet has made their search easier and more convenient.

Al Napier is a top-producing Realtor in the greater central Connecticut area, specializing in assisting first-time buyers and sellers accomplish their goals. Mr. Napier has been working in this capacity for most of the past decade and is well versed in the financial disciplines of the real estate profession.

Mr. Napier has served on both the professional standards and technology committees of the Connecticut Association of Realtors and the Greater Hartford Association of Realtors. In addition, he is also considered by many to be a bonafied tech-head and early adopter of technology in general (and the Internet in particular), as well as something of an authority on real estate agency. He also builds and maintains Web sites as a hobby; you can view Mr. Napier's personal Web site, www.alnapier.com, and use it as an example of how effective and helpful a local real estate site can be.

Howard Savage, Ph.D., is a supervisory economist at the U.S. Department of Commerce. He received a B.A. from Oklahoma City University, an M.A.S. from The Johns Hopkins University, and a Ph.D. from the University of Texas at Austin. He has earned a Master's Certificate in Project Management from the George Washington University. He has taught at the University of Oklahoma, Hood College, The Johns Hopkins University, and the University of Maryland.

Dr. Savage's background includes work in the private sector as an owner of a mortgage banking company, a portfolio manager in an investment firm, a certified financial planner and registered general securities principal in an investment firm, and extensive financial consulting with over 300 growing firms in the Mid-Atlantic area and Latin America. He has also done real estate and financial research for the Governor's Office of the State of Texas, the U.S. Department of Housing and Urban Development, and the Scottish Office (Great Britain). His current work with the U.S. Department of Commerce involves analyis of mortgages, residential mortgage markets, and financial analysis of multifamily properties.

Timothy Thompson is a real estate developer and builder in the metropolitan Baltimore area. For more than two decades he has been developing property and constructing residential homes, commercial office buildings, and shopping centers. Mr. Thompson is also a partner in TeleTechnologies, Ltd., which specializes in new digital signal processing technology, including digital image and sound compression. In addition, he has introduced computer technology into various business applications, most recently in the ownership and development of several Internet projects, including www.homebuyerfirst.com, www.compressit.com, and www.comicfind.com. Mr. Thompson has graciously agreed to help make your home search easier by posting all the Web sites mentioned in this book at www.homebuyerfirst.com.

Mr. Thompson is a past president of the local chapter of the Homebuilders Association of Maryland and remains active in the Association. He holds a B.A. from Loyola College and resides with his wife and two children in Glen Arm, Maryland.

Introduction

On average, Americans change residences once every five years. Some areas are more transient; for example, in the Washington, D.C., metropolitan area, 20 percent of all residents change their zip codes each year. This indicates that tens of thousands of individuals are seeking new housing all the time. If you are one of these people, *The Unofficial Guide to Buying a Home Online* is for you.

If you are a first-time or experienced homebuyer and haven't checked out the real estate market in the past three years, you're in for an entirely new experience. You can now find your dream home next door or in the next state (and the financing you'll need to purchase it) without leaving your computer. *The Unofficial Guide to Buying a Home Online* is a comprehensive manual that's loaded with Internet-based money- and time-saving home buying techniques that will show you the most viable and cost-saving ways to buy a home online. *The Unofficial Guide to Buying a Home Online* provides streetwise tips and warnings, savvy facts, and insider secrets to help you manage the anxiety that goes with making the purchase of a lifetime.

New, easy-to-use electronic commerce methods have toppled the old ways of home buying and created new ways of purchasing homes at record-breaking cost savings. Besides saving you a bundle on your mortgage (1 percent of the loan amount is standard), the convenience of the Internet can't be matched—you can shop 24 hours a day, 7 days a week. We'll show you how to electronically check out the neighborhood, whether it's in the next block or the next state. To come to the point, we'll show you Web sites that cover every aspect of the home buying process. These are the latest and greatest Web sites available and they will provide you with low-cost or free resources that can save you money, time, and effort.

The Internet makes home buying easier then ever

It's hard to believe, but you can begin shopping for your dream home over the Internet and finish with FedEx delivering your loan documents. In 1998, about $800 million in online mortgages were originated. Forrester Research of Cambridge, Massachusetts, predicts that online originations will jump to $25.5 billion by 2001, and by 2003 to 2005 will constitute about 10 percent of the entire mortgage market.

Currently, the World Wide Web lists about 1.3 million homes for sale and includes over 30,000 real estate–related Internet sites. It's easy to get confused in this real estate cyberspace. *The Unofficial Guide to Buying a Home Online* is your practical guide to making certain you don't get lost, whether you're a new homebuyer or an experienced one.

The Unofficial Guide to Buying a Home Online is designed for individuals of all ages, incomes, and education levels. It's a comprehensive, results-oriented reference book. You'll get expert advice on

- Exploring the possibilities of home ownership and finding out where to start researching the Internet for home buying information and online tutorials.

- Organizing your online house hunting and finding and using online tools to get prepared for the home buying process.

- Discovering online databases for finding homes around the corner or across the nation.

- Uncovering Internet-based information about neighborhood schools, crime, and area demographics.

- Finding high quality, low-cost sources for mortgages.

- Getting prequalified for an online mortgage loan and receive financing from an Internet lender.

- Pinpointing Web-based tips and advice on how to negotiate, inspect a house, and close the deal.

- Locating appraisers, inspectors, and other professionals who can make your purchase safer.

- Learning the tax implications of being a homebuyer and owner.

- Using the Internet for a hassle-free move.

- Making improvements to your home and
  knowing how valuable they will be when it's time
  to sell.

The Unofficial Guide to Buying a Home Online is
designed for Internet users who want to buy a
house. Today there are still some people who wonder if this can be done. Can buying a home online
actually save you money, time, and effort? The
answer is yes, and this book provides all the information you'll need to know.

What are researchers saying about buying a
home online? Independent research survey data
indicates that the Internet is where most consumers
will begin researching their real estate transactions.
Killen & Associates of Palo Alto, California, forecasts
that within the next six years, 30 percent of all individuals seeking home loans will start by looking for
them on the Internet.

Cashing in with online home buying

Statistics indicate that individuals with three or
more years of experience on the Internet are more
likely to tackle purchasing their dream home
online. After purchasing books, stocks, CDs and
other items, consumers are likely to reach a certain
online comfort level. The strongest appeal of buying
a home online is the deep discount and convenience. According to Chuck Williams, president and
CEO of Brightware, of the top 75 mortgage-lending
Web sites, 2.7 percent of the guests converted their
visits to actual mortgages.

The disadvantage of buying a home online is the
lack of face-to-face meetings with loan officers or
other lending representatives. If you need a high
level of personal assistance, face-to-face meetings,

and telephone consultations, buying a home online may not be for you. However, this doesn't mean you can't be a "looker" and gain a better understanding of the home buying process.

Consumers now accept the Internet as a standard tool for researching and conducting even the most major transactions. In the RealEstate.com Online Home Survey, a national survey by RealEstate.com (www.realestate.com), results indicate that nearly 90 percent of all consumers who are planning to buy a home in the next year are likely to use an online real estate service. Almost 80 percent will search for home listings, and just as many will research their home loan online. Four in 10 will apply for a mortgage loan on the Internet.

This means that if you're looking for convenience, saving time, money, and effort using the Internet is for you, even is you're not ready to apply for a mortgage online.

Not just for beginners

Over three million people in the United States will purchase homes this year. Often, owning a home is the achievement of a lifetime and a major part of the American Dream. It's also the cornerstone of the wealth-building plan of many people. There are two primary capital accumulation benefits. First, the equity in your home is likely to appreciate over the years. Second, the interest portion of your home mortgage payment is tax deductible.

The Unofficial Guide to Buying a Home Online is designed for Internet users who want to get a head start on their wealth-building plan by saving as much money as possible when purchasing a home. Independent research surveys indicate that if you're not using the Internet to research real estate–related services now, you will be soon. In each chapter of this book you'll discover substantive tips for saving time and money. The chapters are organized in the exact order of the home buying process.

The Internet is making the home buying experience easier and more efficient. Thousands of people are using the Internet to complete real estate transactions each day, and the number of visits to real estate service Web sites is growing at a phenomenal rate. *The Unofficial Guide to Buying a Home Online* is an essential guide that can effectively direct you through real estate cyberspace.

Welcome to the new frontier of home buying!

So You're Thinking About Buying a Home

GET THE SCOOP ON...
How buying a home online differs from buying
a home in the traditional way ▪ Being a savvy
real estate consumer ▪ Determining what you
need to do and when ▪ Understanding what
homebuyers can and can't do on the Internet

PART I

Preparing to Buy a Home

Chapter 1

B uying a home online represents new opportunities for first-time and experienced homebuyers. According to Forrester Research (www.forrester.com), in 1998, online home loan originations totaled about $725 million. This is about 1 percent of the total residential loan market. Forrester predicts that online originations will jump to $25.5 billion by 2001, and by 2003 (to 2005), they will constitute about 10 percent of the entire home loan market.

Now more than ever, the Internet provides homebuyers with comprehensive, personalized, and results-oriented information, resources, and tools. *The Unofficial Guide to Buying a Home Online* provides you with expert advice to guide you each step of the way to home ownership. This chapter is your starting point.

In this chapter, you'll discover the right reasons for beginning the home buying process now. You'll learn how you can save money by shopping and comparing interest rates online. You'll also discover some of the latest and greatest real estate Web sites available. This chapter helps you get started with the process of buying a home online by showing examples of how the Internet can help you buy your dream home. Later in the book, these topics are expanded with step-by-step instructions, directions to online resources, checklists, worksheets, and online calculators.

Should you purchase a home?

Buying a home—whether using traditional or online resources—can be an exciting experience. People have many reasons for wanting to purchase a home. Some of them are rather unrealistic, such as the desire for a simpler lifestyle, a need to get back to nature, or the notion that a better house will foster a better marital relationship. These are generally not good reasons to jump into buying a home.

However, if you fall into one or more of the following categories, it might be time to get rolling and begin the home buying process:

- Changes in your financial requirements, such as the following:

    - You think your finances are in order and it's time to buy your own home.

    - Interest rates have gone down.

    - You want to pay a lower interest rate on your mortgage.

- Changes in your physical requirements, such as the following:

    - Your personal living situation has drastically changed due to marriage, retirement, divorce, the death of your partner, or the addition of your elderly parent.

- You are expecting a child (or another child) and you currently don't have enough room for everyone. Additionally, you want a safer neighborhood and a better school system for your children.

- Your current house is too large and too old. All your children have grown and moved away. You want to travel, but maintaining the house and yard is taking up all your leisure time.

- Your company has offered you a job that you can't refuse and you need to relocate.

- Your work location has changed. Your daily commute now takes several hours and you are often stuck in the middle of rush hour traffic.

If you fit any of these categories, it might be time to move to a home that meets your physical and financial requirements.

Can you save big bucks by buying a home online?

You may have seen the commercial where a couple drives by a new housing development they didn't know existed. The couple looks disappointed and indicates that they didn't know that these homes were available. The commercial leads you to the conclusion that the couple probably bought the wrong type of house and paid too much money for it. The couple may have bought the house without knowing about other new housing developments in the area they might have liked better, possibly even with a lower price. With the Internet revolution, this scenario does not have to happen. With more than 30,000 real estate–related Web sites available, you

Moneysaver
When you purchase a home, you can deduct the cost of your mortgage loan interest from your federal income taxes, and usually from your state taxes, too. This adds up to hefty savings at the end of each year.

can do your own home buying research without leaving your home or office. Now you don't have to depend on someone else's so-called expertise.

If you've picked up this book, you're either using the Internet already or are ready to start. Whether you're already on the Internet or not, you probably already know that being connected to the Internet means being connected to the largest information repository in the world. It connects every continent, thousands of companies, and millions of people into a 24-hours-per-day buzz of questions, answers, ideas, and inspirations. Don't worry if you feel a little lost—everyone does at first. This section gets you into the Internet and gives you the tools to make the most of its vast research capacity for buying a home online.

Without a doubt, the Internet can help your home buying experience be less time-consuming, less costly, and more convenient than ever. The Internet can assist you in doing the following:

- Outlining your game plan for buying a home online. You can go online and easily determine whether you are ready to buy a house and gain valuable insights about the right time to buy.

- Finding the best neighborhoods, real estate agents, and homes.

- Getting a grip on those tricky mortgage terms and products with online tutorials, mortgage advice, and online financing.

- Getting the biggest bang for your real estate buck with online house defect finders and Internet advice about how to negotiate and close the deal. The buyer could look for items such as aluminum wiring, synthetic stucco, and polybutyl plumbing as examples of potential problems in some homes. More detailed analysis of the house should be done with a live home inspection.

■ Making a smooth move to your new home by using online relocation and moving resources.

The World Wide Web (also called the Web, or the WWW) is a big part of the Internet, but in terms of age, it's the little brother of the online world. The Internet has been around since the 1960s, and the Web wasn't launched until the 1990s.

Getting connected and going online

When you start your subscription you'll be joining between 30 and 50 million people who are already using the Internet. Getting connected basically takes three easy steps:

1. Get a computer (or a WebTV unit that connects to your television set). Make sure your computer has a modem and access for a telephone line.

2. Get an Internet service provider (ISP), such as America Online, Earthlink, or one of the many other local or global providers (check the Yellow Pages). Costs average around $10 to $20 per month, and most ISPs charge a one-time connection fee. Many ISPs offer their products with a free one-month trial and usually provide all the software you need for free. This even includes e-mail, which will likely reduce your telephone bill. (But make sure you find an ISP that has a local number, or each time you connect, you will be charged long-distance rates.)

3. Start house hunting and purchase your dream home! This book shows you many of the pitfalls you should be aware of and shares some

> 66
> Banks will lend you money if you prove you don't need it.
> —Mark Twain
> 99

valuable tricks of the trade. After all, you don't want to waste time, money, and effort.

If you're new to the Internet, you might want to get *The Internet for Dummies,* 6th Edition, by John R. Levine, Carol Baroudi, and Margaret Levine Young (published by IDG Books).

What does buying a home online mean?

Unofficially...
Companies like E-Loan (www.eloan.com), the National Urban League (www.nul.org), and Black Homes Online (www.blackhomes.com) provide free computers to those with low incomes in poor economic areas so they can take advantage of the benefits of buying a home online.

Whether you're just thinking about buying a home or have to quickly relocate to another state, you'll find that the tools available online can save you time, money, and aggravation. The world of real estate has changed greatly in the past several years. In the not-so-distant past, if you wanted to buy a house, you checked out newspaper classified ads or talked with a Realtor. Now you can access online full-color photographs and detailed property facts for more than 1.3 million homes for sale. Once you know how to search, you'll be able to view many homes without venturing outdoors.

For example, to capture this growing market, *aggregators* (that is, loan marketplaces) provide enticing sites that get between 15,000 and 20,000 hits per day. You can go to an aggregator's Web site and complete home loan application forms, which are then screened and sent to multiple lenders. These firms then render a decision on the application. Lenders find that the benefits of using aggregators include reducing the costs of prospecting for customers and increasing the firm's approval rate. Consumers also benefit because they receive faster approval times and lower loan costs. Here are a few examples of aggregators:

> *Quicken Mortgage* (www.quickenmortgage.
> com) provides information about mortgages,

compares different types of mortgages with your financial profile, and helps you get pre-qualified and apply for mortgages from over 10 major mortgage lenders.

E-LOAN (www.eloan.com) lets you shop for rates, apply for a home loan online, and monitor the progress of your loan application.

iOwn (www.iown.com), formerly named Homeshark, provides comprehensive resources for homebuyers, sellers, and owners.

LendingTree (www.lendingtree.com), shown below, is an online service for mortgages, home equity loans, auto loans, student loans, debt consolidation, and credit cards.

At LendingTree online loan marketplace, lenders compete for your business and you choose the loan that's right for you.

What you can do online

For many people, purchasing a home is the achievement of a lifetime. It represents personal and financial success, the freedom to do what you want with your property (within limits, of course), and it's a valuable investment. For many individuals, home ownership is the cornerstone for building personal wealth. The rewards of home ownership often include a greater participation in local events and a sense of community, tax savings, greater stability for you and your family, and an investment in the future.

You can become a homeowner by purchasing your home online. Buying your home online means that you can:

- Save money on your home purchase.

- Easily relocate from one part of the country to another.

- Save time by researching your housing options via your computer.

- Avoid the hassle of being driven by your agent from one unacceptable house to another.

- Take advantage of the benefits of electronic purchasing.

- Hire a home inspection company to inspect the house you are interested in buying.

What you can't do online

Although you can go through virtually the entire home buying process online, there are a couple of things that you can't (or shouldn't) do online:

- You can't visit the property and walk through the house, grounds, and neighborhood. (You'll learn more about this in Chapter 4, "Finding a Neighborhood Next Door or Across the Country," and Chapter 6, "Finding Your Dream Home Online.")

- You can't accompany an inspector during the property inspection or make sure that all the utilities are turned on. (For details, see Chapter 9, "Online Help with Appraisals, Inspections, and Insurance.")

■ You can't negotiate all the items of the sale, and you cannot close escrow online. However, this is one area which may change in the next few years.

Where should you start online?

The Web is more than just a place for personal homepages. When you're setting out to buy a home online, you need to do lots of research before making what might be the biggest purchase of your life. You will want to contact sources with data on local market conditions. They will be able to tell you the names of local organizations or companies in the area in which you are looking to buy a home. They may have other tools to help you in your search, such as sources of financial assistance in buying a home, if you qualify for that assistance. It's a good idea to start your real estate research by using some of the four major types of online research sites:

■ **Academic centers.** There are literally thousands of colleges and universities online. Many of them also have their card catalogs online, in addition to the work, papers, and ideas of many of their students and faculty.

■ **Libraries.** Many public libraries have their catalogs online as well. Another benefit to online libraries is that librarians are professionally trained to know where to look for information. Many of them have applied that savvy to their Web pages and compiled great lists of reference links.

- **Associations.** Sometimes you need the experts as well as their expertise. Web sites for a variety of associations are available online, including many Realtor and mortgage associations. These Web sites publish FAQs (lists of frequently asked questions, with answers), position papers, articles written by members, and other items that can help you with your research.

- **Reference guides.** When you hear the word "reference," you probably think of things like dictionaries and encyclopedias. Yes, you can find those online. But you can also find things like national phone books, Yellow Pages that encompass the United States as well as several other countries, subject guides to Web pages, full-text search engines for Web pages, tax forms, maps, translators, and currency calculators. All kinds of things that would have required special printed reference guides before are now available online.

Finding real estate Web sites

The Internet offers tons of free advice for homebuyers: Everyone has an opinion about when and what type of house someone should purchase. The Internet provides authoritative information to assist you in your decision making. One good example is the Consumer Information Center Web site (shown below), located at www.gsa.gov/staff/pa/cic/housing.htm. This is an excellent online source for government publications and offers free literature to help new and experienced homebuyers shop for real estate and mortgages.

When you access the Information Center, you see a broad listing of booklets that explain different

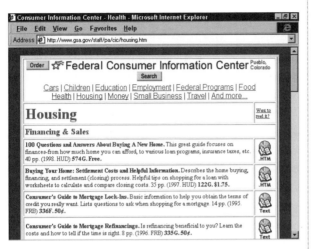

The Consumer Information Center provides free, reliable information online for homebuyers.

issues faced by homebuyers (definitions of adjustable rate mortgages, homeowners insurance, appraisers, and physical inspecting services, to name a few). Select the brochure you want to read, and either print it out or save it on a floppy disk so you can read it at your convenience.

Getting a mortgage is central to purchasing a home. A mortgage is a serious issue, and an educated consumer is less likely to have their home loan application denied. Additionally, knowing which mortgage is best for your financial situation and how to shop for the best mortgage rates can help you buy the best house you can afford. The mortgage process has radically changed over the past few years.

Becoming knowledgeable about mortgages is easy with the Internet. First-time homebuyers can visit homes online and learn about the real estate market in their local areas. (For more information, see Chapter 6, "Finding Your Dream Home Online.") Unless you're paying cash for your dream home, most new homebuyers need to learn about mortgages. Mortgage Mart (www.mortgagemart. com) provides detailed information about the process of shopping and obtaining a mortgage. (For additional information about financing your dream home, see Chapter 7, "Online Mortgage Advice and Lending.") You'll discover which loan is right for you and how you can get almost instant online home loan preapproval. Chapter 8, "Avoiding the Down Payment Cash Crunch," shows how you can purchase a home with little or no down payment. You'll also learn how to take advantage of creative financing options.

The Web can help you deal with the paperwork you'll need to complete a loan package. The business of getting a mortgage means filling out forms. The best way to handle this paperwork is to use the Internet to learn about real estate terminology and mortgage procedures. Mortgage lending is a well-established process. However, the way in which different mortgage lenders approach this process varies. You'll need to supply lots of financial documents, such as income tax reports, pay stubs, and copies of your bank account statements.

To purchase the property of your choice, you'll need to order a title search, appraisal, and a physical inspection. The Real Estate Library (www.relibrary. com) has all the major real estate topics listed and provides links to informative articles that can help you get a handle on what sometimes looks like an arcane process. For legal matters, Nolo Press (www.nolo.com) is a source of forms and legal information. Of course, depending on your specific situation, you may need the advice of an attorney in the area in which you are buying the house.

It's important to determine how large a home mortgage you can afford before you go shopping. Today, there are around 3,000 online mortgage lenders. Many of these Web sites have online calculators so you can enter your personal information and learn the maximum amount that you will be able to afford. Many local Realtor Web sites also have calculators, as well as locally tailored information specifically for their area. You can also use the online calculators at home buying supersites like Financenter.com (www.financenter.com), shown below, by following these steps:

1. Go to the Financenter.com homepage and click on Homes.

2. When the next Web page appears, in the ClickCalcs box, select How Much Can I Borrow?

3. Enter the required information.

4. The calculator uses a formula based on your total income, your long-term debt, and the

Watch Out!
Keep in mind that calculators are just estimators. If a lender believes that the house you selected is worth less than what you want to pay or if your credit report indicates that you may not be a good credit risk, you may not be able to obtain the mortgage amount you expected.

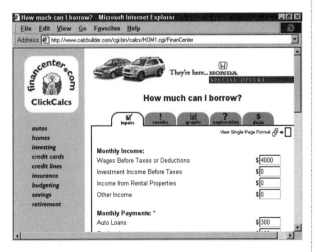

Find out how large a loan you can afford at Financenter.

cost of the property (including property taxes) to determine how large a home loan you can afford.

If you use different online calculators you may get a variety of amounts you can afford, but they will all be in the same price range. This is because different lenders have different loan policies, so you may not be able to get the same size mortgage from every lender—whether you use online calculators or talk to live people at a variety of lending institutions.

When you know how much home you can afford, you can go online to shop for the best rate, which can save you thousands of dollars over the course of the loan term. The cost savings can allow you to purchase a larger home, improve the quality of your lifestyle, or help pay for your child's college tuition.

Many people use newspapers to find interest rates. Web sites such as Bankrate (www.bankrate. com) compare rates nationwide. This is valuable because many small banks don't advertise their rates. With the Internet you can shop for lenders of all sizes and select the ones that offer the best rates.

The process of buying a home online

Imagine that it's Saturday morning. You've decided that today is the day you'll start the process of buying a home online. You don't know exactly what you're looking for and are uncertain about what you can afford. If you want to be an online homebuyer, follow these general steps to get started:

1. Turn on your computer and go to a general real estate site such as realtor.com (www.realtor. com), which is shown below. Realtor.com has a wide variety of online real estate tools and resources to help you assess your finances.

Moneysaver
On a 30-year fixed $150,000 mortgage, monthly payments at 8 percent are $1,100 (not including taxes and insurance). If you can acquire a 7 percent loan with the same terms, you'll pay $1,000 a month. This would save you $36,000 over the life of the loan!

Use their online calculators to compare what you'll spend if you buy or rent. Calculate the amount of down payment you can afford and determine how much you can actually pay for a house. (For more on this, see Chapter 3, "Is Now the Right Time to Buy a Home?")

Realtor.com can help you start the process of buying a home online.

2. Study local economics, demographic trends, and the real estate market in general at real estate supersites like Yahoo! Real Estate (yahoo.realestate.com). As a savvy consumer, you'll avoid scams and frauds.

   Discover the neighborhood you're looking for (for example, planned urban communities, historic, urban, or suburban areas) with iOwn (www.iown.com). Compare local school districts and learn about other communities. For details, see Chapter 6, "Finding Your Dream Home Online."

3. If you need a real estate broker, you can find the best Realtor in your area by checking out

sites such as realtor.com (www.realtor.com). Find out more about signing the real estate agent agreement and discover how you can avoid conflicts of interest in Chapter 5, "Using a Real Estate Agent."

4. Get help finding your dream home on the Internet with a site such as Real Direct (www.realdirect.com). See Chapter 6, "Finding Your Dream Home Online," for assistance in selecting the type of housing (single family, co-op, condominium, etc.) you need and determining what's right for you.

    Use Internet *update bots* (small programs) to monitor changes in multiple listings of available homes in neighborhoods in which you want to live. These update bots will automatically let you know when someone wants to sell a house in your desired neighborhood. For example, Cyberhomes (www.cyberhomes.com) includes "homes by e-mail." Cyberhomes, which lists 900,000 homes for sale, will save your home search criteria and notify you by e-mail when it receives a new listing that meets your requirements.

5. Create your own game plan and mortgage hunting strategies. This will allow you to make major financial decisions based on your own online research. Use the Internet to find news about the latest interest rates. (Shopping for and comparing interest rates online is one of the easiest tasks of the home buying process.) Find online sources for mortgages at sites such as Homefair (www.homefair.com). Compare interest rates and determine which mortgage fits your financial profile. For more details, see

Chapter 7, "Online Mortgage Advice and Lending."

6. Use the Internet to get a good understanding of your down payment options by going to a site such as Coldwell Banker (www.coldwellbanker.com), which has plenty of helpful tips for low payment loans. You'll learn about the 20 percent solution in Chapter 8, "Avoiding the Down Payment Cash Crunch."

7. Take advantage of online real estate opportunities that you didn't know existed before you became an online homebuyer. Check out how to make an offer by referring to the online resources provided by sites such as Century 21 (www.c21homepros.com/faq/16.html). For more information, check out Chapter 10, "Negotiating and Closing the Deal."

8. For a smooth move, check out the many online moving and relocation companies, such as Movers.com (www.movers.com). This site and others provide free estimates, change of address help, maps, storage, checklists, and other types of assistance. For details, see Chapter 14, "Getting Moving Help Online."

These eight steps cover the main points of buying a home online. Purchasing a home may seem complicated, but millions of people from all walks of life do it every day. Consumers who are armed with detailed information and practical tips find that they are less likely to make mistakes or get frazzled by the process, and they can complete the process faster and move into their new homes sooner than others. Using online calculators, worksheets, and other Internet resources can significantly reduce your stress level. You don't have to be an Internet guru to access all the available data. You don't even have to be an experienced homebuyer. With *The Unofficial Guide to Buying a Home Online* as your guide, you'll discover how to buy a home with less money, time, and effort.

Real estate supersites

In real estate, as in many areas, what you don't know could get you into trouble. The Web can assist you in protecting your wallet and finding the home of your dreams. All of the following Web sites provide high-level information for free. Industry professionals, trade associations, and businesses sponsor many of these government and real estate supersites. The following are some good starting points:

> *Home-Links.com* (www.home-links.com) is a comprehensive group of links and resources about everything related to buying a home, from Realtors to landscaping.

> *MSN HomeAdvisor* (homeadvisor.msn.com) shows you each step of the home buying process. This Web site gives you information about how to get started and how to find reports about neighborhoods. It provides tips on home buying, shows how to find financing, and suggests how to make an offer and close the deal.

> *MSN Sidewalk Real Estate Buyer's Guide* (national.sidewalk.com/buyersguide/ realestate) is an online tutorial for first-time homebuyers. Discover how to find a home, a neighborhood, and links to lots of high-quality real estate resources on the Web.

> *Realtor.com* (www.realtor.com), as mentioned previously, is a valuable resource for both

consumers and Realtors. A visit to the resource center is worth your time. This online home buying source has a wide variety of worksheets and calculators to help you with the math of home buying.

Using the Internet to be prepared

Satisfied homebuyers are individuals who have the most information—and use it to their advantage. This is why using the Internet is so important. There are definite "rules of the game" when it comes to purchasing a home. It's not like purchasing a car, buying groceries, or anything else you have ever previously purchased.

If you don't know the rules of the game because you're a first-time homebuyer or you haven't purchased a home recently, you may find home buying a mysterious and sometimes frustrating process. Here are some insider tips that can make the process easier:

- Familiarize yourself with the entire home buying procedure. Know what each step is and what to expect (like the old Boy Scout motto says, "Be Prepared"). Make certain that you don't get blindsided at the last moment and have to spend the night (or several weeks) in a hotel.

- Be an educated consumer. Take advantage of all the resources, tools, worksheets, and checklists available on the Internet. In later chapters, you'll find the most up-to-date and best real estate sites on the Web so that you can efficiently complete your research. While you're researching, don't just skim the surface, but really dig in. Don't let others

Bright Idea
Many federal, state, and local first-time home-buyers' programs are available. A good place to start your search is with your state's housing finance agency. For a nationwide directory, see the National Council of State Housing Agencies (ncsha. org/NCSHA/ ncshal1/ncshal2/ directry/statindx. html).

make decisions for you. If you're not sure about something, stop the process until you're satisfied with the answers to your questions.

- Make certain that your financial house is in order. This means taking control of your finances by checking your financial position, reading a copy of your credit report, and knowing exactly what you can afford.

- Keep your bank account records, financial statements, and tax returns in good order, since you may need to provide copies when you apply for the mortgage. If you are currently a homeowner and are buying another home, you should keep your previous mortgage loan documentation together in one file, as you will need to refer to it.

- Sometimes a small investment can bring a bigger reward. For example, spending a few dollars by hiring your own appraiser or building inspector can save you thousands of dollars.

There are so many things to remember when you start the home buying process that a checklist may help you get organized. The following checklist can help you avoid common and (often expensive) mistakes:

FIRST-TIME ONLINE HOMEBUYER CHECKLIST

☐ Keep track of your credit report.
☐ Get your financial house in order.
☐ Determine your housing needs and wants. Decide what type of house you want to buy.
☐ Check out how to apply for an online loan.
☐ Find a real estate agent you can trust and who respects you.

☐ If you find your dream home, make a written offer to the seller.

☐ If the seller doesn't accept your offer, he or she may make a counteroffer. Find out what contingencies you can include in an offer.

☐ If the seller doesn't accept your counteroffer, repeat step 6.

☐ Open an escrow account with your real estate agent. (Escrow accounts usually have a life of about 45 to 60 days.)

☐ Have a professional home inspection.

☐ Arrange for home insurance.

☐ Compare moving company prices and take advantage of online tools to plan your move.

☐ Make your walk-through of the property for a final inspection.

☐ Arrange for a closing agent or attorney to make certain that all the paperwork is properly signed, sealed, and delivered.

☐ If you completed all the previous steps, you get possession of your home and the key. Move in and begin enjoying your new home!

Just the facts

▪ You don't have to be computer savvy to be an online homebuyer.

▪ The Internet offers tons of free advice for homebuyers.

▪ If you are exploring the possibility of home ownership or are seriously looking for another residence, the Internet can save you time, money, and aggravation.

- Real estate industry professionals, trade associations, and businesses sponsor many high-
  quality sites that are excellent starting points
  for online homebuyers.

- First-time (and experienced) homebuyers
  often need a checklist to make certain they
  cover all the bases of the home buying process.

GET THE SCOOP ON...
Financially preparing for home ownership
▪ Using software and the Internet to take
control of your finances ▪ Understanding the
credit reporting system ▪ Correcting errors on
your credit report ▪ Getting online financial help

Creating a Financial Game Plan

Chapter 2

If you are considering purchasing a home this year or in the next few years, you need to look at your financial situation very carefully. If you don't know your net worth and spending patterns, you may be in for a surprise when you apply for a home loan.

Keeping track of your finances can also help you determine if you're ready to be a homeowner. Remember that there are extra costs to home ownership, such as property taxes, maintenance, security, homeowners association or condominium fees, and landscaping.

This chapter covers the basics of developing a personal financial plan for home ownership. You'll learn how to determine your starting point, develop a workable budget, and evaluate your credit situation. And speaking of credit concerns . . . could your credit report include something that might make a lender hesitate about approving your loan? If your credit situation needs some work, you can use several online resources that can help you repair your credit (without paying a hefty price).

Getting your financial house in order

The average middle-class American in the 1950s used few financial instruments—primarily savings accounts, savings bonds, home mortgages, and life and car insurance. Over the past 50 years, the U.S. middle class has grown and the financial options available to it have increased. Today, Americans are more financially sophisticated. Many individuals use cash savings, stocks, bonds, mutual funds, insurance, home real estate, 401(k) retirement plans, IRAs, estate planning, and fixed and variable annuities. (An *annuity* is an even cash flow stream, like social security benefits.) The interplay of the amounts and timing of these devices is what financial planning is all about.

Financial planning helps balance incomes, inheritances, real estate investments, retirements, and extended business interests. According to the Institute of Financial Planning (www.laicfp.org/myths.html), most people recognize the importance of financial planning, yet many don't understand or have misconceptions about who benefits from financial planning (specifically, how financial planning best benefits them). Here are several of the commonly held financial planning myths:

- **Myth:** Financial planning is for the wealthy. **Fact:** Even individuals with a small amount of assets need to be financially organized.

- **Myth:** Financial planning is just about investing. **Fact:** Financial planning covers all the bases of your personal financial situation.

- **Myth:** Financial planning is another term for retirement planning and isn't necessary until you're older. **Fact:** The younger you start, the more likely you can retire early or have a more comfortable retirement.

- **Myth:** Financial planning requires a big plan. **Fact:** You don't need a big plan, but just planning from paycheck to paycheck won't help you reach your financial goals.

- **Myth:** Financial planning is a one-time effort. **Fact:** As you go through different life stages you'll require different financial plans.

- **Myth:** You can get along without financial planning. **Fact:** Putting off making a financial plan or planning from paycheck to paycheck can result in missed financial opportunities because you aren't prepared to take advantage of them.

Moneysaver
One perk of having your financial ducks in a row is that you'll be ready to take advantage of low interest rates. For example, if you borrow $100,000 at 7.5 percent for 30 years, your monthly payment will be $699. At 7.75 percent, the payment would rise to $716.41. Over the course of the loan, that's an extra $6,267 in interest.

The personal financial planning process

People without financial plans generally do not achieve their financial objectives. When should you start your financial plan? You should start this very moment. In this chapter, you'll find all the guidance, online tools, and directions you'll need to get started.

You may not have a formal plan, but you probably do some financial planning, even if it's only noting the bills that need to be paid on the back of your paycheck envelope. Equity Analytics, Limited (www.e-analytics.com/fp1.htm) says that there are four steps to developing a financial plan:

1. **Determine what you have.** There's no way you can achieve your financial goals (that is, get to

the finish line) if you don't know your starting point.

2. **Ascertain what resources you need for living.** Your financial health doesn't depend on how much you make, but how much you spend. Individuals who make a lot of money but spend more than they have are as broke as those who never had any money to begin with.

3. **Determine your financial objectives.** What do you want in the future? Do you want to purchase a house in the next year, three years, or five years? If so, you'll need a workable plan.

4. **Decide how you are going to reach your goals.** Some people use investing in securities as the cornerstone of their personal wealth. Others use the equity they acquire in their homes. The best method is the one that meets your personal goals.

It's important to write down your financial plan so you can work out any inconsistencies. Make certain you set specific milestones so you can achieve your goals. For example, you might decide to start a down payment account, with a goal of having saved $15,000 two years from now.

Determining your net worth

The first step in getting where you want to go is knowing where you are now. In financial management, no plan can be implemented without knowing the starting point. Professional financial planners say that most people don't know their net worth and when potential customers make a ballpark guess, they usually aren't even close. Table 2.1 provides a net worth worksheet that can assist you in quickly calculating your personal assets.

TABLE 2.1: YOUR PERSONAL NET WORTH WORKSHEET

ASSETS	Amount	LIABILITIES	Amount
Cash & Cash Equivalents		Home mortgage	$
Savings account	$	Other mortgages	$
Cash management account	$	Other real estate debts	$
Money market account	$	Automobile loan(s)	$
Certificates of deposit	$	Insurance payments	$
Other	$	Student loans	$
Stocks & Bonds		Credit card debt	$
Stocks	$	Other installment debts	$
Bonds	$	Margin loans from brokers	$
Mutual funds	$	**Tax Liabilities**	
Other	$	Income taxes	$
Insurance & Retirement		Property taxes	$
Cash value of life insurance	$	**TOTAL LIABILITIES**	$
Surrender value of annuities	$		
IRA	$		
Keogh	$	**Net Worth Calculation:**	
401(k)	$	**Total Assets**	$
Company insurance plan	$	**Less Total Liabilities**	$
Profit sharing	$	**Total Net Worth**	$
Real Estate & Other			
Value of your home	$		
Value of a second home	$		
Rental properties	$		
Real estate partnerships	$		
Other	$		
Partnerships	$		
Ownerships in businesses	$		
Personal Assets			
Collectibles	$		
Automobiles	$		
Boats	$		
Recreational vehicles	$		
Household furnishings	$		
TOTAL ASSETS	$		

You can also use online worksheets to determine your net worth; in some cases, they do all the math for you and you need only fill in the important values. A few examples of sites that offer online worksheets are:

MoneyWeb Net Worth Calculator (www.moneyweb. com.au) is an Internet financial directory and resource center. Each category of the net worth calculator is explained.

BYG Publishing (www.bygpub.com/finance/ calculators.htm) provides a net worth calculator that can assist you in tallying up your personal wealth.

Iowa's News and Information Network (www. fyiowa.webpoint/finance/clcnet.htm) has a handy net worth calculator that includes unique categories, such as the value of your certificates of deposit (CDs).

How are you using your income?

What resources do you need to support your current lifestyle? Whatever your situation, you need to understand and take command of your finances. In Chapter 3, "Is Now the Right Time to Buy a Home?" I'll discuss the pros and cons of renting and buying, but for now let's focus on understanding how much you're spending each month. You'll need to know your annual gross income, your monthly debt payments, family living expenses, savings, and investments. If you want to work out your budget using a pen and paper, you can use the worksheet in Table 2.2.

TABLE 2.2: DEVELOPING YOUR NET CASH FLOW

INCOME	Amount	EXPENSES	Amount
Annual Income		**Home**	
Salary	$	Mortgage or rent	$
Spouse's salary	$	Utilities	$
Commissions	$	**Family**	$
Spouse's commissions	$	Groceries & sundries	$
Bonus	$	Clothing	$
Spouse's bonus	$	Laundry & dry cleaning	$
Royalties		Medicine	
License fees	$	**Transportation**	$
Income from business	$	Gasoline	$
Dividends	$	Auto expenses	$
Interest earned	$	**Tax Liabilities**	$
Rent paid to you	$	**Miscellaneous**	$
Income from trusts	$	Installment loans	$
Gifts to you	$	Payroll savings	$
Alimony received	$	Retirement contributions	$
Pensions	$	Professional fees	$
Social Security	$	Charitable contributions	$
Tax refunds	$	Religious contributions	$
Other income	$	Other	$
TOTAL INCOME (A)	$	**TOTAL EXPENSES (B)**	$

TOTAL INCOME (A)	$
LESS TOTAL EXPENSES (B)	$_____
TOTAL SURPLUS (SHORTFALL) (C) (A – B = C)	$

The Internet offers a wealth of resources that can make this job easier for you. Here are some examples:

The editors at *Money* magazine (www.money. com) have created interactive lessons to assist you in making a budget. The budget lesson can be covered in about 10 minutes. The following figure shows Money.com's *Instant Budget Maker* tool (www.pathfinder.com/ money/101/).

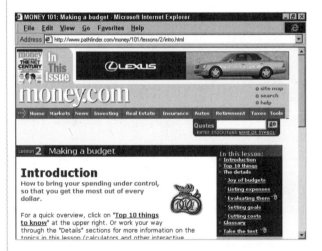

MetLife's Budget Maker (www.metlife.com/ lifeadvice/money/docs/budget4.html) uses Snoopy cartoon characters to help you with each step of the budgeting process. This makes creating a budget less tedious and more fun.

When you complete the worksheet in Table 2.2 or use the budget helpers online, you may discover that more money goes out than comes in. This is called a *shortfall*, which means that you are living beyond your means and may need some assistance with debt management. A *surplus* means that you have excess funds. This is the money that's available for your financial objectives.

Making a budget based on your goals

Strategic financial goals can be stated in broad terms, such as, "I want to retire early." Tactical goals are specific and short-term: "I want to save $20,000 by 2002." In other words, your goals and objectives are the finish line, and creating and implementing a financial plan is how you get there. To start your financial plan, write down your goals, which for most people are in the following order of importance:

1. **Emergency fund.** It's important to have an emergency fund to protect yourself from unexpected situations—for example, uninsured medical costs and unemployment. (The average unemployment period for many white-collar workers is now six to nine months.) Some conservative financial planners suggest that an emergency fund should equal four years of expenses.

2. **Insurance.** It's a good idea to have adequate insurance to cover disability, health, life, automobiles, and property.

3. **Expendable income.** If you can pay the monthly bills without stretching, you can begin spending your extra money on things like planning for your children's college tuition, taking care of your parents, or helping your children with the down payment for their first automobile or home. Or you can use the extra money on things like vacations, purchasing a

Bright Idea
The agony of budgeting occurs mostly at the beginning. After you have a budget in place, you can fine-tune it by comparing your budget to your actual spending. Analyze your household spending in a businesslike fashion, and don't forget to use the great tools available on the Internet.

vacation home, making home improvements, or purchasing a new home.

4. **Retirement.** You might want to work toward an early or a comfortable retirement. Most people want to maintain their standards of living during their retirement years.

5. **Maximizing wealth.** This goal is to maximize your personal wealth. Some individuals may want to capitalize on their own business or engage in philanthropy. All estates need some planning, although most people don't need to hire professionals to do this.

Creating your financial plan

After you have articulated your financial goals, you need to complete your plan with specific amounts, time frames, and other details. Go one step further than saying, "I am going to draw up a will next month. Then I'll decide who will get what," or "I'll set up an emergency fund next year." Actually write down some solid numbers and dates.

Your financial plan must provide the details of how you will reach your goals and objectives. It should include your home or proposed home purchase, investments, car purchases, insurance, tuition costs for you or your children, and retirement and estate planning. Each of these goals needs a plan and a spreadsheet or worksheet articulating that plan. Then all the plans are coordinated.

These coordinated plans are the blueprints of your financial future. At first it may sound overwhelming, but don't get worried, because there are many online tools and offline resources to assist you. Remember that no one is better qualified and more interested in maximizing your net worth than you.

Using personal finance software

For some individuals, the best approach to creating a financial plan is to use personal finance software. The two most popular brands, both of which cost less than $100, are Quicken and Microsoft Money. These programs, although considered stand-alone software applications, are integrated with the Internet. This means that you can also use them for PC banking, PC bill paying, and downloading your brokerage statements. All this information is then integrated into your net worth and budget reports:

Microsoft Money (www.money.msn.com) makes keeping accurate financial records easy, so you can stay on top of your expenses and well under (or close to) your budget. Among other things, Microsoft Money can assist you in determining your net worth and tracking your day-to-day financial affairs. The software can quickly summarize how you use your money and create guidelines for future spending.

Quicken (www.quicken.com), over the years, has evolved from being simply an electronic checkbook into something much more. In its current incarnation, Quicken not only tidies up your monthly bills but also helps you organize and manage almost every aspect of your personal financial life. With Quicken's built-in budgeting, you can create a realistic budget based on the previous year's figures. You can develop as many budgets as you require, so you can take into consideration best- and worst-case scenarios.

How much can you afford?

Each lender develops its own credit policy, but there are some general guidelines, called "qualifying ratios." Qualifying ratios may be eased if you make a large down payment. However, most lenders (except for the Veterans Administration) for conventional mortgages will not grant loans to borrowers who have debt (house payments and personal long-term debt) in excess of 36 percent of their gross income. Non-conforming lenders, however, may allow higher percentages of debt. In your effort to get your financial house in order, you'll need to know if you have any serious debt problems. There are many online tools that can help you determine your debt ratio. For more information about qualifying ratios, see Chapter 3, "Is Now the Right Time to Buy a Home?"

Your debt ratio measures the percentage of monthly income that is used to pay previous obligations. If you discover that your debts are greater than your monthly income, you'll want to start developing a plan to get out of debt as soon as possible.

For example, Credit Union Land (www.culand. com/debt.html) points out that all financial institutions, including credit unions, use various methods to help determine your ability to repay the loan. Credit Land provides an online calculator to help you determine if you are "loaned out." If you'd like to know what your debt ratio is, fill out the online form and click on the Submit It button. You'll get the results almost instantly. The online results (which are anonymous) indicate your debt ratio rating. This can alert you to any serious debt problems that could prevent you from receiving mortgage approval.

Timesaver
If relatives are giving you financial assistance for your down payment, make sure they provide you with a "gift letter" in advance. Gift letters show lenders that the funds do not have to be repaid. The financial institution you select may, however, require you to complete the gift letter on their particular form when you complete an application for a mortgage.

Keep in mind that a total debt ratio of 40 percent or more may indicate that you are carrying too much debt. For an FHA mortgage, total debt limits are 41 percent, and possibly slightly more if your credit is very good. However, each financial institution calculates this ratio slightly differently because they take different factors into consideration. For example, lenders sometimes consider factors such as the following:

- How long you've held the same job—this is 2 years of continuous employment if you have a part-time job, or if you have changed the type of work you are doing.

- Other liquid assets that enable a higher down payment to housing price ratio.

- The amount of cash reserves you'll have on hand after the deal closes.

If you want to figure your debt ratio with pen and paper, here's how. First, divide your total monthly debts (the housing expenses for the proposed loan plus other monthly credit obligations) by your total monthly income. For example, if your total obligations are $1,300 ($1,000 for housing expenses and $300 for other credit obligations), the debt ratio would be 32.5 percent ($1,300 ÷ $4,000 = 32.5 percent). Remember, a low debt ratio results in a higher credit grade. In contrast, a high debt ratio means a lower credit grade.

A quick and dirty way to determine if you're carrying more debt than lenders like to see is to add up all your monthly debts (car payments, student loans, and other obligations) and divide by 12. If the result is higher than 10 percent of your income, debt is an area of concern. If your monthly debt is between

5 and 9 percent of your income, this should not prevent you from getting a standard mortgage. If your debts are less than 4 percent of your annual income, your debts should not cause a problem when applying for a home loan.

If you want the Internet to do all the work, go to the Homefair Web site (www.homefair.com). In the left column is a listing that includes the category Tools & Calculators. Click on Mortgage Qualifier. A few other online sources that can provide you with a quick idea of what you can qualify for are Excite (www.excite.com), Yahoo! (www.yahoo.com), and most online mortgage lenders, such as AppOnline. com (www.apponline.com) and Mortgage.com (www.mortgage.com).

Some lenders and mortgage brokers work with borrowers with blemished credit histories. Many of these "sub-prime" lenders will allow the following:

- Your total debt load can be 50 to 60 percent of your gross monthly income (instead of the 36 percent guidelines used for "A" grade credit borrowers).

- The only proof of income you'll need is six months of bank statements (instead of tax returns, W-2 forms, or pay stubs). With 30 percent down, some lenders will only ask for a statement of income—called a "no documentation," or "no doc" mortgage.

Borrowers with less-than-perfect credit generally pay higher-than-market interest rates for their past mistakes and are required to pay a minimum 20 percent down payment. If you have a steady income but a poor credit history, you may want to consider a sub-prime loan with its higher-than-market interest rate. If you make each mortgage payment on time for the following year, you might be able to refinance at a lower rate. Shop online for sub-prime lenders with programs specifically designed to help individuals finance or refinance their homes. A few examples of sub-prime lenders are:

> *Delta Funding* (www.deltafunding.com) specializes in non-traditional mortgage lending.

> *Eastern Mortgage* (www.eastern-mortgage.com) focuses on sub-prime mortgages and home-equity loans.

> *Hanover Mortgage Company* (www.hanovermc. com) gives attention to mortgages for people with not-so-perfect credit.

> *Southern Pacific Funding* (www.sp.funding. com) concentrates on sub-prime loans for homebuyers.

Understanding the credit reporting system

A credit report includes information about your borrowing and how you have managed your credit in the past. The credit report is based on facts collected from public records, such as court documents, and your creditors. Credit rating agencies compile this information for potential lenders, employers, and others who have a legitimate reason to ask for it.

There are two types of credit reports lenders may request. The first type is an "in-file" report, which instantly shows a fairly reliable picture of your credit history and costs between $8 and $25. The second type, a full residential mortgage credit report, is comprehensive and draws from the three largest credit rating agencies; these reports may take

Unofficially...
Credit reports can also be used when you apply for a job or rent an apartment, so it's important to make certain the information in them is correct.

several weeks to be processed and cost between $30 and $80.

Lenders use credit reports in their credit scoring systems to determine mathematically whether they think you will be able to meet all your financial responsibilities—including the loan you're trying to obtain. Overall, having a good credit history means you'll have an easier time when you want to purchase a home.

What credit reports do and don't contain

Credit reports can contain the following:

- Your name and any past name you might have used.

- Your current and previous addresses.

- Your employer.

- The number of credit accounts you have, the date they were opened, the highest credit limit or current credit balance, and payment history (the number of missed payments, late payments, or timely payments). Additional information includes accounts in collection, bankruptcy, tax liens, and so on.

A credit report does not contain information about:

- Checking and savings accounts.

- Medical history.

- Major cash or check purchases.

- Business accounts, unless you are personally liable for the debt.

- Credit scores.

- Your race, gender, religion, or national origin.

If you have an excellent credit history, you can purchase a home with a 5 percent down payment and debt ratios as high as 38 percent for the housing ratio and 44 percent for your total debt ratio. In some areas, local or state assistance programs permit no money down.

Individuals with good credit histories will likely require a 10 percent down payment and ratios such as 39 percent for housing and 40 percent for total debt.

A poorer credit history means that you'll have to make a larger down payment and your current debt ratios will have to be lowered.

Credit bureaus

Credit bureaus are record-keeping companies that track the credit histories of consumers. The credit bureau keeps records of when you pay on your loans, mortgages, rental agreements, and credit cards. There are three primary credit bureaus:

> *Experian* (www.experian.com), formerly TRW, provides credit advice as well as information about its products, real estate, customer services, awards, consumer credit, and business credit. To get a copy of your credit report, print a copy of their Consumer Credit Report Order Form and mail it, along with a check, to the address listed at the site. Prices vary by state, so check the Web site for the correct price.

> *Equifax* (www.equifax.com) provides Equifax links, a consumer center, investor services, company news, job opportunities, and information about community affairs. You can order your credit report online by charging it

Bright Idea
Getting a loan if you have spotty credit or as a self-employed person with un-provable income used to be sub-prime lending. Now if you have 30 percent down and provide a "statement of earnings," you may get a no doc mortgage with a good interest rate.

to your credit card. The company will send you the report by U.S. mail within two weeks.

Trans Union Corporation (www.tuc.com) provides a company profile, information about credit reporting and a consumer credit report review, a fraud victim assistance department, information about their products and services, and employment opportunities. To get a copy of your report, send your request, along with all the information listed at the site and a check for the fee, to the address listed at the site. Fees vary by state, so visit the Web site for the correct price.

Keep in mind that credit bureaus do not grant or deny your application as a potential credit risk. The lender or creditor makes the credit approval decision.

Checking out your own credit report

It's a good idea to order a copy of your credit report before you apply for a mortgage so that you can find out if it shows any problems and clean up any mis-understandings or errors. (You'll learn about clean-ing up problems later in the chapter, in the section "Correcting errors on your credit report.") There are many Internet sources for credit reports. Here are a few examples, with approximate prices:

QuickenMortgage (www.quickenmortgage.com/tools/creditassess/creditquery.asp) has a variety of services, including one that allows you to self-assess your credit at no charge.

CreditReport-Net.com (www.creditreport-net.com) provides online reports that range from a single report for $8 to a detailed credit report for approximately $30. You can view your report online or have it sent by U.S. mail.

CreditMedic (www.creditmedic.com) allows you to select the components you want to investigate in your credit report. Total charges are shown at the bottom of the page as you add and remove components. You must order at least one report to obtain a credit score. Prices for components vary from free to $8 per report.

Real Estate Digest Credit (www.ired.com/dir/tools/credit.htm) provides links to Internet consumer credit sites.

iCreditReport (www.qspace.com/qspace) offers three types of credit reports. The first type is an online report that appears in 30 seconds ($8). The second type is a three-in-one report ($30) that consolidates and compares the credit reports from the three major credit reporting agencies; this report is mailed to you. The third type of report is a quarterly e-mail credit monitoring notification ($50) that tells you about any new activity on your report.

Consumer Info (www.consumerinfo.com/n-cgi/index.pl?02614001) offers a 30-day free trial in which you get a credit report as well as the CreditCheck Monitoring Service, which regularly sends you information about your credit rating so that you never have any surprises. The fee after the trial period is about $60 per year.

Often, if you can do any of the following, you can receive a free credit report:

- Certify that you are unemployed and currently seeking employment.

- Certify that you are receiving welfare assistance.

- Show that you have been denied credit, employment, or rental housing based on your credit report.

- Show that an inaccuracy has been made in your credit report due to fraud. (In this situation, you will likely have to provide your fraud case number to the credit bureau.)

- Show that you have received a financial adverse action, such as an increase in your interest rate or a decrease in your credit limit based on your credit report.

- Show that you have been denied credit. Within 30 days of being denied credit, you are entitled to a free report from the same credit bureau that the inquiring company used.

Note that each credit bureau has slightly different rules about releasing free credit reports. Check with each credit bureau for specific requirements.

FICO scores

Lenders consider credit scores predictors of the borrower's willingness to pay and the likelihood of the borrower defaulting. If a borrower misses credit payments due to illness, divorce, or injury, time will heal the credit problem. There is no set standard, but usually two years is long enough for the ills of collections and judgments. (Credit reports can also indicate foreclosures and bankruptcies that stay on your credit report for 7 to 10 years.) Overall, credit injuries can be healed with the reestablishment of a good payment history.

Your credit score often determines whether you'll get a loan. It's impossible to know your credit score. Credit scores are proprietary information that belongs to lenders and others that use the services of credit scoring companies. Even relatively simple credit scoring systems use 10,000 to 20,000 different possible combinations to determine a credit score.

In general, though, lenders base their credit scores on the information contained in the credit report and primarily on the borrower's mortgage payment history. If the borrower is a first-time homebuyer, the lender often prefers that the customer have at least five credit accounts for two years.

Some of the criteria used for credit scoring are obvious. A higher wage earner is a better risk than a low wage earner. Fewer credit cards are better than more credit cards. A stable employment history, including time on the job at one employer, also increases your score. Of course, paying your bills on time is a must. A property foreclosure is likely to be the most damaging item on your credit report. What all this means is that it's important to protect your credit rating. However, if you already have a bad credit rating, don't despair; you can always rebuild your credit and improve your score.

Some lenders use their own proprietary software to evaluate potential borrowers. Many companies use the Fair Issac & Company (FICO) scores provided by the major credit bureaus. Some credit bureau scores are numbers, some are letters, and others are classes (such as accept plus, accept, referred to underwriting, and caution). The lender does not release these scores to applicants.

> 66
> Americans don't understand the consequences of having a poor credit rating. Less than one-half of American adults consider a history of extremely late bill payments to be an obstacle to their being able to finance a home.
> —Franklin D. Raines, Chairman and Chief Executive Officer of Fannie Mae
> 99

Unofficially...
According to Harvest Mortgage (www.harvest-mortgage.com), there are eight good loans for each loan which eventually will default for individuals with FICO scores below 600; for scores of 700–719 there are 123 good loans for each loan that eventually will default; and for borrowers with scores of 800 or more, one loan will eventually default for every 1,292 good loans.

FICO scores can be called by different names by each of the major credit bureaus. Because the credit information recorded at each bureau is rarely the same and each credit bureau places a slightly different emphasis on distinct credit factors, you will probably have a different credit score from each of the major credit rating agencies. For more on FICO scores, refer to the following sites:

The Northern California Credit Service (www.nccredit.com/understanding.html) has an excellent article on understanding credit bureaus and FICO scores.

Fair Issac & Company (www.fairisaac.com/servlet/sitedriver/content/924) gives you information on what the company that started it all has to say about credit scoring.

Keystroke.com (www.keystrokenet.com/mortgage/homefinance/buying/fico_score.html) explains how FICO scoring is an automated process used to speed up the evaluation of credit reports. Use Keystroke's Credit Rater to assess your credit quality score online.

FICO scores range from 365 to 840 points. The lenders believe that the higher your FICO score, the less borrower risk. A FICO score of 660 or higher is considered "A" credit; "B" credit usually starts at 620. Credit scores of "B," "C," and "D" are considered impaired, sub-prime, damaged, or blemished.

Improving your FICO score

Some lenders reduce your interest rate by one-quarter of a point if your FICO score is between 700 and

724. Other lenders establish a base rate, then add on costs for borrowers with lower FICO scores. There are also sub-prime lenders that specialize in loans to "B" and "C" level borrowers. Of course, these loans have a higher interest rate than those to "A" level or prime borrowers. You will want to get more than one quote on your interest rate, if possible, to make sure you are getting a competitive interest rate.

Don't despair if you have a low FICO score. There are some compensating factors for low FICO scores, such as the following:

- A larger down payment.

- Low debt-to-income ratios.

- An excellent history of saving money.

- Reasonable explanations for items that negatively impact your credit history. For example, you may have had a divorce, been sick for a long time, or been laid off of work for a while before getting back on your feet. If you have a bankruptcy in your past, lenders look at when the bankruptcy was discharged and the kind of credit you have reestablished since then.

As stated earlier, each credit rating agency scoring system is slightly different. However, there are some general rules to improving your credit score. Table 2.3 shows the 15 top things that impact your credit score and result in a low credit score. Getting a perfect score on any of the items listed in Table 2.3 can significantly improve your likelihood of loan approval.

Unofficially...
Credit reports and scores aren't always accurate. For example, one woman had a foreclosure in her recent credit history but still received a FICO score of 728. Additionally, credit agencies can be slow in removing negative time-sensitive entries and incorrect information. Scores may also account for one-time occurrences, such as a change in your financial situation due to a job loss, divorce, or death in the family.

Note! ➡
Adapted from
Harvest Mortgage
(www.harvest-
mortgage.com/
ficoscoring.htm),
September 23,
1999.

TABLE 2.3: DO-IT-YOURSELF CREDIT REPAIR

Code Description	Equifax	Trans Union	Experian
Too few accounts currently paid as agreed	19	19	19
Time since derogatory public record or collection	20	20	20
Amount past due on accounts	21	21	21
Serious delinquent derogatory public record of collection filed	22	22	22
Too many bank or national revolving accounts with balances	23	N/A	N/A
No recent revolving balances	24	24	24
Proportion of loan balances to loan amounts is too high	33	33	33
Lack of recent credit information	32	32	32
Date of last inquiry too recent	N/A	19	N/A
Time since account opening too short	30	30	30
Too few revolving accounts	26	N/A	26
Too many revolving accounts	N/A	26	N/A
Number of established accounts	28	28	28
No recent bank balances	N/A	28	N/A
Too few accounts with recent payment information	31	N/A	31

Correcting errors on your credit report

When you review your credit report, check for any errors. If you find inaccuracies, look at the last page of the credit report for instructions on how to correct the errors. Some errors can be easily fixed, such as your address, date of birth, and name of employer. Accounts that are paid up but don't belong to you should also be corrected. Accurate but negative information cannot be changed. For example, bankruptcies and foreclosures can remain on a credit report for 7 to 10 years. Information that is no longer true can be updated. For example, if bankruptcy information is still on your credit report after seven years, you can inform the credit rating agency that the notation is outdated and should be removed.

To avoid unpleasant surprises, a consumer should order a copy of his or her credit report at least once a year and have the reporting agency correct any errors. Sometimes items like an unpaid telephone bill that is over 7 years old can remain on your current credit report. You have a legal right to question any item on your credit report. If the credit bureau cannot establish the validity of the data in a reasonable period of time, the item must be removed from your credit file.

To request corrections or dispute items on your credit report, write to the credit rating agency. You don't need anyone to do this for you. Some Internet fraudsters charge up to $29 per line that they correct. Credit bureaus actually encourage consumers to correct inaccurate information and suggest that you review your credit report every three years.

The Credit Infocenter (www.creditinfocenter. com), shown below, provides good advice about your credit profile. If you are seeking more information about correcting credit problems, they are an excellent information source.

The Credit Infocenter provides a wide variety of credit advice.

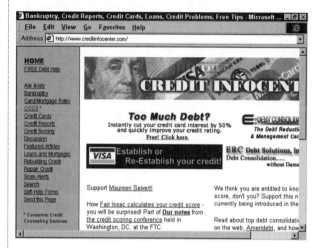

The Credit Infocenter discusses how to get approvals for legitimate credit cards and order credit reports. It also provides information on bankruptcy, credit rebuilding, and credit repair. The following is their advice for correcting errors on your credit report:

- Don't lie to credit bureaus or on credit applications. This is a crime in certain states.

- Dispute inaccurate information in writing (verbal requests don't count). Indicate exactly what is inaccurate. If you don't own the account, write that it is "not mine" or, if you paid the account on time, write to the credit bureau that it is "not late." The credit bureau is required by law to investigate your assertions.

- Provide the reason for your dispute. You must have an explanation for everything that you are claiming is inaccurate. Provide written evidence whenever possible. Copies of cancelled checks (both front and back) are always good.

■ Use inaccuracies and inconsistencies as examples of how the credit listings are wrong. You can use your two other credit reports to show the inconsistency you are reporting.

■ Become more insistent with each dispute. Don't threaten to hire an attorney, complain to the Federal Trade Commission (FTC), or your state attorney general immediately. Don't bombard the credit bureau with your disputes, but don't ignore the problem.

At the end of the credit rating agency's investigation, they must notify the other two major credit agencies about the corrections they have made. Additionally, they must provide you with a written list of their corrections and a new copy of your credit report.

If the credit bureau will not correct the inaccurate information, they should include a copy of your statement of dispute in your credit file and should enclose this attachment with future reports. If you request, the credit bureau will also provide a copy of your statement to anyone who received an old report. (There might be a fee for this service.)

Deleting credit inquiries

Every time you apply for credit, the lending company checks with a credit rating agency. This is called placing a credit *inquiry*. If you respond to a mailed credit offer, the lending company makes an inquiry. Credit inquiries remain on your record for about six months.

Too many credit inquiries indicate that you might be in financial trouble, your payment-to-income ratio might be higher than you reported, or for some other reason you are desperate for credit. If a lending company sees lots of inquiries and no one giving you credit, they might not want to give you credit either.

To erase inquiries, order credit reports from all three of the credit rating agencies. The inquiries are listed at the end of the report. Some are promotional and don't mean anything to lending companies, some are legitimate inquires that you authorized, and some could be from some unknown origin that you did not authorize. To erase inquiries from an unknown origin, find the address of each unauthorized inquirer. Experian reports list the inquirers' addresses. The other credit bureaus do not include the addresses of the inquirers in their reports; contact the credit rating agency that lists the inquirer you want to contact. Write a letter to each organization that you did not authorize.

Your letter will challenge whether the inquiring entity had the proper authorization to obtain your credit report. Ask the inquiring organization to remove their inquiry from your credit report. Send the letter by certified mail. Ask for verification that the inquiry was removed. State that if they did have your permission to please present proof.

If you don't get a response within 30 days, send another certified, return-receipt letter and demand a response. Not all your inquiries may be removed, but the majority should be.

To stop unwanted inquiries in the future, there are several approaches. You can contact an "opt-out program" by calling 1-888-567-8688. You may request to be removed from the credit reporting agencies' lists to receive non-requested solicitations for credit cards and other lending offers. This can be done with a two-year renewal process, or one could opt-out indefinitely. To get off direct mailing lists, write to Direct Marketing Association, Mail Preference Service, P.O. Box 9008, Farmingdale, NY 11735, and request that your name be removed from unsolicited mailing lists.

Getting financial help

The following table is the "You Know You're in Trouble If..." checklist. If you check off any one of these seven items, you might be headed for a serious debt problem. If you answer "yes" to several of these questions, you need to resolve your financial problems as soon as possible.

THE "YOU KNOW YOU'RE IN TROUBLE IF..." CHECKLIST

☐ You bounce checks on a fairly regular basis.

☐ You can only afford to make your minimum monthly payments.

☐ You don't know exactly how much money you owe.

☐ You have more than 10 department store, gas company, and bank credit cards.

☐ You have to ask a relative or a friend to co-sign a loan.

☐ You take cash advances on one credit card to make payments on another.

☐ Your monthly credit card and installment loan payments are greater than 20 percent of your after-tax income.

Getting help with your credit problems

There are many advantages to using credit. Credit can enhance your lifestyle by making buying quicker and more convenient. It can even establish a credit history so you can obtain a loan for a large-ticket item like a home. The major disadvantage of credit is that you commit your future earnings to paying finance charges and other fees. Also, credit cards can get lost or stolen and can make spending too easy. If you have credit problems, you can end up with a poor credit history, the inability to pay creditors, and possibly bankruptcy.

There is no formula to determine what amount of credit is right for you. However, you always have the choice of using credit or cash. If you use cash, you have to save until you can afford the item. If you use credit, you get your purchase immediately, but make payments and pay finance charges with your future income.

Usually, credit problems can be easily fixed. With a checking account and a combination of one or two secured credit cards, you can often build a good track record in 12 to 18 months that will allow you to get an unsecured credit card. For people who have damaged credit, it could take 18 to 36 months to restore credit.

Realizing that you have a credit problem is the first step in getting control of your finances. The National Foundation for Consumer Credit (www.nfcc.org) is a not-for-profit organization that provides free professional counseling and some low-cost services, including budget counseling, debt management planning, educational services, housing counseling, and counseling by phone and mail.

Bright Idea
If you need some help in getting your finances under control, avoid "credit repair" kits and advisors that charge upfront fees. Seek not-for-profit organizations like Debt Counselors of America (www.dca.org) for offline and online help.

The National Foundation for Consumer Credit also has debt management counseling to help you determine how much you really can afford to pay on your bills. They will assist you in arranging affordable repayment plans that creditors will accept and can help you develop a personalized budget that meets your needs.

Avoiding getting into credit trouble

The Better Business Bureau (www.bbb.org/alerts/ credicorp.html), shown below, provides the following advice to individuals who are considering credit card offers:

- If you have a poor credit history, be skeptical of companies that offer you a preapproved card without checking with a credit bureau.

- Avoid offers for a "guaranteed" MasterCard or Visa. These offers usually require upfront fees for a secured credit card. All you might get for your money is a list of telephone numbers— usually 900 numbers, so they're not even free calls—for banks that issue secured cards.

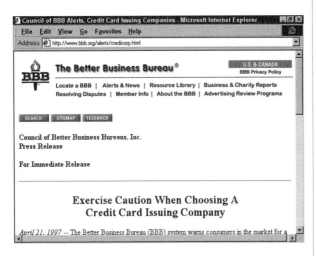

The Better Business Bureau can show you how to avoid credit repair scams.

- Be certain you understand the terms of the credit card (interest rates, annual fees, grace period, minimum payments, and credit limit).

- Don't sign anything until you are certain of all the facts. If the company does not provide you with a full explanation, walk away from the offer and go to another issuer.

- Determine if the card is a "general purpose" card or only good for merchandise in the issuer's store or catalog.

- Check with the Better Business Bureau to find any complaints against the issuing company.

Just the facts

- You can use the Internet to track your personal finances to be ready to purchase a home this year or in the near future.

- The Internet provides many online sources to assist you in determining how much you can afford to pay for a home.

- Most mortgages are underwritten using credit-scoring formulas.

- There are many things you can do to improve your credit score.

- Use online tools to evaluate your creditworthiness and to get financial help.

GET THE SCOOP ON...
The characteristics of typical homeowners
▪ Does your financial profile meet the test for
home ownership? ▪ The rent vs. buy dilemma
▪ Determining the price range you can
really afford

Is Now the Right Time to Buy a Home?

Chapter 3

The Internet can help you make what might be the biggest financial decision of your life—whether or not to purchase a home. The Web provides vast amounts of information on selecting and financing your dream home. In this chapter, you'll see how savvy homebuyers look at their finances and the market before buying. You'll also learn how changes in your personal and financial situation have to be considered when you are shopping for your dream home.

You'll be able to find online tools for analyzing the rent vs. buy decision and calculating how much you can afford for a home. If you prefer to use pen and paper, you can use the included worksheets to figure out if you're carrying too much debt, sort out your housing needs and wants, and determine the maximum monthly payment you can afford. Armed with these tools, you can go online for home loan preapprovals and prequalifications to speed up the home buying process.

Financial profiles of homeowners

In the United States, home ownership is at an all-time high. According to the U.S. Department of Urban Housing and Development (HUD), nearly half of all central city dwellers and about 70 percent of suburban residents currently own homes. Low interest rates and affordable housing have spurred this increase.

Not only are there more American homeowners than ever before, but the demographics of the typical homeowner have changed. Recent studies indicate the following:

- About 66 percent of all naturalized U.S. citizens own homes. In contrast, about 33 percent of the individuals awaiting citizenship own homes.

- More single people than ever are buying homes. Both men and women are marrying later in life. They have careers that provide the resources for purchasing homes.

- If you're married, home ownership appears to be within your reach sooner and more often than if you're single, regardless of whether you are a U.S. citizen or not.

- Many home purchasers are looking for houses that can accommodate their technological needs, including home offices.

According to Newsday.com writer Kenneth Harney, in his column "Nations Housing" (August 1998), as you might expect, older homeowners are more likely than younger homeowners to be mortgage-free. Homeowners in the western states are more likely to carry a mortgage than in other places in the nation. The higher your income and education, the more likely you are not to have a mortgage. Harney provides the following information:

- Nearly 40 percent of all homeowners have no mortgage debt whatsoever—no first deed of trust, no home equity line, no second mortgage.

- Around 38 percent of homeowners use home equity lines of credit to buy a car. Other uses for home equity lines of credit include consolidating credit card debt and paying off medical bills. However, the majority of homeowners use their equity lines for home improvements.

- About 5 percent of homeowners with mortgages have second mortgages. These individuals state that the tax deductibility of their loans is the big attraction. About 40 percent of homeowners with second mortgages use the money to consolidate credit card debt, and about 20 percent buy a car.

Where do you stand?

There are many reasons for wanting to buy a home, and your profile might or might not be different from those of the homeowners just mentioned. Some changes in your financial and personal circumstances that could affect the timing of your home buying might include the following:

- You have to relocate due to a job change.

- You have just saved enough for a down payment.

- Your family got bigger (or smaller) and you need more (or less) room.

- You need a house that has one level or other features that can accommodate your or an elderly parent's physical disabilities.

Moneysaver
Although the tax savings may seem attractive when you use a home equity or second mortgage loan to pay for a car, there is one drawback: You'll pay interest on your loan for 10 or 15 years, and the car will likely be long gone by the time you've finished paying for it. To avoid this problem, you should pay it back in the normal length of time you would pay back a car loan—3 to 5 years. You will get the advantage of the tax deduction of interest on the mortgage loan and possibly a lower interest rate.

Moneysaver
Although personal factors may make you inclined to forget general market conditions, don't act hastily. Home buying is also an investment. If your personal situation again changes quickly, you may discover that selling your property will put a dent in your wallet due to repairing the property, commissions, and closing costs.

- You have just been promoted and can afford a bigger house.

If you're trying to decide if now is the best time to buy a house, you'll need to consider your personal financial profile and the real estate market. These areas are discussed in the following sections.

Looking at your finances

Not considering the real estate market and other factors, but just looking at your finances, now is a good time to buy if you meet the following criteria:

- Due to your tax bracket, you are paying an excessive amount of taxes and need a tax break. Mortgage interest is deductible, and that can make home ownership a viable option.

- You can invest in your home long enough to counteract the transaction costs involved in buying and selling, which is generally between three and five years. If you don't stay in the house long enough for appreciation to cover your transaction costs, you'll lose money.

- You can easily handle property taxes, maintenance, landscaping, and other home ownership costs, as well as dips in your home's value. (Unfortunately, these dips can last for up to 10 years.)

Looking at the market

It's always difficult to tell by analyzing the real estate market if now is the right time to buy. However, several factors can influence your decision:

- **House prices.** The real estate market moves in cycles. In a *buyers' market,* a home purchaser may buy a home that is still dropping in price.

In a *sellers' market,* homebuyers may have to pay more than the fair market value of a home because of consumer demand, because there are more buyers than houses for sale. If you purchase at the beginning of an upward-moving market, your home may be worth more next year than this year. However, if you purchase near the top of an upward market, when the market declines, your home will be worth less than what you paid.

Unofficially...
Pay attention to your local real estate market. Housing markets are regional. This means that prices may be up in Illinois and down in California. National statistics aren't always very helpful when judging the market trend in your local area.

- **Annual timing.** Usually home sales are lowest in the fall and winter, especially between the Thanksgiving and Christmas holidays. Home sellers who list their homes or keep their homes listed during this time are frequently desperate to sell, so generally the best time to make an offer is in December. Spring and early summer months are the peak selling months: About 30 to 35 percent of all homes sold in a year are sold between April and June.

- **Interest rates.** When purchasing a home, of course you want to pay as little interest as possible. Interest rates change all the time and experts agree that it's impossible to forecast rate changes. However, you can get some help by looking at interest rate trends. Check out Realty Time's Industry Trends (www.realtimes.com/rtnews/trcpage/industry-trends.htm), where you'll discover news on the latest interest rates and home prices.

For more information on interest rate trends, check out Mortgage.com (www.mortgage-net.com/trends/). This Web site has links to articles, data on current and historical interest rates, bond rates, the Shirmery Report on interest rate movements, and the U.S. Department of Commerce, Bureau of Economic Analysis reports.

Sorting your housing needs and wants

Before beginning your search for a dream home, you need to sort out your priorities. What about parking? Can you walk up two flights of stair with groceries? Do you need a basement that has a separate entrance into the house? Do you need at least two bathrooms? Determine the parameters of your search. Housing that adds an extra hour to your commute time may cause additional stress that you don't need or want.

Many homebuyers create a list of what they consider absolutely necessary in a home and what features would be nice to have (a want). Table 3.1 lists some examples of needs and wants.

Bright Idea
Over time, many of your wants can be added to a home. So if the house doesn't have a feature you want now (for example, stained glass windows in the front door), you can add or change it later.

TABLE 3.1: EXAMPLES OF NEEDS AND WANTS

Examples of Needs	Examples of Wants
Enough room for you, the family, your office, furniture, pets, and other things necessary to live comfortably	Neutral colors or specific colors for carpeting, walls, the exterior, roof, etc.
Enough bedrooms for the family and maybe a guest or two	Whirlpool in the master bathroom (unless necessary for medical reasons—then it could be considered a need)
The right number of bathrooms to accommodate your family	Hardwood floors in specific rooms or throughout the house
An eat-in kitchen	Bay windows or special window treatments
Storage space (in a basement or attic) or ample closets	Built-in bar or entertainment center
A backyard or enough room on your lot so the children can play outside	Brass lighting fixtures, faucets, door handles, etc.
The ability to adapt the house to the handicapped	Skylights

Examples of Needs	Examples of Wants
Central heating and air conditioning	Swimming pool
A garage	Built-in bookshelves
Close to the school you want your children to attend	A good view

Housing options

The following is a list of the most popular types of homes available. When you have compared your selection criteria to the types of housing available, you'll have a better idea of the right type of home for you:

- **Single-family residences** or dwellings are defined as one home per lot. This is the most typical kind of property. Single-family dwellings can be one-, two-, or three-story buildings that are completely separated from any adjacent housing. These freestanding buildings are often surrounded by a front- and backyard. Homeowners are responsible for all landscaping, repairs, maintenance, and improvements. Generally, existing homes maintain their market value and often increase in value over the years. Single-family homes offer homeowners the greatest amount of ownership and control, but are frequently the most expensive housing option.

- Duplexes, triplexes, attached, or cluster housing arrangements are sometimes called **multi-family homes.** Often this type of housing is selected by first-time homebuyers. (The rental income can help offset the cost of the home.) Veterans Administration (VA) and Federal Housing Administration (FHA) loans can be used for multi-family homes with up to four units if the buyer occupies one of the units. The disadvantage is that you are easily accessible for maintenance requests at inconvenient times.

■ **Condominiums,** sometimes called condos, are very different from single-family homes. Homebuyers own "from the plaster in" as in a single-family home, but the exterior, landscaping, roofs, etc. are considered common elements. A homeowners association oversees these items. Your condominium fees cover the cost of insurance, taxes, repairs, and maintenance on common elements. Condominiums are generally less expensive than single-family dwellings, but in some situations, condominium fees can be higher than your mortgage.

One advantage of condos is that owners don't have to spend leisure time with home maintenance and landscaping. However, owners can't make any major changes to their homes without approval of the condominium's board of directors. The disadvantage of condos is that their value is slower to rise than single-family homes. In a soft or sluggish real estate market, the value of a condo may even decrease. In some areas of the nation, the condo may be difficult to sell because more people want to rent them than own them. Additionally, the condominium association has the right to refuse a buyer if you decide to sell your unit.

■ **Co-ops** are cooperative apartment buildings that are often located in large cities that have a housing shortage. Here the buyer purchases shares in a corporation that owns the whole apartment building and receives a lease to his or her own apartment. A board of directors supervises the management of the building. Maintenance charges are included in your share of the overall mortgage on the building.

Because a corporation owns them, co-ops are more selective about who lives there than the other housing options. However, this selectivity can sometimes be an advantage. Where else can you have a say in selecting your neighbors?

■ **Townhouses** are owned by individuals, but have shared walls to other units. Often townhouses have two or three levels and a small front- or backyard. In general, townhouses are less expensive than single-family dwellings, but they have less privacy. Townhouses may also have a homeowners association that contracts for items like garbage removal or snow removal for the entire group of townhouses. Of course, all services involve fees, so find out how much it will be before you buy.

When selecting your new home, it's wise to keep a few things in mind. A large percentage of homeowners sell their homes after five years. This means that when you select a housing type, you should also consider its resale value. Realtor.com (www.realtor.com) provides these suggestions:

■ The most popular single-family home has three bedrooms and two baths.

■ One-bedroom condominiums are harder to sell than two-bedroom condominiums.

Bright Idea
There are many housing options and home styles. The *Chicago Tribune* has a style of homes index at chitrib. webpoint.com/ homes/gloss_hs. htm. To choose a style, click on the name of the style that interests you. A sample drawing of the home style and a definition will then appear.

- Two-bedroom/single-bath homes are harder to sell than three-bedroom homes with two baths.

- Houses on very busy streets or next to commercial buildings are often harder to sell and may sell for less money.

In addition to these housing options, you may have other special requirements, such as needing space and facilities for someone who is physically handicapped, a senior citizen, or someone with a learning disability. Here are some samples of available online resources for out-of-the-ordinary housing requirements:

California Department of Developmental Services (dds.cahwnet.gov/ah01.htm) provides online information for individuals with developmental disabilities who want to purchase their own homes. This organization also provides assistance to individuals with any type of disability who are looking for a home to rent or buy.

American Association of Homes and Services for the Aging (www.aahsa.org) provides tips on choosing facilities and services for consumers and family caregivers. The Web site provides a searchable directory, up-to-date reports, insurance, financing, technology, and more.

HUD for People with Disabilities (www.hud/gov/disabled.html), an agency of the U.S. Department of Housing and Urban Development (HUD), provides information on government-sponsored initiatives, news, resources, general information, and related links. This Web site is an excellent starting place to find out about the HUD assistance programs for the disabled or elderly.

Rent or buy?

There are many reasons that purchasing a home may be in your best financial interest, though two stand head and shoulders above all the others. First, you can deduct the annual amount of mortgage interest you pay from your income tax bill. Second, the equity in your home may appreciate at a faster rate than your other investments (that is, if inflation doesn't increase faster than your home's value).

However, there are also costs involved in owning that renters do not face. According to the research conducted by the National Multi Housing Council (www.nmhc.org), an apartment industry organization shown below, many first-time homebuyers fail to understand the total costs of home ownership, including property taxes, utility bills, and home maintenance and repair costs. Some industry professionals estimate that for every $1.00 paid for housing by a renter, a homeowner pays $1.50.

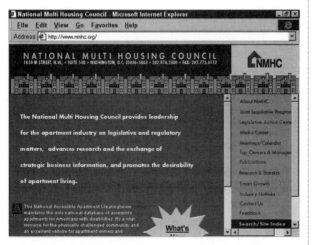

The National Multi Housing Council is a non-profit organization that provides useful research and statistics on renting.

The high cost of housing and low appreciation rate of residential real estate in some areas of the country may make home ownership a poor investment. Recent studies indicate that some wealthy people in America rent their primary homes and own vacation property in areas where the cost of living is relatively low, such as Arkansas or Montana.

Why rent?

Owning a home, as I've said, can be expensive. Home ownership involves paying a mortgage, maintenance costs, and property taxes. Transaction fees are also added to the mix. This is the cost of real estate agent commissions, escrow fees, title insurance, transfer tax fees, and loan origination charges (which include prepaid interest, points, and appraisal fees). Normally these costs are amortized over the time you live in your home. If you plan to stay in your house for 20 years, the transaction expenses are low. If you only stay in your house for a few years, these expenses are high.

Another concern is the amount of cash paid as a down payment. If you wisely invest your down payment money in the stock market, your investments may appreciate at a higher rate than if you invest the money in the equity of your home. Housing prices fluctuate over time. The shorter the ownership period, the more likely you'll be forced to sell in a less-than-perfect market and lose money on your investment.

There are several reasons why home buying may not be for you:

- If you plan to move in the next three to five years, you may be better off renting. The costs of buying and selling a house can make it an expensive proposition.

- Renting might make more sense financially: Your current rent might be especially inexpensive, and you have no property taxes or hefty flood and environmental insurance premiums.

- Home ownership means that you are responsible for landscaping, home maintenance, and repair. As a homeowner you can be subject to surprise bills, such as needing a new water heater or furnace.

- If housing prices are declining or level in your geographic area and you buy now, you may pay more than what the house will be worth in the near future.

Why buy?

When you buy a home, you can do anything you like to it. For example, you are free to paint the walls black or install a purple countertop in the kitchen if that's what you want. The personal satisfaction that is part of home ownership can be your best reward for buying a home. Additionally, buying a home can increase your net worth in three ways:

- The value of your home may increase with the rate of inflation.

- With every monthly payment, your home becomes a source of emergency cash (in the form of an equity loan) for family emergencies, college tuition, etc. Additionally, you don't have to sell your home to take advantage of its profit.

- The mortgage interest you pay is deductible when preparing your income taxes. This can lead to substantial savings.

As you can see, for many individuals, home ownership is often their largest asset.

The math aspects of the rent vs. buy decision

Sometimes it's useful to calculate the price of a house you can afford. You never know when a home ownership opportunity may come your way. For example, you may be offered a job in another part of the country and your company will pay for the down payment on a new home. Or one of your relatives may want to move and sell his or her house to a family member. Knowing what you can afford can help you make a financial decision about home ownership.

Remember that you can deduct the mortgage interest and many of the closing costs you'll pay. For more information on tax savings, see Chapter 11, "Costs and Tax Benefits Associated with Buying a Home."

Let's look at a more sophisticated way to calculate the financial aspects of your rent vs. buy decision. The Internet offers many rent vs. buy online calculators. The online calculator at the Financenter provides serious homebuyers with immediate results, graphs, and an easy-to-understand explanation of what the results mean. Start out at the Financenter Web page (www.financenter.com), and then follow these steps:

1. Click on Homes.

2. From the ClickCalcs list, select Am I Better Off Renting? Click on ClickCalcs.

3. Enter all the values the page asks for, such as your rent amount, rent-related expenses, home purchase price, and home loan–related costs.

4. Click on Results.

On the next page you'll see your results. The calculator provides charts of the total cost at loan

Unofficially...
When I used Financenter to compare the average rental rate for my type of home to my mortgage rate, I discovered that the rental was cheaper than my mortgage rate. Further analyses indicated that owning was better only if my loan's interest rate was 2 percent less than it currently is.

payoff or home sale, the total cost at various appreciation rates, and shows exactly what owning will
cost you over the holding period in today's dollars.
Total tax savings are calculated, as are maintenance
costs, selling price, equity upon sale, and selling
costs. A monthly comparison of principal and interest payments, taxes, insurance, and mortgage insurance are derived. This is compared to your rental
rate. (Click on Explanation for a narrative of your
results.)

You can find similar rent vs. buy online calculators at the following sites:

> *QuickenMortgage.com* (www.quickenmortgage.
> com) can give you a general idea of whether
> you should rent or buy. At the homepage,
> click on the hyperlink Rent vs. Buy. This
> handy online calculator only requires a few
> inputs: your monthly rent, purchase price of
> your dream home, down payment amount,
> your pre-tax income, how long you plan to
> live in the house, and your tax filing status.

> *Homefair* (www.homefair.com) has articles and
> online calculators to provide information and
> ideas for the prospective first-time home-
> buyer to consider. At the homepage, click on
> Buying Your First Home. Next you'll see a
> page with many tools. Click on the Rent vs.
> Buy hyperlink and follow the instructions.

Setting a realistic price range

You can roughly figure that you can afford to buy a
house that is between two and a half to three times
your annual salary. Each lender develops its own
specific credit policies, but all lenders use *qualifying
ratios* to determine how much money to loan

you. Most lenders (except for the VA) do not grant loans to borrowers who have debt (house payments and personal long-term debt) in excess of 36 percent of their gross income. However, a lender might be lenient about the qualifying ratios if you make a large down payment. Table 3.2 shows the debt qualification ratios for conventional and FHA home loans. (For more information, see Chapter 2, "Creating a Financial Game Plan.")

TABLE 3.2: QUALIFYING FOR A CONVENTIONAL OR AN FHA LOAN

Loan Type	Home Payment as a Percentage of Gross Income	Home Payment and Long-Term Debt as a Percentage of Gross Income
Conventional	26–28 percent	33–36 percent
FHA	29 percent	41 percent

For conventional loans, your monthly mortgage payment should not exceed 26 to 28 percent of your household gross monthly income. For FHA loans, your monthly mortgage payment should not exceed 29 percent of your household gross monthly income. (These guidelines may be more lenient for low- and moderate-income families.) So, for a conventional loan, if your total household gross monthly income is $5,000, you could afford a monthly mortgage payment of $1,400 ($5,000 × .28). For an FHA loan, you could afford a monthly mortgage payment of $1,450 ($5,000 × .29).

Next, you need to consider your monthly housing costs and any debt that requires payments longer than 11 months. All long-term monthly expenses (car loan payments, student loan payments, revolving or installment credit), monthly expenses, and your monthly mortgage payment (with property taxes, utilities, maintenance, and insurance) should be between 33 and 36 percent for conventional loans. So, if your gross monthly income is $5,000, your total expenses should not exceed $1,800 per month ($5,000 × .36). For FHA loans, the maximum allowable monthly housing costs and long-term debt together can't exceed 41 percent. And for an FHA loan, your total expenses should not exceed $2,050 ($5,000 × .41).

Many online calculators can assist you in determining how much of a house you can afford. For example, most online mortgage lenders have this tool. Here is a sampling of the most popular sources for this information:

> *Financenter* (www.financenter.com) offers several online calculators to assist you in your financial decision making. For example, one online calculator can help you determine how large a home loan you can afford.

Discover the home loan you can reasonably afford with HomeAdvisor.

MSN HomeAdvisor (homeadvisor.msn.com), shown above, has an online calculator called How Much Can You Borrow. It's simple to use and does all the math online.

QuickenMortgage.com (www.quickenmortgage. com) has a Home Affordability online calculator. Here, you'll get a quick idea of the home sales price and loan amount you can reasonably afford using a conventional mortgage.

Avoiding the time crunch

According to Neal Gendler, a staff writer for the *Minneapolis Star Tribune,* about one homebuyer in five is moving between metropolitan areas. The Employee Relocation Council goes on to estimate that each year corporations relocate about 125,000 households, and another 375,000 households move on their own for new jobs. The Employee Relocation Council (www.erc.org) states that a typical transferee is a 38-year old man with a median income of $55,000. Transferees usually have between several days and a week to find a new residence.

Often, getting organized and prequalified for a home loan can help lessen the time pressure trap that many homebuyers feel they are caught in. Start by getting organized. It's wise to keep all your records in one place and start a home buying file. Information you should have in the file includes the following:

- **Credit data.** Get a copy of your credit report from each of the three major credit-reporting agencies. Check for anything that might make a lender hesitate in approving a loan. If the report needs correction, start the process immediately. (See Chapter 2, "Creating a Financial Game Plan," for details on how to make corrections to your credit report.)

■ **Loan documents.** In addition to information on your current home loan(s) and car loan(s), start collecting all the data your mortgage lender will request when you complete your application. (See Chapter 7, "Online Mortgage Advice and Lending," for more information.)

■ **Real estate listings.** The Internet lists more than 1.3 million homes for sale. Start checking the home listings that are relevant to you. Print out the information that you'll need and include it in your file. (For more information, see Chapter 6, "Finding Your Dream Home Online.")

■ **Physical inspection reports.** When you are selecting a new home, make certain you have a copy of the Home Inspection Checklist with you. (See Chapter 9, "Online Help with Appraisals, Inspections, and Insurance," for how to download and print a copy of the checklist.) Collect all the inspection reports about your current home and keep them in a file. If these reports are up-to-date, they may speed up the time it takes to sell your current home.

■ **Area maps of neighborhoods that interest you.** These free neighborhood maps can save you hours of driving around. (For Internet help, see Chapter 4, "Finding a Neighborhood Next Door or Across the Country.")

■ **Residential insurance information.** Spot the best insurance quotes online. This is valuable for getting a handle on the housing expenses for your new house. (For more details, see Chapter 7, "Online Mortgage Advice and Lending.")

Just the facts

- The right time to purchase a house depends on your financial position and your local real estate market.

- To improve your decision making, make two lists: one that includes your housing needs and one with your housing wants.

- Before you decide if you should buy a house, check your personal situation using one of the Internet's rent vs. buy calculators.

- You can avoid running into a time crunch by starting a home buying file and collecting the data your lender will require.

Shopping for a Home Without Leaving Your Computer

PART II

GET THE SCOOP ON...
The U.S. regions with the most possibilities
▪ Determining which state and city are best for
you ▪ Using online cost-of-living calculators
▪ The best neighborhood for your situation

Finding a Neighborhood Next Door or Across the Country

Chapter 4

Today, more Americans own homes than ever before. A strong economy, low mortgage rates, and affordable housing mean that now is the time to start preparing to purchase a home or to start looking for a home. Careful online research will allow you to discover which towns have the strongest job growth and the most reasonable house prices.

I'm certain you have heard this before and you're likely to hear it again as you research the optimum place to live: In real estate, what matters most is location, location, location (with affordability thrown in for good measure). However, location, location, location means something different to each person. For example, some individuals will only consider living in the country, while others like the hustle and bustle of big cities.

Bright Idea
The Internet is not limited to U.S. neighborhood finders, employment trends, housing, and economic information. If you plan to relocate to a foreign country, you can still research your options online. For example, check out the Country Commercial Guides (www.state.gov/sss/about_state/business/com_guides/omdex/html).

One of the best ways to begin the search for your dream home is to start your research on the Internet. This chapter will guide you to the most useful articles and reports about the best regions, states, cities, and neighborhoods in which to live.

Nationwide and regional housing trends

The National Association of Realtors (NAR) points out that because of the current economic expansion and low unemployment and mortgage rates, now is an excellent time for individuals to find their fortunes in another area of the city they currently live in, in the next town, or even in the next state.

The NAR surveyed all 50 states in the nation. In 1998, it reported that the five states that experienced the greatest increases in housing prices were Michigan, South Dakota, Nebraska, Massachusetts, and Kentucky. These price increases ranged from 9 to 10 percent. The five states with the lowest median price increases were New Mexico, Maryland, Delaware, Vermont, and Hawaii, with the first four states only increasing around 2 percent and Hawaiian home prices actually decreasing 2 percent.

Overall, sales of homes hit an all-time high in 1998, with nearly 5 million single-family homes sold. In the first quarter of 1999, nearly 2 million units were sold. By the year 2000, the NAR expects to see over 5 million existing homes sold, and nearly 2 million new homes are projected to be built.

According to Realty Times (www.realtimes.com/rtnews/rtcpages/industrytrends.htm), housing prices vary from region to region. Table 4.1 illustrates the differences in housing prices for the four regions into which Realty Times divides the nation. Housing statistics for these areas indicate that the most expensive region to live in is the West, that home prices are increasing the fastest in the Midwest, and that more homes are selling in the South than in any other area of the country.

TABLE 4.1: REGIONAL HOUSING TRENDS AND YOUR STANDARD OF LIVING

Region	Average Single-Family Dwelling Costs (per Unit)	1998 Sales Price Increase (Percentage)	Units Sold (Million)
West	$166,400	1.8	1.1
South	$115,700	4.1	1.97
Midwest	$115,400	7.1	1.12
Northeast	$155,300	6.6	0.72

← **Note!**
Source: Realty Times (realtimes.com/rtnews/rtcpages/industrytrends.htm), November 16, 1999.

In their December 2, 1999, report, the Office of Federal Housing Enterprise Oversight (www.ofheo.gov) notes that due to the predicted strength of the New England economy, the New England region is the strongest in the nation. Over the past year, Massachusetts homes have appreciated at a rate of 7.9 percent, and over 23.3 percent in the past five years.

For more online information about national and regional housing trends, see these sites:

> *The Bureau of Economic Analysis* (www.bea.doc.gov) is an agency of the U.S. Department of Commerce, considered the nation's economic accountant. Among other things, this site offers regional data, articles, and surveys, and allows you to compare this data to national gross domestic product, industry, and income/wealth data.

> *Economic Statistics Briefing Room* (www.whitehouse.gov/fsbr/employment.html) provides statistical snapshots of the civilian labor force, unemployment, employees on

Unofficially...
Since 1980, homes in Massachusetts have appreciated 257.9 percent. However, this past performance does not predict future appreciation values.

Bright Idea
Recent legisla-
tion requires the
federal govern-
ment to make
its research
available to the
public. After all,
you and other
taxpayers have
paid for it. Much
of this informa-
tion is posted on
the Internet,
which means
that you can
now access high-
level, quality
housing informa-
tion 24 hours
a day, seven
days a week.

non-farm payrolls, average weekly hours, average hourly earnings, employment cost index, and productivity.

Federal Reserve Bank of Boston Regional Economic Information Links (www.bos.frb.org/economic/ reglink.htm) provides economic data on New England.

Relocating to a different state

There are several online sources that provide an overview of the states with the fastest job growth. Many of these overviews paint a bright picture of economic growth across the nation and focus on trends in specific states. To discover the best state to live in, or to discover which states offer the highest salaries, check the median income by state at the U.S. Census Bureau (www.census.gov/hhes/income/ income98/in98med.html). You can also find information about all 50 states and all the counties and sizable cities in them at Yahoo! (www.yahoo.com)— simply type in the state or city name. For insights and economic briefs about job gains, see the Bank of America Economic Analysis and Research Web site (corp.bankofamerica.com/research/e_ economic_analysis_research.html).

State governments and the city and town chambers of commerce sponsor many Web sites that provide information on relocating to specific states and cities. The following are a few examples of what you'll find:

> *Homefinders Inc. Real Estate* (www.nwdir.com/ relo.htm), located in Washington state, includes market analyses of any home within the United States. You'll also find information

about communities, price trends, neighborhoods, and crime trends. The cost is approximately $10 for comparable home sales in the
area.

Employment & Unemployment (www.labor.state.
ak.us/research/research.htm), located in
Alaska, provides information on Alaska's
largest employers, economic snapshots of the
state, and offers state profiles and overviews,
employment forecasts, employment earnings
and summary reports, occupational outlook
surveys, unemployment rates, and more.

Iowa Economy (www.state.ia.us/trends) provides employment reports, state industry
trends, worker data, consumer data, business
data, and farm economic data. For example,
to demonstrate how the state is growing, at
this Web site you'll learn that in the first
quarter of 1999, existing Iowa home sales
were 56,400, compared to 55,000 sold in the
same quarter in 1998.

Nebraska Databook & Economic Trends (info.
ded.state.ne.us), located in Nebraska,
provides links to the Nebraska Quarterly
Business Condition Survey, recent Nebraska
economic trends (revised monthly),
Nebraska's economic performance (annual
report), and other selected state and local
statistics.

Doing Business in Rhode Island (www.riedc.
com/start.html) provides information about
Rhode Island business programs, job training, economic trend information, taxes, business incentives, and more.

Finding the right city

Your research may indicate the best area of the
nation to live in and which state has the best employment opportunities. Now it's time to discover which
city is best for your personal situation. Don't feel
alone in your search—each year thousands of individuals relocate with hopes of finding better jobs
and an improved lifestyle in another city. The U.S.
Bureau of Labor Statistics Regional Information
(www.bls.gov/regnhome.htm), shown below, divides
the nation into 10 regions. At this site you can find
information about employment and unemployment, prices and living conditions, compensation
and working conditions in a specific city. For example, you may discover that individuals in your field
are paid 10 percent more than in another city and
the cost of living is lower. In this situation, you
might be able to give yourself a raise by moving to a
new city.

Careful research helps you discover which cities
have particularly strong job growth. You may have to

If you're thinking
about relocating
to find better
job opportuni-
ties, the Bureau
of Labor Sta-
tistics can tell
you where you'll
be paid the most
for your job
skills.

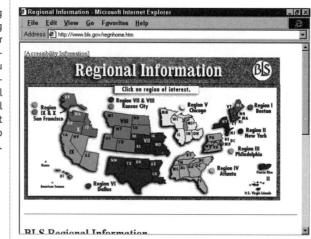

sort through a lot of statistics to find exactly what
you're looking for, but the payoff can be worth it
(and it's free). Here are some places to get started:

> For information about the community you
> are planning to move to, see *RPS* (www.
> rpsrelocation.com/community.htm), which
> is an online relocation resource. This Web
> site has a city comparison tool that lets you
> analyze over 1,000 U.S. cities with side-by-side
> comparisons in 30 categories.

> *The Bureau of Labor Statistics* (stats.bls.gov/
> newrels.htm) provides monthly information
> about employment in more than 300 metro-
> politan areas. This information includes the
> most recent statistics for civilian labor and
> is divided by state and metropolitan area.
> For each metropolitan area, you'll see
> employment statistics for the last two months
> compared to the same months for the
> previous year.

> To find out which locality has the fastest job
> growth, check out the *Regional Financial
> Association* (RFA), which offers fee-based
> information about metropolitan areas and
> cities. RFA demonstrates its products at www.
> rfa.com/free.stm. Discover the highest-city
> ranking of civilian employment, which metro-
> politan areas are at their business cycle peaks,
> and what the probability is of an area-based
> recession.

Comparing the cost of living for different cities

While a given city might offer more jobs with higher
salaries and new opportunities, it also might have
a higher cost of living. For example, according to

Unofficially...
Recently, a major moving company completed a customer study. The results indicated that 53 percent of job candidates who rejected relocation offers did so because they could not reconcile cost-of-living differences with what their employer proposed to pay.

RFA (www.rfa.com), the average home in San Jose, California, costs more than $370,000. In Santa Fe, New Mexico, the average cost for a house is $173,000. So if you're planning to move from Santa Fe to San Jose to take a job that offers a terrific new salary, you might end up using all your extra money to finance your new home.

The differences in the cost of housing from one area to another aren't the only things to be concerned about. For example, the amount of income tax you pay differs in various regions of the nation— seven states don't have state income taxes. Other costs vary by region and state as well, such as the costs of food and transportation, and the sales and property tax rates.

This means that when you move to a new area, you might need to make more money than in your old location to cover increased costs. On the other hand, if you move to an area where the cost of living is lower, you might find that you end up with more money in your pocket.

Small things count when you relocate. The Bureau of Labor Statistics shows that there is a significant difference in the cost of goods and services between the nation's top 25 metropolitan areas. This means that you may pay more for the things you regularly use, such as milk, gasoline, and dry cleaning.

Table 4.2 shows the results of Money.com's 12th annual survey of the best places to live in the United States. Money used 65 factors in its rankings, including measures of education, arts and culture, leisure, transportation, health, housing, the economy, weather, and safety. It indicates that San Francisco, California, is the best city to live in, with Austin, Texas and New York City, New York, as the runners-up. However, when the reporters divided the country into four sections, interviewed 512 households across the nation, and used metropolitan statistical reports to rank 300 cities, they came up with a different answer. According to this analysis, the best large cities to live in are Minneapolis, Minnesota, Washington, DC, Seattle, Washington, and Norfolk, Virginia. The best medium-sized cities are Madison, Wisconsin, Trenton, New Jersey, Boulder, Colorado, and Richmond, Virginia. The best small cities are Rochester, Minnesota, Manchester, New Hampshire, Fort Collins, Colorado, and Charlottesville, Virginia.

TABLE 4.2: THE BEST PLACES TO LIVE IN THE UNITED STATES

Location	Large City	Medium City	Small City
Midwest	Minneapolis, MN	Madison, WI	Rochester, MN
Northeast	New York, NY	Trenton, NJ	Manchester, NH
West	San Francisco, CA	Boulder, CO	Fort Collins, CO
South	Norfolk, VA	Richmond, VA	Charlottesville, VA

← Note!
Source: Money.com (www.pathfinder.com/money/depts/real_estate/bestplaces/winners.html), November 17, 1999.

Using online cost-of-living calculators

You can use online cost-of-living calculators to accurately compare cost-of-living differences between U.S. cities and negotiate a mutually acceptable compensation match-up. The Internet offers a variety of online salary comparison calculators. Some of the best are:

DataMasters (www.datamasters.com) includes the 1999 U.S. cost-of-living comparisons for 399 U.S. cities and metropolitan areas. Enter the state you currently live in. Select the state you plan to move to and click Go! to Step 2. Select your present city and the city you plan to move to. Enter your current salary or a

Bright Idea
You can contact
your alumni
association to
obtain the
names of alumni
living in the
area you're
considering.
Telephone them,
introduce your-
self, and ask
them a few ques-
tions about
where they live.
Don't worry
about appearing
too nosy. Most
people are will-
ing to share
their knowledge
about their
neighborhood.

hypothetical salary amount. Click Go! Perform Analysis. For example, when I compared Richmond, Virginia, to Baltimore, Maryland, using a hypothetical salary of $100,000, the results indicated that in Richmond, the hypothetical $100,000 was equivalent to a salary of $93,990 in Baltimore. (That's about a 6 percent decrease in buying power. Therefore, if someone living in Richmond only received a 5 percent raise, they would lose money by taking the job offer and moving to Baltimore.)

Homefair (www.homefair.com/homefair/ cmr/salcalc.html) allows you to enter the country and state you are from, as well as the country and state to which you're thinking of relocating. Click on Show Cities and select the appropriate cities. Click Calculate to see how the two cities compare.

Money.com (www.homefair.com/calc/ citypick.html) lets you enter the city you are moving from and the city you are planning to move to. Enter your current salary and the salary you'll receive in your new job. Click Compare to find out if you'll be richer or poorer if you take the job offer. If you leave one salary blank, you'll discover how much you need to make in order to maintain your current standard of living.

Finding the right neighborhood

Finding the right neighborhood is often harder than finding a home that meets all your requirements. The neighborhood you select can be in the country, a city, or a suburb. The house you select in

the neighborhood is more than a building. Your
selection will become *home,* and home is a major
part of every individual's life. Where and what type
of home you purchase will affect your life for as long
as you live in your house.

Learning about a neighborhood firsthand

Neighborhood search strategies begin with your
financial resources. First, you need to select the type
of home that meets your primary needs, and then
select the best neighborhood that is within your
price range. If at all possible, you should physically
visit your prospective neighborhood. Do neighbors
take care of their property? How are the landscaping and garbage removal services? Are there any old
wrecked cars in the driveways? Enlarge the area you
are investigating. What about the area two blocks
away? How is that neighborhood? Make a second
visit after dark. Find out if the neighborhood
changes. For example, does a restaurant offer valet
parking in the office building next door? Does the
traffic pattern change?

Learning about a neighborhood online

Whether you currently live far from your prospective neighborhood and can't physically visit it or
you simply want to gather some statistics that might
help you decide which neighborhood to choose,
the Internet is there to help. Realtor.com (www.
realtor.com) recommends that you select your location, carefully choose your housing criteria, and get
detailed reports about the neighborhood. Each
neighborhood has its own personality. Here are
some factors you should consider:

- The statistical material provided is a snapshot
  of the neighborhood. This includes the

number of schools, the education and income level of the residents, crime risk, type of urbanization, access to cultural events or facilities, and average age and number of children.

■ Average home qualities include median home prices, average age of the housing, average square footage of homes in the neighborhood, and lot sizes. A neighborhood map shows how close the neighborhood is to freeways and other cities.

■ The school area information provides the names of the local schools and total number of students per school. Average SAT scores for math and verbal are compared to state and national averages. The percentages of students attending four-year and junior colleges are shown, as well as the number of National Merit Finalists per school.

■ Crime statistics are illustrated on a scale and ranked as below, average, or above the standard crime risk.

■ Educational profile statistics provide neighborhood characteristics such as level of education, level of employment in professional and other white-collar occupations, how many residents tend to be renters, and how many live in large, multi-unit dwellings.

Analyzing and understanding a neighborhood report
Neighborhood reports are offered by a number of Web sites and vary in price from free to over $25. The type and depth of information you'll receive also varies. These reports, which may be mostly statistical, can sometimes seem overwhelming. The following is designed to assist you in understanding

what all this information means so that you can
make informed decisions about your next neighborhood. (Please note that the following listing is
not comprehensive, nor is it listed in order of
importance. What's critical to one family may not
matter to another.)

- **Day care facilities.** Is your new dream home
  close to your day care provider? Does dropping
  off the children in the morning require you to
  backtrack to where you work? Many day care
  providers charge high fees for late drop-offs
  and pick-ups. If you have an additional distance to drive before and after work you may
  discover that you have to pay day care late fees.

- **Schools.** How close are the children's schools?
  Is one school close and the other far away
  from your new home? If so, this may cause
  problems for you and your spouse.

- **Transportation.** How close to your new home
  is your place of employment? An extra half-
  hour with your family may not sound like
  much now, but it can really count later on.
  How is traffic congestion in the morning and
  late afternoon? Coping with rush-hour traffic
  can add extra stress to your life.

  Is public transportation available? If you live
  in a large city and don't drive, this can be an
  important consideration when selecting a new
  home. Safe and reliable public transportation
  for teens and seniors is an important issue
  when selecting your next home. Visit the
  Bureau of Transportation Statistics (www.bts.
  gov), shown below, for more information
  about transportation.

The Bureau of
Transportation
Statistics gives
information
about the
availability of
transportation
in your new
neighborhood.

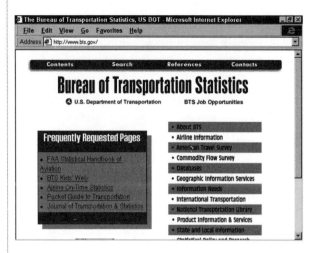

■ **Churches.** If you're active at your church, a long commute to Sunday and mid-week activities can eat up a lot of your time and a significant portion of your weekend.

Unofficially...
I had to laugh
when my hus-
band told me
that one of the
top reasons he
liked our new
home was
because it was
close to a large,
highly rated
medical facility.
He believed that
if anything went
wrong, all he had
to do was just
roll down the
hill to their
emergency room.

■ **Medical services.** How far are medical facilities from your new home? Recently, the proximity to medical services has become more and more important to the aging baby-boomer population and those individuals who are caring for their elderly parents and relatives.

■ **Crime.** Does your new neighborhood have a crime watch organization? What do your instincts tell you about the area? Do you feel safe? For more information on crime statistics, see the Bureau of Justice Statistics Sourcebook of Criminal Justice Statistics Online (www.albany.edu/sourcebook).

■ **Civic organizations.** What types of municipal services are available? In my neighborhood (Alexandria, Virginia), for example, the city landscapes the trees (this includes trimming

and adding mulch at the base), and sweeps
and lays new brick sidewalks regularly.
Additionally, there are two historic societies
that oversee homeowner maintenance and
improvements. You won't find a shiny aluminum roof in my historic neighborhood.
However, if you want the freedom to put a hot
tub in your front yard, this area might not be
for you.

■ **Homeowners associations.** Many housing
developments have homeowners fees for the
outside maintenance of houses, landscaping,
recreational facilities (such as a pool and tennis courts), and security. Membership fees
paid to homeowners associations are often
mandatory. Fees can start at reasonable
monthly prices and increase to hefty sums
over the years.

■ **Taxes.** What is the tax rate for the neighborhood? The effective tax rate is the annual
property tax bill divided by the value of the
home. Is this higher or lower than the other
homes you're considering? Also, are there any
deed limitations? Discover what they are and
how they are enforced.

■ **Shopping.** Find out where the grocery store
and shopping areas are. Can you walk to the
corner and get a quart of milk and go to the
bank? Or do you need to drive 20 miles to get
to the grocery store? For those folks who don't
drive, this is an important question. No one
wants to feel stranded.

A few of the online resources for neighborhood
reports include:

Bright Idea
Online neighbor-
hood reports
use crime informa-
tion from national
sources. This is
usually second-
hand information
that has gone
through several
organizations.
You'll get a
better idea of the
crime risk in the
neighborhood
by checking
CrimeCheck
(www.crimecheck.
com) online,
talking with
neighborhood
residents, or
checking with
the police for
any reports of
crimes in
the area.

Dataquick (www.dataquick.com) provides a variety of reports at their consumer information center:

- Homes sales reports (approximately $10) can assist you in determining your property's current market value. These reports are extensive. They include the property's address, characteristics, sales comparables, how characteristics may vary by state or county, and a sales comparables map.

- Neighborhood demographic reports (approximately $5) include property information, housing statistics, changes in the neighborhood and county since 1990, number of owner- and renter-occupied households, number of units, and when they were built. Information about people who live in the neighborhood includes median age, per capita income, median household income, education level, characteristics of the families, and types of employment since 1996. In addition, these reports provide information about shopping and public services.

- Local crime reports (approximately $5) use statistics that are determined by dividing the number of crimes into the number of people in the area to determine the ratio of crimes to people. For comparison purposes, the report includes crimes in the neighborhood, county, state, and nation.

Monster Daata.com (www.monsterdaata.com) provides four types of neighborhood reports.

The property tax assessment report (approximately $5) determines the value of your home or the one you are considering buying. The report includes the latest tax assessments, building features, valuations, and comparable sales. Comparable sales reports are approximately $5, property valuation reports are approximately $5, and a full report is approximately $9. Full reports include snapshots of up to five neighborhoods at once. Schools, demographics, lifestyle characteristics, and cost-of-living statistics are included.

For specific online information about neighborhood schools, see *2001 Beyond* (www. 2001beyond.com). Prices for a one-year subscription to their national school database vary; check the Web site for details. These lengthy reports (about 20 pages) are divided into eight sections: school directory, school overview, curriculum, upper school curriculum, interscholastic sports, upper school extracurricular, senior statistics and school awards, and personnel directory.

The *U.S. Census Bureau* (www.census.gov) provides information, surveys, and statistics on people (housing, houses sold by type of financing, current construction reports, etc.), businesses (economic surveys, foreign trade, etc.), geography, news, and hot topics. The Web site has a search engine, catalog, access tools, and links to related sites.

Fedstats (www.fedstats.gov) is a fee-based service that searches more than 70 agencies in the U.S. federal government that produce

Watch Out!
It's not always financially wise to purchase the best home in the best neighborhood. You may get a better return on your investment if you purchase the least expensive home in the most expensive neighborhood.

statistics of interest to the public. Get the
statistics you seek from agencies and special
programs.

USDA Economics and Statistics Search (usda.
mannlib.cornell.edu/usda/ess_entry.html)
contains nearly 300 reports and datasets from
the economic agencies of the U.S.
Department of Agriculture. This material covers national and international agriculture and
related topics. Almost all reports are in text
files that are time sensitive.

Just the facts

- If you move, your standard of living may
  improve or decline due to additional taxes
  (state, local, and city), elevated housing prices,
  and higher costs for goods and services.

- Online cost-of-living calculators can help you
  determine if relocating offers you financial
  benefits.

- It's important to investigate a number of neighborhood factors, whose importance depends
  on your personal situation, before making a
  decision.

- Whether you are moving across town or
  across the nation, you can use an online
  neighborhood report to evaluate your new
  neighborhood.

GET THE SCOOP ON...
What a real estate agent can do for you
■ Types of agents ■ Locating and selecting a
real estate agent ■ Evaluating your agent

Using a Real Estate Agent

Chapter 5

So you've decided to buy a home. Now you need to decide whether to find a person to help you or to go it alone. Real estate can be a very complicated business, and buying a home can be one of the most important financial decisions of your life.

A recent survey by Home Buyer Agents (www. homebuyeragents.com/presentation/slide7txt. html) indicates that many consumers know little or nothing about how to choose a real estate agent. About half of the homebuyers surveyed reported that they selected a Realtor based on a recommendation. Another 19 percent indicated that they called the agent because they saw a sign or advertisement, and 11 percent reported that the agent "found" them. The remaining 20 percent of consumers surveyed met their agents at an open house, contacted them because of a flyer or mailer, knew the agent from a previous experience, or forgot exactly how they selected the agent. Very few homebuyers interview their real estate agents.

Working with a licensed real estate agent provides you with the services of someone who specializes in this field. This chapter covers what type of real estate representation is available and helps you decide which type is right for you. You'll find pointers for selecting a real estate agent, as well as suggestions on using the Internet to find the best agent in the community you selected and online help for evaluating your real estate agent's performance.

How a real estate agent can help you

Most homebuyers start searching for a home by reading the classified ads in the weekend newspaper, checking free real estate magazines offered at grocery stores, and doing research using the Internet. Online sources like HomeWEB (www.homeweb. com), shown below, offer an industrywide network that allows homebuyers to browse through local or national listings.

HomeWEB offers free online listings of homes for sale.

Doing your research online is a good, safe way to start your house-hunting search. The more educated you are about housing, the less likely you are to make a mistake or to get involved in a fraudulent transaction. Using the Internet, you can get a good understanding of:

- Price ranges for specific neighborhoods
- The types of houses that are available
- Who the top-rated agents are in your area of interest

It's not necessary to use a real estate agent to purchase a home. It might seem that the Internet would put an end to the need for real estate agents, but the opposite has happened. The Internet has made real estate agents more important than ever; agents can advertise their access codes in newspaper ads so potential customers can see their listings and contact them by e-mail, telephone, or pager. Agents can help you leverage the information you receive over the Internet. They provide market expertise and fill in the missing information that flat Internet pictures provide.

Individuals who don't use agents often drive around the neighborhoods they want to live in, looking for "for sale" signs. (The signs usually stay up longer than the newspaper ads because there is no expense to the seller.) All this driving around can be very time-consuming. A real estate agent can often shorten the time it takes to locate the perfect house.

Real estate agents and brokers have a thorough knowledge of the real estate market in their geographical locations. They know which neighborhoods meet their client's needs and budgets. They act as intermediaries in negotiations between buyers and sellers, assist in the title search and closing

Timesaver
Studies show that individuals who research homes online visit 6 to 8 homes before purchasing. Homebuyers who rely solely on their agents often visit 12 to 21 homes before buying. This indicates that using the Internet can be a big time saver for homebuyers.

meeting, and provide homebuyers with information about real estate financing.

Good agents will listen to your needs and desires, then search through the appropriate listings of available properties from both their own listings and those of the Multiple Listing Service (MLS). The MLS includes more than 1.3 million Realtor listings. All MLS participants (both listing agents and agents for homebuyers) agree to share the real estate commissions for the home listed.

Your real estate agent will weed out the inappropriate homes in this listing. Next, he or she will probably show you several properties to get your feedback, repeating the process until you find the home that's right for you. Additionally, the agent is informed of new properties as they become available and may know about homes that are for sale by owner (FSBO).

Your real estate agent should save you time and money. Using an agent should let you view more properties than you would have access to otherwise. The following are some of the things a good agent will do for you:

- Create a profile of your needs and wants.
- Assist you in getting prequalified for a home loan. This way you'll both know how much you can afford.
- Help you find the necessary financing.
- Get details on ads you might see in the newspapers that are offered by another brokerage.
- Coordinate appointments for home showings, then drive you from one showing to another.
- Provide specific information about the community that interests you.

- Present your offer to the seller and act as intermediary for the negotiation. However, unless
the agent is a "Buyers Broker," all real estate
agents work as an agent of the seller, not the
buyer.

- Make certain that everything is ready for closing the transaction. This may include recom-
mending home inspectors, appraisers, and a
title company for the settlement, and making
sure all the local disclosures of rights and
obligations relating to the property are known
to you before the actual settlement.

It's important that you trust and feel comfortable with your agent. The Internet offers some valuable advice in this area. One example is the South
Coast Oregon Directory Real Estate Guide (www.
presys.com/shopper/cities/realeatate/rightagent.
html), which can help you find out what to do if
things don't work out and you need to hire another
agent. It can also help you understand what to
expect if things go smoothly.

Types of real estate professionals

According to the *1998–1999 Occupational Outlook
Handbook* (stats.bls.gov/oco/ocos120.htm), all U.S.
states and the District of Columbia require real
estate agents and brokers to be licensed. In general,
prospective agents must be high school graduates,
at least 18 years old, and pass a two-part written test
(national and state). There are different levels of
agents. The written examination is more comprehensive for brokers than for agents.

Overall, states require candidates for the general
sales license to complete between 30 and 90 hours
of classroom instruction. Individuals seeking broker

Unofficially...
In 1998, the
average age of
first-time home-
buyers was 32.
The average age
of a real estate
broker was 52.
This means that
real estate bro-
kers may have a
difficult time
relating to and
understanding
the needs of
their young
clients.

licenses are required to complete between 60 and 90 hours of formal training in addition to a specified amount of experience in selling real estate (generally one to three years). In some states, the requirement for selling experience is waived for the broker's license if the applicant has a bachelor's degree in real estate. Usually, state licenses must be renewed every one or two years, typically without a reexamination. Many states, however, require continuing education for license renewal.

Each state governs how real estate agents work. In brief, a real estate agent is a person licensed to negotiate and transact the sale of real estate on behalf of the property owner, unless the buyer has signed an agreement with the Realtor to act as a "Buyer's Broker." A Realtor is a member of the National Association of Realtors (NAR) and subscribes to a code of ethics and standards that is detailed at HomeAdvisor (homeadvisor.msn.com/ gettingstarted/NARCode.asp). Check out this Web site to find out what your Realtor is obligated to do, so you can accurately judge his or her performance.

The responsibilities of real estate professionals

The following is a list of the different types of real estate representation that's available. It's likely that one of these types of agents will be the best for your home buying needs:

- **Listing agent.** A listing agent has no commitment to the buyer, uses the Realtor's code of ethics mentioned earlier in this chapter, offers buying and selling assistance to clients, has access to the MLS. Assists consumers in shopping around town. Often specializes in particular areas of a city or rural area and represents the seller.

- **Subagent.** A subagent brings real estate deals to the buyer but represents the seller.

- **Dual agent.** A dual agent plays the role of mediator. The dual agent does not represent either the buyer's or the seller's interests; the objective of the dual agent is to close the deal. This means that the dual agent receives a commission from the both the buyer and the seller. (In this situation, it's difficult for the agent to be unbiased.) Currently, there are several lawsuits in progress about these dual agent activities. Therefore, hiring a dual agent may not be in the best interest of the homebuyer.

- **Buyer's agent.** Until the late 1970s, real estate agents were the legal agents of the seller. That means that even when you carefully selected an agent, the agent was still representing the seller. New estate laws allow "buyer's agents," who represent only the buyer.

  Today, there are three types of buyer's agents. In most cases, buyer's agents always act as buyer's agents, and never list properties for sale, but there are some exceptions to this. First, if the buyer's agent is unable to sell a personal listing, occasionally he or she acts as a listing agent or dual agent. Second, if a part-time buyer's agent discloses all listings to a consumer first as a seller's agent, if there is no match, he or she acts as a true buyer's agent (not as a dual agent). The buyer's agent provides the buyer with focused real estate services and is often the best representative for homebuyers.

- **Real estate broker.** A broker is licensed by the state. Most of them own or manage real estate offices; others work in the marketplace, listing, showing, and selling homes. A broker is the principal person in charge of a real estate selling office, supervising real estate agents. Other brokers in the same office are called Associate Brokers.

▪ **Real estate salesperson.** A salesperson also licensed by the state, but who works for a real estate broker. When you work with a real estate salesperson, you are also working with the firm he or she represents.

The following are some online resources for finding out more information about types of real estate agents:

The *Chicago Sun-Times* (www.suntimes.com/ realestate/homebuyingfaq1.html) has a frequently asked questions section that provides useful information about which party (sellers or buyers) agents really represent.

National Association of Exclusive Buyers Agents (www.naeba.com) has a list of questions that should be asked of any real estate agent.

The awful truth about commissions

In 1998, more than $20 billion were paid in real estate agent services. However, when consumers were surveyed, most believed they overpaid for the real estate services they received. As a general rule, the seller pays all commissions with the buyer's cash. That is, the seller includes the cost of the real estate commission in the sales price of the house. Commissions are negotiable by law and from area to area. For example, a commission may be 6 percent of the purchase price. This means that if a home sells for $120,000, the 6 percent commission is $7,200. About $3,600 (3 percent) goes to the brokerage for listing and marketing the property. The other $3,600 (3 percent) goes to the selling agent or buyer's agent for finding a buyer.

Often, uninformed consumers don't understand how commissions are paid, what services are supposed to be provided, and what value they should receive for their money. The following are a few examples of real estate professionals' services and what they typically receive in payment:

- **Builder's agent (for new construction).** This person may or may not be a licensed real estate agent (it varies by state) and gets paid a commission by the builder for every new home he or she sells. In other words, the agent is paid to move the builder's inventory as quickly as possible.

- **Limited-service broker.** This type of broker has unbundled typical brokerage services and provides a wide menu of specific services to consumers. Charges are either a flat fee or a percentage of the home's sales price for each type of service provided. Services and fees vary by geographical location.

- **Discounting broker.** This is often a new brokerage or one involved in a price war. The broker is forced to discount listings in order to attract business. Be suspicious of the real reasons behind discounted prices. You may not get the service you expect. Usually a "discount commission" means that you, as a buyer, agree that you will do certain things usually done by the real estate agent. In other words, you save money, but get less service.

Moneysaver
Don't pay fraudulent real estate fees. In real estate, there is no such thing as a referral fee. If you don't close, your real estate agent does not get a commission or a referral fee.

- **Full-service broker.** This is a typical MLS real estate agency. The company lists sales contracts, which stipulate, for example, a 6 percent commission. Usually half (3 percent) is paid to the listing brokerage, and the remaining 3 percent is paid to the buyer's real estate agent.

What to look for in an agent

It may seem that the Internet will put an end to the need for real estate agents, but the opposite has happened. Agents can help you leverage the information you receive over the Internet. They provide market expertise and fill in the missing information that flat Internet pictures provide.

It takes about three years to really understand and learn the real estate trade. Part-time agents tend to miss things that full-time professionals use to their advantage. These folks will usually be technically savvy and use computers, answering services, pagers, car phones, or assistants. Additionally, you'll want someone with expertise in a specific area. An agent who works and lives in or very near the towns that interest you is a plus. When choosing a real estate agent, there are several characteristics that you should look for:

- **Experience.** Make certain that the agent is familiar with the neighborhood and real estate market. He or she should know regional economic trends. You may need someone who has the local expertise that only long-term residents have.

- **Knowledge.** Find out if the agent is familiar with the area's schools and parks, current taxes, utilities, banks, and stores. Is he or she familiar with the required legal contracts?

How will the agent protect your interests? Does he or she have a real estate specialty (new construction, condominiums, rural properties, etc.)?

▪ **Support.** Is the agent a full-time employee of a brokerage? Is he or she an employee in a real estate company that is part of a national conglomerate? Will this affect the agent's business relationship with you?

▪ **Credentials.** Only hire a Realtor who is licensed as an agent or a broker in the correct state. The agent should show evidence of continuing education and accreditation in real estate disciplines. Some specific credentials to watch out for are:

> **CRS:** A Certified Residential Specialist is someone who has undergone a rigorous, specialized course of detailed training aimed at making residential transactions as smooth and worry-free as possible.

> **GRI:** A Graduate of the Realtors Institute is someone who has undergone an intensive period of detailed training in general real estate transactions, not just residential housing sales.

> **ABR:** An Accredited Buyers Representative is a designation of excellence in buyer representation. The Real Estate Buyer Agent Council (REBAC) of the NAR awards this designation to real estate practitioners. Individuals with this designation meet specified educational and practical experience criteria.

Licensed real estate agents or broker real estate agents are licensed by their state to help people buy and sell property. Typically, people licensed by the state must have completed courses in real estate, including coursework in real estate law, real estate financing, and listing. (A *broker* is a person licensed to own a real estate firm.)

- **Reputation.** The agent should provide references. Contact the last five or six customers and find out if the agent was responsive, thorough, professional, and demonstrated industry knowledge. Buying a home involves many significant decisions. Get the most reputable advice you can to help you make the best decisions.

In addition to establishing a rapport with agent candidates, you should interview prospective agents about their experience and availability to commit the time needed to meet your expectations. Consider yourself an employer conducting a job interview. Meet at least three candidates before hiring. The following are some of the questions you should ask:

- Does the agent have access to the MLS? It's a good idea to work with agents who utilize the MLS because you'll get access to a wider selection of homes for sale.

- Is the agent licensed? Work with agents who are registered with the local Board of Realtors. Most of these agents also belong to the NAR. This means they are bound by a code of ethics that protects you and your family.

Watch Out!
Don't let your real estate agent persuade you to buy a home you really can't afford or that doesn't meet your expectations or requirements.

■ Will the agent provide references? Ask for a list of recent buyers and sellers represented by the agent. Call them and ask about the service they received.

■ Does the agent specialize in residential rather than commercial real estate? How are the agent's fees structured? Can you have that information in writing?

■ Does the agent work primarily with buyers or sellers? How objective is the agent? Does the agent work primarily with one builder? Does he or she have a financial interest in any certain housing developments? (If so, what's in the agent's best interest may not necessarily be in *your* best interest.)

■ Is the agent familiar with the neighborhood—the schools, traffic patterns, future construction plans, etc.?

■ How will the agent assist you? How will he or she advise you of new listings, and approximately how many showings will he or she take you to each week of your search?

■ Is the candidate a full- or part-time real estate agent? Does he or she have full access to the MLS? What about access to FSBO and foreclosed properties?

■ How many buyers and sellers are currently clients of the agent? Does the agent have a self-imposed limit on the number of customers he or she can adequately represent at one time? Determine how much time the agent can commit to your needs.

■ What are a few real-life illustrations of the agent's successful negotiations? Ask the agent to provide some examples of his or her negotiating skills. What are some of the more difficult purchase agreement negotiations the agent completed?

- How does the agent close a sale? Ask the agent to demonstrate some of his or her closing tactics.

All these items are important, but they don't guarantee that the agent is a real winner. However, real estate agents who provide clear answers are more likely to be ethical and competent than others who cannot provide sufficient answers. For more online suggestions about how to choose a real estate agent, see:

The Motley Fool (www.foolcom/shouse/ findingahousestep8.htm) has suggestions about selecting the best real estate agent for your needs.

The Memphis Area Association of Realtors (www. maar.org/findarealtor.htm) knows that buying a home can be both exciting and stressful. They provide some helpful guidelines for choosing an agent and real estate company.

The Chicago Tribune Online Edition has a section called Real Estate Essentials. On the homepage are helpful checklists (chicagotribune.com/marketplaces/homes/ ws/0,1246,16622,00.html). Click on the Agent Checklist for questions you should ask an agent. This is another great way to keep a record of the candidates you have interviewed.

You want an agent who works hard and can close your transaction. Like other parts of the business

Bright Idea
Many real estate brokerages have responded to the changes in their clientele. Go to the Century 21 (www. century21.com) homepage and click on Office Search. Here you can find an office that speaks any of over 70 languages in addition to English, thus meeting the needs of many homebuyers who want to work with real estate agents who speak their primary language. You can find similar information at RE/MAX (www. remax.com).

world, the real estate field tends to follow the 80/20 rule: Twenty percent of the sales force does 80 percent of the work. Things are more likely to go smoothly if you're working with a real estate agent who is in the top 20 percent.

The best agent in your local area may be a "top producer." Some of these individuals buy or sell over 100 homes per year. These agents often have more listings and a better understanding of the housing market than other agents. The disadvantage of hiring a top producer is that he or she may not have enough time to commit to your specific needs. For profiles of specific agents in your area, see Real Estate Profiles—The Web Magazine for Real Estate Professionals (wwwrealestateprofiles. com/rep/rephome.html).

Finding an agent

Suggestions for finding an agent range from reading advertisements and selecting the agent with an eye-catching ad to getting recommendations from friends. (Some Realtors attract customers by providing access codes in their newspaper advertisements so homebuyers can read their listings on the Internet.) Some people read the real estate section of their newspapers for articles about specific agents who have earned recognition for outstanding performance.

Some online sources for finding real estate agent candidates include:

> *Open House America* (www.openhouse.net/realtors.html) can assist you in locating a real estate agent or service that focuses on the neighborhood in which you want to relocate. The Open House America directory shows

Unofficially...
The demographics of real estate are changing. The Fannie Mae Foundation has stated that, while the number of white homebuyers in 1997 dropped 1.3 percent from 1996, the number of minority buyers increased 27.7 percent. Many of these minority homebuyers are looking for real estate agents who come from similar cultures or who speak their native languages.

who's who in online real estate. All you need to do is complete the online form and click on Submit. Results show links in alphabetical order by city.

Homeowners Online (www.homeowners.com/new35.html) is a real estate mega-source Web site that provides mortgage calculators, current interest rates, related links, and the Realtor Connection. To locate a Realtor in the area that interests you, click on the state in which you wish to purchase property. You'll be provided with a long, alphabetical list of counties and Realtors for those counties. This listing frequently includes the Realtor's Web site and e-mail address in addition to his or her name, address, and other contact information.

Finding a buyer's agent

As mentioned a bit earlier, real estate commissions are negotiable between the real estate agent and the seller, and if there is a buyer's agent, between the buyer's agent and the buyer. Many states have recently changed their laws to protect homebuyers. The buyer's agent may receive a similar commission to the traditional agent (generally about 3 percent). However, you can often negotiate the amount of the fee. For example, you can negotiate a contract with a buyer's agent that offers a 2.5 percent commission and a $100 bonus for every thousand dollars you pay under the asking price.

Buyer's agents only represent buyers. They have a legal and ethical obligation to put the home-buyer's interest first. In general, they perform the following duties:

- Negotiate on your behalf.

- Provide unbiased facts about the true value of the home, the market and neighborhood, and obvious housing defects.

- Suggest that you hire a home inspector (see Chapter 9, "Online Help with Appraisals, Inspections, and Insurance," for details).

- Help you with financing alternatives and suggest that you get preapproved by a lender (see Chapter 7, "Online Mortgage Advice and Lending").

Remember to spell out your conditions in the agent's contract. Additionally, you'll want to make certain that the agent's contract is only for 90 days. If he or she can't find your dream house during that period of time, you'll need to move on to another agent. Or, you may choose to have a longer contract with the agent, but have a cancellation clause that can be executed after a certain period of time if you are not happy with his or her efforts on your behalf.

The Internet provides a vast array of information about buyer's agents. For a few examples, you can visit the following:

Exclusive Buyers Agents.com (www. exclusivebuyersagents.com) provides listings of buyer's agents by geographical area. You can discover buyer's agents in your state with this nationwide listing.

National Association of Exclusive Buyer Agents (www.naeba.org) gives you information about how to search for an agent near you, types of buyer's agents, suggested interview questions for a buyer's agent, the standard practices of buyer's agents, and links to other relevant Web sites for homebuyers.

District of Columbia: Buyer's Edge (www.
buyersagent.com) provides information about
the benefits of a buyer's agent, how you can
contact a buyer's agent, suggestions about
how you can save money by using a buyer's
agent, articles, and community links.

Oregon: Realty Consultants (www.rltycon.com)
offers an explanation of the buyer's agent
duties, answers to frequently asked questions,
contact information for buyer's agents,
related articles, and more.

1Agent (www.1agent.com) is a company
designed to find the best real estate agent
in the area in which you want to live. The
company inquires into the educational background of the agents they recommend. The
brokerage agents pay 1Agent's fees, so the
services are free to you.

Finding an out-of-state agent

According to HomeBuyer Agents (www.homebuyer-
agents.com), selecting the right out-of-state real
estate agent is one of the most important parts of
successfully completing the home buying process. A
good real estate agent can save you time and money,
and help you obtain the biggest bang for your buck.
When selecting the best agent, try to be as objective
as possible. Once you make your decision, try to follow up with him or her on a regular basis to make
sure he or she is making progress in helping you
find a home. Here is some advice on choosing a
good out-of-state agent:

- If you're moving out of state, you might find
  you need two real estate agents: one to sell the
  house you currently live in, and one who is a
  market expert in the area you plan to move to.

- Try the Residential Referral Network (www. galaxymall.com/realestate/referrals/works. html). Complete the online request form that identifies your real estate needs, and this nationwide referral service will recommend an agent in the area you specify. There is no charge for this service, and you are under no obligation to use the agent.

Here are some examples of sites that can help you locate good agents in other states:

Colorado Real Estate (www. coreferral.com) can assist you in finding qualified real estate agents throughout Colorado. The company is independent, so it is not obligated to use agents from a specific brokerage. If you are unhappy with the agent, you can call for another agent at any time (unless you have signed a contract with that agent).

Relocation Scout (www.relocationscout.com) is a free service that can assist you in almost every aspect of relocation—whether to the new house next door or to a house in the next state. Finding an agent at this site is simple: Just enter the desired city's name and click Go.

American Relocation Center (www. buyingrealestate.com) promises to save you time and money by providing user recommendations for using a buyer's agent and checking out a neighborhood in another state. It also provides tips on how to save money when relocating and selling your home. American Relocation Center divides its services into standard, first-time buyer, military, and retirement services.

Better Homes and Gardens (www.bhg-real-estate. com/consumer/realserv/relocate/relocate. html), shown below, has an online relocation network that you may find useful. You can preview neighborhoods across the country, determine your housing needs, and make housing cost comparisons. Additionally, you'll find helpful information about how to have a successful garage sale and develop a calendar to help make your move less stressful.

Better Homes and Gardens provides a valuable online relocation service.

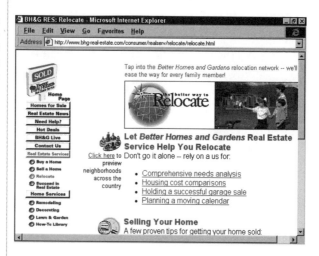

United Van Lines (www.unitedvanlines.com) offers a variety of relocation services. One of these services is locating a real estate agent in another state.

U.S. Relocation (www.usa-relocation.com/ index_main.htm) helps individuals find a Realtor by providing a national map and a listing of all the states. Click on a state to find a Realtor. The Web site also provides a mortgage calculator, links to Realtor.com for home buying advice, and a helpful relocation package.

Is your real estate agent doing the job?

Your real estate agent is your "house hunting partner." He or she is doing a good job if you're getting the type of service described here. A good agent knows the neighborhood inside out and has a good grasp of your financial situation and your housing needs and wants. If you have questions about working with an agency, see Buying a House—About Agency Relationships (www.ourfamilyplace.com/homebuyer/agency.html).

Your agent should put you in touch with lenders, attorneys, home inspectors, and insurance companies. He or she should provide reports about the neighborhood, general information, and what laws are in the works that may affect the property you're interested in.

Your real estate agent should also treat you with respect. You should feel comfortable talking frankly with him or her about your home buying criteria. Be specific and take advantage of all the services your agent has to offer.

If you have a good relationship with your real estate agent, the stress that often accompanies the home buying process will lessen. If it's an unhappy match, you may want to stop your agreement before the 90- or 120-day buyer's agent contract is automatically terminated. If you make this move, you are likely to be liable to the real estate broker for the money and time spent on your behalf.

You may want to change real estate agents, but you have a contract with a buyer's agent that states you'll work exclusively with that agent to find a

Watch Out!
Even if you have a terrific relationship with your real estate agent, be wary. When making your final house selection, it's not wise to rely solely on the advice of a person who has a significant financial stake in the sale. Use the Internet to become a knowledgeable consumer so you know how to assess the neighborhood, your needs and options, your legal rights, and comparable prices.

house. The contract may require you to pay a broker fee even if you buy the house through another agent.

Reading the fine print of real estate contracts is very important. You can use a non-exclusive contract so if you find a FSBO (see Chapter 12, "The Internet and Do-It-Yourself Real Estate") or a builder with a new home you won't be encumbered with a commission. Make sure that any buyer's agent agreement you sign states that you can cancel the contract if you're dissatisfied with the service. The contract should also include a termination clause for a date within a certain period of time.

Just the facts

- Recent legislation protects homebuyers more than ever before by allowing exclusive buyer's agents.

- The Internet provides a vast array of recommendations and checklists to assist both first-time and experienced homebuyers in selecting a real estate agent.

- It's helpful to use online questionnaires to interview several real estate agents before signing any agreements.

- Use the Internet to discover how your real estate agent should be working with you, and to find the services, information, and other types of assistance you deserve.

GET THE SCOOP ON...
Organizing your search for a home
■ Online house hunting strategies ■ Determining
whether to buy a new or existing home ■ How
the Internet can help you avoid overpaying for
your home ■ Comparing housing prices

Finding Your Dream Home Online

Chapter 6

The Internet lists more than 1.3 million homes for sale. One of those homes may be the place where you want to spend the rest of your life, or maybe just a few years. This chapter focuses on how you can find your dream home online. It covers how you can organize your online house hunt and use Internet-based scorecards to whittle down the actual number of possible houses. You'll see how you can focus your search by deciding on housing types, styles, and sizes. I'll also discuss the benefits and limitations of purchasing a new home, fixer-upper, or resale house. The result is that you'll save time and effort when you start looking at homes with your real estate agent.

The average homebuyer looks at 21 houses before buying one. The average house hunter who uses the Internet to view and evaluate homes only looks at approximately 12 homes. Cutting your house hunting time in half is definitely efficient. Even better, all the information you receive over the Internet is free!

Organizing your search

Looking for a new house can be both nerve-wracking and exciting. Often this reaction is the same for both the first-time and experienced homebuyer. One way to avoid getting confused after visiting half a dozen homes in an afternoon is to develop a checklist before you start house hunting. The following are some things you should do before you start finding your dream home online:

- Make certain your financial house is in order. Get a copy of your credit report and check your personal finances to make certain that you are ready to buy. For more information about getting money wise, see Chapter 2, "Creating a Financial Game Plan."

- Determine your annual budget (include everyday and occasional expenses such as insurance, medical expenses, auto repairs, and one-time expenses). Know what you can comfortably afford.

- Check out the different types of housing that are available. Make a list of your housing wants and needs (see Chapter 3, "Is Now the Right Time to Buy a Home?").

- Check out the neighborhood you want to live in (see Chapter 4, "Finding a Neighborhood Next Door or Across the Country"). Get a neighborhood report about schools, crime, and the general characteristics of your new neighbors and neighborhood.

Timesaver
One easy way to organize your house hunting is to purchase a three-ring binder and an accordion folder. You can use the binder for the different documents you'll receive, and the folder for the real estate brochures you collect as you visit different houses.

Using a scorecard to compare houses

It's easy to get confused about the attributes of this house and that one after viewing three or four homes in one day. You can use a scorecard to compare the homes that you think you might be interested in. The Internet provides several types of scorecards that you can print out and use when you visit a house. Here are a few examples:

> *Our Family Place* (www.ourfamilyplace.com/ homebuyer/scorecard.html) has a scorecard that allows you to list the features of each individual house.

> *HomeAdvisor What You Want Checklist* (www. homeadvisor.msn.com/ie/homes/ whatyouwant.asp) can help you define the features that are important to you. Check off general requirements, specific requirements, and add your comments to the form.

> *House Hunter's Helper* (www.hypervigilance. com/househunt.html) is a checklist that provides specific information about the house. Items include price, age, square footage, address, and school district. General information includes traffic, community, power lines, pool, and amenities. Exterior items include driveway, storage, patios, and decks. Interior items include floors, ceilings, and plumbing. The checklist totals five pages and will help you make certain you don't forget that one critical item.

> *Realtor.com Worksheet* (www.realtor.com/ aspcontent/compare.asp) is a home comparison worksheet that includes enough space to compare three homes side by side. You can rank the houses you are viewing, then tally up the scores.

The *Chicago Tribune* (wysiwyg://39/http://
chicagotribune.com/marketplaces/homes/
ws/item/0,1308,22220-25170-22693,00.html)
provides a checklist to use when you are tour-
ing condominiums.

Focusing your search

To focus your search, you need to get your priorities
in order. This doesn't have to be a painstaking and
detailed task. Just take 5 or 10 minutes from your
hectic schedule to jot down a few things about
choosing your new home. For example:

- Where do you want to live? In the next block or
  in the next state? How important is the school
  district? If you don't have children or are an
  "empty nester," it probably doesn't matter at
  all. If you do have school-age children, it might
  be the top factor on your priority list. (You
  began making this decision in Chapter 4,
  "Finding a Neighborhood Next Door or Across
  the Country.")

- What type of house are you looking for?
  Traditional single-family, duplex, condo, or a
  co-op? By now you should have made up your
  mind. If not, refer to Chapter 4, "Finding a
  Neighborhood Next Door or Across the
  Country."

- Housing comes in a variety of styles. When I
  moved from the West coast to the East coast, I
  was surprised to find very few contemporary
  homes. For more information about housing
  styles, see About.com's (www.about.com)
  Architecture page. At About.com, you'll find
  many hyperlinks to Web pages that show

Bright Idea
HomeAdvisor
(homeadvisor.
msn.com/ie/
homes/seehome.
asp) provides a
checklist of the
questions you
should ask when
viewing a home.
This can help
reduce the likeli-
hood of getting
an unwanted
surprise after
you buy a house.

everything from Byzantine to today's most fashionable housing styles.

▪ How many bedrooms and baths do you need? How about a garage or a basement? Is your family getting bigger or smaller? Do you plan to work from a home office? Deciding on these factors can help you determine what size house you'll need today and five years from now.

▪ What's the maximum amount you can and want to pay for a home? It's a good idea to decide this upfront, because much of your decision making will center on the answer to this question. The amount you can and want to pay per month will determine the amount of your mortgage, but this will vary with the length of the mortgage and other related housing costs.

▪ When focusing your search, keep a few things in mind. If you have a budget of, say, $200,000, do you want a larger basic home or a smaller home with lots of upgrades and amenities?

Correctly evaluating what you want and need in a home is one of the most important things you'll do in your house hunting. For more about getting focused, check out the following sites:

HomeBuyerPower (homebuyerpower.com/ powerful/main01.htm) includes information about how you can narrow your focus and prioritize your housing needs and wants.

NewHomeNetwork (www.newhomenetwork. com) has a lifestyle questionnaire that can help you target your housing needs.

Determining whether to buy a new or an established home

Do you want a new house or an established home? New houses have hidden additional costs but usually require little maintenance. Established houses are often less expensive than new houses, and they often have charm and mature landscaping. However, they may have maintenance problems due to sagging walls, cracked floor supports, and the lack of a sufficient number of electrical outlets.

Deciding to purchase a new home or an established home is a major decision. It's not like deciding between a new or used car. New cars have greater value, better warranties, and can be a lot flashier than an old jalopy. Deciding between a new home and an established home is a lot different.

In the next several sections, you'll uncover the advantages and limitations of purchasing a new home or an established home, including fixer-uppers. You'll soon discover that there are many housing options and ways that the Internet can assist you in your house hunting.

Purchasing a new home

For some people, owning a new home is the realization of their ultimate dream. However, most individuals are unfamiliar with the process of buying a new home and don't know what to expect. Moreover, due to the Internet, new legislation, and changes in the real estate industry, buying a new home has radically changed. This means that even experienced homebuyers can run into some unexpected glitches. You don't need a degree in real estate law to comprehend what's involved in buying a new home, but understanding the important points can help you avoid unwelcome surprises.

The advantages of a new home

Homebuilders can provide you with more reasons for purchasing a new home than you could possibly imagine. However, when everything is said and done, there are three primary advantages to buying a new home:

- **Appreciation.** New homes, depending on local economic conditions, generally appreciate faster than established homes. This appreciation often occurs in the first seven to eight years. If you're concerned about the future value of your home, a new home may be the way to go. All housing price appreciation is based on higher demand than supply. If there are fewer buyers or more new houses than buyers, prices may be flat or down for a while.

- **Warranty.** New homes have better warranties than established homes. New-home warranties generally cover almost everything—from appliances to carpeting—for the first few years. Structural problems are covered for a longer period of time. The length of time of such warranties will vary by area. Additionally, new homebuilders must disclose more to the consumer than a home seller. For example, many builders specify the type of materials to be used in construction, and consumers can watch as their home is being built to see where workmen may make errors and corrections. This means that there is less risk when purchasing a new home.

- **Better technology in construction.** Better construction inspections and constructing homes with new uniform building codes that require energy conservation for lower utility bills are a real benefit to consumers. Floor plans are usually designed to meet the current needs of households. Additionally, new homes use better construction technology to prevent future problems (such as window leakage, noise, and other related issues).

Unofficially...
The upgrades in a model home can cost up to $100,000. Make certain you compare the builder's brochure to the model home to make sure you know exactly what everything will cost.

The limitations of a new home

When evaluating a new home, be sure to ask the builder's representative what features in the house are upgrades and decorator items. In short, you need to determine the basic package. Often, model homes have lots of built-ins and other amenities that are not included in the standard home, so if you opt to include these items in your home, the price could be considerably more than the list price of the basic house.

Very few buyers of new homes get all the upgrades and options they need or want. Choosing from a long list of options is often confusing. Additionally, real estate agents and others often allow homebuyers only one chance to select all the new home's upgrades and options.

You might forget to choose an upgrade that is essential for your particular lifestyle, maybe because it wasn't on the options list. There might be a cut-off time during the construction period, after which you can't add more options (or there may be a change fee involved in doing so).

On the other hand, you might have ordered upgrades that you decide you don't need after doing a little research and getting helpful advice from your relatives. When you request an upgrade, the builder includes it in the budget. It's likely that the item is purchased right away and you can't change your mind later.

In construction, as in so many things, timing is everything. If you change your mind about a certain amenity, speak out immediately. For example, it's often easy to exchange a built-in microwave oven for a second oven. If you want more lights in the living room, ask for them and get a quote. If you decide you really don't want an elevator, tell the builder. There may be a cut-off time for your upgrade. You may not get all the cost of the option refunded. However, if the builder is constructing similar homes, you may be able to swap or make a deal and sell the option back to the builder.

Checking out the trends in new homes

What's hot and what's not in new homes is an issue you should be familiar with when hunting for a new house. There are several innovative trends in new homes. According to NewHomeNetwork.com (www. newhomenetwork.com) you should be aware of the following:

- New homes have fewer details and more space. Homebuyers are opting for bigger bedrooms and placing less importance on vaulted ceilings and marble foyers.

- Forget the fireplace and large whirlpool bathtub in the bathroom. Unless you are a luxury homebuyer, there is no demand for these types of amenities.

- New homebuyers are looking for homes that have lots of space for storage. Many homebuyers are purchasing homes with three garages. The third garage is not for another car, but for storage.

- Recreation rooms are out, and media rooms are in. Where else are you going to put that large-screen television or home theater?

- More and more individuals are working from their homes. This means homebuyers are very interested in at home office space that isn't tucked away in the corner of a windowless basement.

- As Americans become more technologically savvy, their need for cable modem hookups to fast Internet service, extra electrical outlets in rooms, and enough space in children's bedrooms to accommodate computers and similar equipment has increased.

Unofficially...
When looking at model homes, if you don't like the style of the living room or want to include some of the items listed earlier, don't write off the entire house. The builder may have a similar home with what you want.

- Rooms that can be multi-functional are in big demand. For example, a hot item is a family den that can be converted into a guest bedroom or quarters for a nanny or relative. An apartment over the garage also has great appeal for families with a live-in adult or child.

- Kitchens are now the "nerve centers" of homes and often include desks, computers, and storage areas. Where does this extra space come from? Formal dining areas are less in demand; casual eating areas that double as formal eating areas are more in demand.

Getting the right stuff in a new home

Try to ignore the pressures of the home buying process and keep in mind that the most often overlooked options are:

- **Insulation.** You might choose to reduce your utility bills and soundproof your house by upgrading the basic insulation.

- **Triple-paned or tinted windows.** One side of your new home may get lots of sun exposure and require some special upgrades.

- **Extra doors.** What about a door from the master bedroom to the back deck? How about putting in extra headers so that walls can be easily made into doors later on?

- **"Pre-plumbs" and "pre-wires."** If your home has three or more levels, you may want to "plumb" the area for the elevator you plan to install later. Other preparations can include pre-plumbing or pre-wiring for a whirlpool tub, a fireplace, electrical enhancements, or a central vacuum cleaner system.

- **Concrete walkways.** You might want to add a concrete area to store your boat or to function as a walkway from the garage to the back or front deck.

One way to be sure you select the right upgrades is to check out other homes built by your builder. Talk with the owners to find out what they overlooked and what they think is terrific.

Using the Internet to locate new homes

Here are a couple of online resources for locating new homes. These sites list homes nationwide and provide additional recommendations and tips for new homebuyers:

> *NewHomeNetwork.com* (www.newhomenetwork. com) allows you to search by region, using a minimum and maximum price. This Web site also includes news about new homes, financing, tips and advice, and a links directory.

> *HomeBuilder.com* (www.homebuilder.com/ mainmap.asp) offers information on more than 100,000 models, plans, and delivery of new homes offered by more than 7,000

You can search
for new homes in
the next block
or in the next
state without
leaving the
comfort of your
computer.

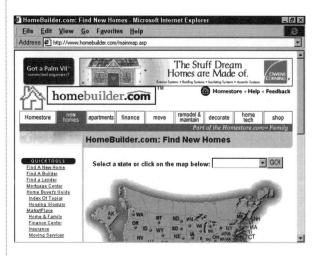

homebuilders in 40 major U.S. cities (see above). A major benefit of this site is that it's updated daily.

Purchasing a model home

Model homes are not quite new. They are similar to existing homes, but no one has ever lived in them. However, there are some disadvantages, such as the fact that you can't choose the color of the hardwood floor or carpet. What the house comes with is what you get.

Most builders design their model homes to stand out from the crowd. Many homebuilders select themes, add amenities, and decorate their model homes to attract the attention of a certain portion of the population (young techno-savvy homebuyers, folks moving up the corporate ladder, individuals interested in the nearby golf course, and so on). These are "memory" features that appeal to a target audience. If you're purchasing a model home, these lovely memory features may turn out to be over-priced gimmicks.

Model homes generally have the best grade of carpeting, but hundreds of feet have already passed by. The builder may freshen up the model home for occupancy, but there may be some damage that can be hard or impossible to fix.

On the plus side, your model home may be the envy of your neighbors and located in the best part of the subdivision. Other advantages of purchasing a model home include the likelihood that the builder will discount all the upgrades and may arrange a purchase-leaseback deal. This means that the builder is now your tenant and rents the home from you until a certain date (usually when most or all of the homes in the subdivision are sold). The tax advantages of this type of deal are usually terrific for both you and the builder.

Purchasing an established home

Many individuals want to live in older neighborhoods that have good reputations. These folks are often seeking the charm of days gone by and are anxious to build new neighborhood traditions. However, purchasing an established home has both advantages and limitations. The following section outlines the key points homebuyers should be aware of when buying an established home.

The advantages of an existing home

Several of the advantages of established homes are as follows:

- **Bigger bang for the buck.** If you purchase an established house, you are likely to get a bigger house in a better neighborhood than if you purchase a new home. New homes are priced by today's cost per square foot. Established home prices don't use the same standard.

- **Higher quality.** Standard materials used in new construction are sometimes of a lesser quality than expected. This means that if you don't want to pay extra for upgrades, you may get a house whose quality is not as good as that of an established house.

- **Mature landscaping.** Landscaping improves with age. Additionally, you don't have to pay a landscaping company to plant your front and back yards.

- **A predictable neighborhood.** Established homes are generally in established neighborhoods. With a new development, you don't know who's going to move in next door. You may also have to contend with homes being built around you as the developer finishes building in the subdivision.

The limitations of an existing home

Established homes can be bargains, but they have some drawbacks. While the home may have matching appliances, window treatments, mature landscaping, and other amenities that new homes don't have, there are other costs to consider. For example, a resale home will likely need to be updated to your specifications.

The cost of updating a home can be staggering. The homeowner has to put in all the built-ins, amenities, and features that are automatically included in a new home. An older home may also have some hidden health risks, such as lead paint, radon gas, formaldehyde emissions from particleboard and vinyl glue, and so on. You'll have to decide what the real costs are of purchasing an established home and how much time you want to spend on home improvements.

Getting the right stuff in an existing home

As you're deciding whether to buy an existing home, you need to think about more than just the look and feel of the physical structure of the house. The following are some things to think about when selecting the house that best meets your needs:

- **Environment.** Are adjoining properties junk-yards, run-down housing developments, rail-roads, etc.?

- **Zoning.** What are the zoning restrictions in the neighborhood? Can someone build a restaurant with a large parking lot and valet attendants next door?

- **Flood plains.** Check the geography of your lot. Flat property may be in a flood plain. Steep lots may require additional drainage.

- **Utilities.** What kind of power do the house's appliances, furnace, and so on need? If the house's furnace and appliances are all electric and the area has expensive electricity, consider how much extra you will spend. Are electric and telephone lines installed below ground?

- **Street maintenance.** Do the streets need repair? Are they laid out in a way that enhances safety and decreases hazards? How are the traffic patterns—is there heavy traffic congestion? Do drivers speed?

- **Municipal services.** Do your property tax dollars pay for water and sewage disposal? What about trash collection and snow removal? Does the house have an adequate well and septic system?

Unofficially... Don't be surprised if you have to buy flood insurance, even if your home isn't on the water. Congressional legislation requires any federally backed or insured mortgage on property in a "special flood hazard area" (SFHA) to have a flood insurance policy in place.

Purchasing a fixer-upper

Sometimes a fixer-upper is the least desirable home in the most desirable neighborhood. If you're thinking about buying a fixer-upper, you need to consider the costs needed to bring the property up to its market potential. Therefore, the cost of a fixer-upper is the price of the house and the required renovations. If you purchase a fixer-upper, make certain that the total of these costs are within your budget.

You can buy fixer-uppers in a variety of states. For example, an existing home listed as being in "good condition" might mean that all the appliances work and everything is okay, but the home needs to be painted (inside and out), the floors need to be stripped and stained, or the carpet needs to be replaced.

"Handyman specials" are homes that can need anything from a few minor repairs to the entire interior being gutted and replaced. However, unless your real estate agent is also in the construction business, don't rely on him or her for an accurate estimate of the time and cost of the renovations.

A home that needs renovations requires cash, and often the exact amount of cash needed is unknown. For first-time homebuyers who often have limited cash, this can lead to disaster. Imagine not having a working kitchen for six months. Additionally, fixer-uppers need owners with the know-how to do the renovations. Many people today don't have the construction knowledge or the time to rewire a home or replace the kitchen floor.

If you get a "203K rehab loan" with a Federal Housing Administration guarantee, you can get money for repairs of an existing home. The funds are paid out as the repairs are made on the home.

Watch Out!
Many people who renovate their homes spend lots of money on their favorite areas, such as expensive gourmet kitchens, hardwood stairways, or picture windows that showcase a special view. These amenities can become white elephants when the homebuyer tries to sell the house later. Remember, you can't sell a $300,000 house in a $150,000 neighborhood!

The amount of the repairs is simply added to your mortgage payments.

There are many advantages to purchasing a fixer-upper. For example, you can get a bigger house in a better neighborhood. Another advantage of a fixer-upper is that you might be able to pay less for the home. For example, let's say that a seller is asking $200,000 for a fixer-upper in a neighborhood of nice houses that also sell for about $200,000. You hire a physical inspector and get a contractor to estimate the work that needs to be done. Renovation estimates are $25,000, and you can count on another $15,000 for cost over-runs and delays. This means that a fairer price for the house would be in the $160,000 range. However, if all the homes in the area are in the same state of disrepair, then $200,000 is a fair asking price. Unfortunately, this means that the real price of the home, including all the work you need to put into it immediately, is around $240,000.

If you're seeking an older home and want to get a handle on renovation costs, you can turn to the Internet for a wide variety of resources. The following is a short list of what you'll find:

> *Old Houses.com* (www.old-houses.com) gives information on how to buy an older home.

> *Building Online* (www.buildingonline.com) provides a building supply directory and a database for renovation research.

> *Building.com* (www.building.com/ communities/communities.html), formerly known as BuildNET, shown below, provides a directory of contractors, architects, manufacturers, suppliers, and more. You can even

Watch Out!
One of the things to consider when purchasing a fixer-upper is the flexibility of your significant other. Many individuals who purchase homes that need a lot of work are surprised when their spouse wants a divorce after six months of dirt, chaos, unexpected costs, and delays. For self-study on this topic, rent the movie *The Money Pit* to learn what *not* to do.

Building.com is one of the most popular Web sites for renovators.

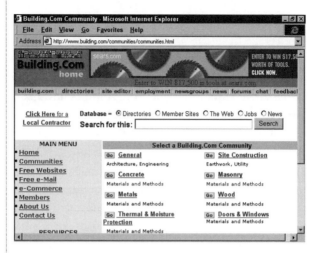

use the Web site search engine to find sub-contractors, news, and related Web sites.

FixerUpper: The Home Improvement Community (www.fixerupper.com) includes assistance for homeowners with questions about fixing up their homes. This Web site offers an online community of folks who are also renovating their homes.

Using the Internet to find the best homes at the best prices

In the not-so-distant past, you had to primarily rely on your real estate agent for all your house hunting needs. Your real estate agent selected which and how many new and existing homes you should see. Now you can visit Web sites and view the actual floor plans and see photographs of homes that your agent disregarded. Once you identify a home that suits your needs, your agent can send you extra information and the property address. He or she can schedule an appointment so you can walk through the house in person.

With the Internet, you can go house hunting
in your neighborhood or in the next state without
leaving your computer. You can use any or all of the
following five resources for house hunting on the
Internet:

- **Local online newspaper ads.** Check out the
  online real estate section of your local newspaper. Look up the ads for the type of home you
  desire. Often the listing agent will include an
  "access code" so you can view homes for sale at
  your convenience via the Internet. A few local
  newspapers have interactive real estate sections. A good example is the real estate section
  of the *Washington Post* HomeHunter (www.
  washingtonpost.com), shown below.

The *Washington Post* has an online local area search engine that makes house hunting easy.

- **National listings of homes for sale.** Two of the
  major national home hunting Internet sites
  are Realtor.com (www.realtor.com) and
  CyberHomes (www.cyberhomes.com). Both of
  these sites include maps of the neighborhood

and links to other useful sites. Each company
will notify you by e-mail of new listings that
meet your search criteria. Many local real
estate company sites may have similar information for the area in which you are looking.

▪ **State listings of homes for sale.** Each state has
its own Realtor organization. These organizations have Web sites that show the available
homes. For example, the Internet site for
California is located at www.ca.living.net. For
access to each state's local Realtor web sites, go
to www.realtor.com. Under Find a Home, select
the state, then the area within the state where
you are looking.

▪ **Listings of homes for sale by owner (FSBO).**
About 10 percent of all homes sold each year
are sold by their owners (for more information, see Chapter 12, "The Internet and Do-It-
Yourself Real Estate"). One of the most popular Web sites for FSBOs is the Owner's Network
(www.owners.com). Just enter your home hunting criteria and let the Internet do the searching for you.

▪ **Real estate agent and brokerage listings on the
Web.** Many large brokerages such as RE/MAX
(www.remax.com), Century 21 (www.
century21.com), and Coldwell Banker (www.
coldwellbanker.com) have Web pages where
you can select a region in the United States
and find agents and listings within that region.
Many area real estate agents have Web sites
that show their listings.

For example, Connecticut Home Online
(www.alnapier.com) in Newington,

Connecticut, offers a look at all its listings online. To make your search more efficient, the area is divided into smaller areas. Next, homes are listed by Multiple Listing Service (MLS) ID number, price, number of bedrooms and baths, and city/area. For more information about a home, you click on the MLS number.

If you need to widen your house hunting geographic search, check out The Real Estate Book Online (www.treb.com). The Real Estate Book Online is a home locating service that covers more than 400 markets throughout the United States, Canada, and Mexico.

Using the Internet to spot overpriced homes

The best way to avoid paying too much for a house is to be an educated consumer. Talk with your real estate agent and take advantage of his or her expertise. Another good way to learn about the real estate market is to research it using the Internet. All real estate is unique, and no two areas in the United States react the same way to events that affect the national and regional economy.

This means that some areas are in a seller's market and others are in a buyer's market. Remember, too, that conditions can change overnight, so keep your finger on the pulse of the marketplace until you close your deal.

Everyone wants to avoid overpaying for a home. As an educated online homebuyer, you'll know the conditions of the real estate market of the area in which you want to live. If you remember four things, you can make certain you don't pay too much for your new home:

Timesaver
Say you want a Tudor-style home in a certain neighborhood. You look up the zip code at www.realtor.com and get 10 results from the search. By checking the photos of the homes online, you discover that only one has the Tudor style you desire. You've just saved yourself hours in a car going from house to house with a real estate agent!

- **Know the local market.** If the seller is asking too much for the house, don't be afraid to walk away from the deal.

- **In a multiple-offer situation, don't panic.** Stick with the prices you feel represent a fair value for the home. To assist you in your negotiations, read Chapter 10, "Negotiating and Closing the Deal."

- **Don't get emotional.** If you're willing to pay more for a house because you love it, you might have a problem with your banker, who is going to use the house appraisal—not your love for the place—to value the property.

- **Don't buy the best house in the neighborhood.** When it's time to sell the house, you may have to take a lower price than you might like because the home will be appraised based on the price of the three most recent sales in the neighborhood, which may not be as nice as yours. In other words, over time your expensive house may have the same value as neighborhood homes that originally cost less.

Pay less by using online comparable market analysis

Each real estate market area has a benchmark called a comparable market analysis (CMA). The results of this data collection are usually available in local newspapers and on the Internet. CMA covers three main points, and all three allow you to compare prices over several years:

- **Average price.** Includes the average price of homes sold. This lets you know the median price for a specific time period.

- **Number of homes sold.** Includes the number of homes sold during a specific time period.

- **Average days on the market.** Indicates the amount of time before a home was purchased. (Keep in mind that this is an average. More expensive luxury homes tend to stay on the market longer than less expensive homes.)

The Internet provides this information and a few other great tools for home price comparisons:

House Clicks (www.houseclicks.com/selling/cma.html) explains how CMA works and includes some excellent examples.

Coldwell Banker (www.coldwellbanker.com) provides an annual Home Price Comparison Index that allows you to quickly approximate housing costs in over 350 markets across North America and beyond. Comparisons are based on a standard single-family dwelling with approximately 2,200 square feet, four bedrooms, two and a half bathrooms, a family room (or equivalent), and a two-car garage. Enter the current market value of your home. Next, select the region where your home is located. Now enter the region where you want to relocate. Click on Submit to see the results of your comparison.

Yahoo! Real Estate (http://realestate.yahoo.com), shown below, provides comparative market analyses in two ways when you click on Home Values. First, you can search by location. You'll discover all the homes that were sold on a particular street, or find the sales history of a specific address. Second, you can search by price range. For example,

Yahoo! Real Estate helps you understand comparable market analysis. (Reproduced with permission of Yahoo! Inc. © 1999 by Yahoo! Inc. YAHOO! and the YAHOO! logo are trademarks of Yahoo! Inc.)

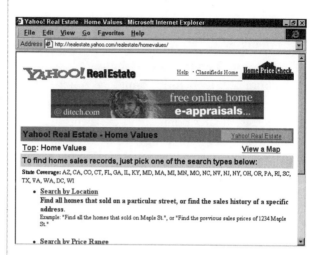

you can find all the homes that were sold in one city between $150,000 and $175,000.

Just the facts

- The Web is the perfect place to start your house hunting search because it lists more than 1.3 million homes.

- The Internet provides a variety of scorecards so that you can properly evaluate the homes you visit.

- Housing comes in three flavors: new, established, and fixer-upper, each of which has advantages and limitations.

- Fixer-uppers can be real money savers, but they require lots of construction know-how and time.

- The Internet can assist you in spotting over-priced homes.

Getting Financing with the Help of the Internet

GET THE SCOOP ON...
Saving money by getting a home loan
online ▪ Shopping online for the best interest
rates ▪ Online prequalification and preapproval
▪ The online mortgage lending process
▪ Selecting the loan program that's right for you

PART III

Online Mortgage Advice and Lending

Chapter 7

M any individuals want to own their own homes, but few can pay cash for them. This means that most people rely on residential financing. Of course, getting financing isn't as much fun a selecting a house, but it is important. Learning about the mortgage process can save you lots of frustration. You don't want to lose your dream house because your mortgage application was denied.

Forrester Research of Cambridge, Massachusetts, predicts that online mortgage lending will grow from $18 billion in 1999 to more than $91 billion in 2003. This means that about 10 percent of all mortgages will originate online. The reasons for this growth are easy to understand. The Internet has quickly become one of the easiest, fastest, and most cost-effective ways for consumers to research and apply for a home loan.

The biggest reasons for applying for a mortgage online are convenience, efficiency, and cost savings. Many homebuyers use the Internet to get the best interest rates. Online lending is convenient and efficient because homebuyers can communicate with their online lenders at lunchtime, during the holidays, or after working hours by e-mail, fax, or mail and delivery services. In the past, getting a home loan often took between 30 and 90 days. Online technology has reduced this waiting period to a few weeks, and new technology will likely reduce this waiting time to a matter of minutes. Of course, the approval is contingent on the appraisal and supplying and confirming your documentation for the mortgage.

What is a mortgage?

Unofficially...
If your credit record shows slow credit card payments, outstanding judgments, lack of established credit, or other difficult situations (for example, self-employment with a short track record), you may want to consider going to a mortgage broker rather than to a direct lender. The mortgage broker can prequalify you based on a wide range of lenders and their criteria. This can improve your chances of being approved for a loan.

A *mortgage* is a loan secured by your property. In other words, your property is used as collateral for your home loan. Monthly payments include interest and principal (see the glossary for definitions). Borrowers can obtain a mortgage from an online mortgage lender or online aggregator (a company that screens loan applications for lenders), traditional banks, or credit unions. For a fee, mortgage brokers (who can be individuals or companies) bring borrowers and lenders together for the purpose of loan origination.

Most lenders require a cash down payment toward the purchase of the home (see Chapter 8, "Avoiding the Down Payment Cash Crunch"), a certified appraisal (see Chapter 9, "Online Help with Appraisals, Inspections, and Insurance"), and your financial profile to meet certain guidelines.

Your financial profile is often evaluated using a Federal Housing Administration (FHA) formula. This guideline is based on FHA findings that most people can afford to spend 29 percent of their gross monthly income on housing expenses. Housing expenses include principal, interest, property-related taxes, and insurance (collectively known as PITI). Therefore, if you multiply your gross monthly income by 29 percent, the result is the PITI. This is the maximum many lenders will allow for your housing expenses. For a conventional loan, the guideline is 28 percent of your monthly gross income, which can be used for total housing expenses.

Lenders require borrowers to sign a promissory note that obligates them to repay the mortgage debt. The borrower also agrees to keep the home insured against fire and other hazards, and to pay property taxes. If the borrower fails to meet these obligations, the home loan is in default and subject to foreclosure.

Monthly house payments are divided into two parts: interest and principal. Interest is the fee for using the lender's money to purchase the house. Principal is the amount of the loan due to the lender. Each monthly house payment includes a portion of interest and principal. There are several types of mortgages available. For more information, see "Types of mortgages" later in this chapter.

Online home loan intermediaries— aggregators

As you first learned in Chapter 1, "Preparing to Buy a Home," aggregators are online intermediaries who connect loan applicants with mortgage lenders. Organizations like QuickenMortgage (www.quickenmortgage.com) can offer online applications for residents of all 50 states and provide real-time mortgage information, online rate lock-ins, and quotes.

Bright Idea
Before you complete an online loan application, determine if you are working with an aggregator or a mortgage banker. If your credit history is spotty, you may have a better chance of getting your loan approved if you go with an aggregator. If you have an excellent credit history, you may get a better deal if you go with a mortgage banker.

Aggregators are not all alike. For example, GetSmart (www.getsmart.net) charges lenders several hundred dollars for each referral, regardless of whether the loan closes. LendingTree (www.lendingtree.com) charges lenders about $10 to review each referral and to bid on a prequalified application. Only if the loan closes does the lender pay LendingTree several hundred dollars for the referral.

Bright Idea
If your credit record is blemished, you can still get a home loan. In this situation, many lenders require a down payment that is 30 percent of the value of the property. You'll likely pay a higher interest rate and more points to get your home loan approved. Some lenders may accept a smaller down payment with blemished credit, but you will pay more interest and possibly more points.

What counts to mortgage lenders

When you're trying to qualify for a home loan, whether online or in the traditional way, lenders usually require the following:

- **Income, assets, and liabilities.** These items indicate your ability to make monthly payments. Give yourself time to gather information on all these areas. Your online mortgage banker will verify all the information you submit.

- **Savings.** Lenders want to see how much cash you have to make a down payment, pay for closing costs, and have some cash reserves for emergencies. Mortgage lenders like to see that your savings equal at least 25 percent of your annual income, indicating that you can probably afford at least a 5 percent down payment. If your savings equal 50 percent of your annual income, you can likely make a sizable down payment.

- **Credit.** This tells lenders how you manage the credit you've received for car loans and credit cards. For more information, see Chapter 2, "Creating a Financial Game Plan."

The mortgage process

The mortgage process differs slightly from lender to lender. However, you can expect the following steps when you apply, either online or in the traditional way:

1. **Complete an application.** This sets the process in motion. You can apply before you find the property or if you have made an offer. At this point you need to be prepared to pay the appraisal and application fees.

2. **Credit check and prequalification.** With your approval and payment, the mortgage lender checks your credit record. This can assist you in determining what type of loan (or loans) you qualify for if you don't know already. However, you should note that each time your credit is checked, there will be a record of it. It may look as if you are applying for loans in different places, which may lower your credit rating in the process.

3. **Telephone contact by a loan officer.** If you have applied for a mortgage online, a representative of your online mortgage company will contact you by e-mail or telephone to verify your loan application information.

4. **Rate lock and appraisal.** Once the loan amount is determined, your loan type and rate will have a "lock-in" that guarantees your interest rate for around 45 days. The lender orders an appraisal of the property.

5. **Loan documentation, verification, and other paperwork.** This is where the fax and U.S. mail come into play. You'll receive a printed copy of

Unofficially...
Once you submit your loan application, you should have a response within 30 to 60 days. (Some lenders promise 7 to 10 days.) If you are denied a loan, the lender is required by law to explain why.

your loan application, disclosure forms, and a document checklist from your lender. The disclosure statements include a truth-in-lending statement (Regulation Z), a copy of the Housing and Urban Development (HUD) guidelines, and a settlement costs booklet (if you are getting an FHA loan). The law requires these statements, so if you don't receive them within three days after submitting your loan application, ask for them. These disclosure forms should indicate the exact amount you will have to pay for the loan and how much you will have to pay out-of-pocket.

At this point, the lender analyzes your loan application for completeness. Then the lender verifies the information submitted, confirms the value of the property with the appraisal, and determines if the property has any encumbrances, judgments, or liens.

6. **Loan submission to lender.** When all the paperwork has been turned in and processed, your loan representative submits the loan package for underwriting.

7. **Lender underwriting and final approval.** A loan underwriter reviews the loan package and faxes an approval and any conditions needed for approval to the loan officer.

8. **Loan documents delivered by express mail.** The lender completes the loan package and delivers it to the escrow agent. The escrow agent contacts you and arranges a convenient time to sign the documents. This event is coordinated with the loan closer, the seller, the real estate agent(s), and the escrow agent.

9. **Settlement meeting or closing.** You go to the office (this may be the first time you have to leave your computer) and sign the documents. The lender reviews the documents and the escrow agent requests a wire transfer of the loan funds, and records and closes the transaction. The closing is a formal meeting between the buyer, seller, real estate agent(s), and escrow agent. It is the day the property changes ownership. The exact procedure may vary from one state to another, but the results are the same. You get the keys to your new home!

Keep a copy of every piece of paper you sign at the closing meeting. In addition to the closing documents, keep your homeowners and title insurance documents in a special file. The settlement form is especially useful when you are preparing your income tax report or if you sell your home. (For more on what's tax-deductible, see Chapter 11, "Costs and Tax Benefits Associated with Buying a Home.")

The paperwork you need to provide

Unfortunately, online home loans are not paperless. The financial documentation that your online lender will want, whether you apply online or through traditional means, includes the following:

- The purchase contract for the new property. (If you haven't selected a house yet, don't worry about this.)

- Checking and savings account statements for the past two to three months. (Make certain they include the bank's name, address, and telephone number.)

Bright Idea
It's a good idea to keep your closing records in a safe place. Make a copy of each piece of paper. Store the originals in a safety deposit box, and keep the copies in a separate file at home.

- Federal tax reports for the last two years, pay stubs, W-2 withholding forms, and other proof of income.

- Any paperwork on divorces, liens, judgments, and bankruptcy discharges.

- Credit card bills.

- Details about long-term debts like car loans, student loans, and revolving or installment accounts that will not be paid off within 11 months.

- If you are self-employed, balance sheets and an income statement of your business.

- Any letters discussing gifts (from a parent or a relative) to help with the home purchase. The notarized letter should state that the amount shown is a gift and not a loan. The lender may have his or her own format or form for the gift letter that you will need to complete.

The fees you need to pay

There are many fees associated with the purchase of a home. Some of these expenses are generally lumped together and referred to as *closing costs*. These costs are paid when the homebuyer and the seller meet to close the transaction. Generally, homebuyers pay settlement costs that are 2 to 3 percent of the house price. This would be in addition to "points" paid for the mortgage.

How and what fees are charged varies from lender to lender. Many lenders only require payment of credit report and appraisal fees during the mortgage process. Other lenders don't charge these fees until the closing meeting. If you get an FHA-insured loan, part of the fees can be financed in the mortgage—check with your lender for details, as the guidelines for the amount will vary depending on your loan. (For details, see Chapter 11, "Costs and Tax Benefits Associated with Buying a Home.") The costs involved with a mortgage include the following:

- **Origination fee.** This is a fee for the work involved in the evaluation, preparation, and submission of a loan application. That is, the fee is paid to the lender for creating the loan. The origination fee is usually stated in the form of points.

- **Mortgage insurance application fee.** This fee covers the processing of an application for mortgage insurance (if applicable). This is usually a flat fee of between $250 and $400.

- **Points.** The lender may charge a certain number of points for the mortgage or for a discounted interest rate. Each point is 1 percent of the loan amount. Most lenders charge 1, 2, or 3 points. Often borrowers are given the option of including these points in their mortgages. However, this raises the annual percentage rate (APR) of the mortgage, making it more costly. For example, a $100,000 mortgage, with 2 points at 7 percent for 30 years, has an APR of 7.197 percent. If the borrower pays the points up front, the APR drops to 7 percent.

- **Processing, underwriting, and document fees.** These are the fees for processing the loan documentation, analyzing risk, and determining an appropriate charge for taking the risk. It involves a review of a borrower's credit, value of security, and certain legal documents.

- **Appraisal and credit report fees.** These are charges for an estimate of value of the house you are purchasing, supported by factual data by a qualified person, and fees for a detailed financial history of a person used by a lender to determine whether to extend credit.

- **Title, escrow, and closing agent fees.** These are the county registrar's recording fees and fees to a third party for acting as the agent for a buyer and a seller of real estate. The responsibilities include handling of paperwork and disbursement of funds.

- **Private mortgage insurance (if applicable).** Mortgage insurance is provided by a private mortgage insurance company to protect lenders against loss if a borrower defaults. Most lenders generally require mortgage insurance for a loan with a loan-to-value percentage in excess of 80 percent.

- **Property and hazard insurance.** This is often a multiple-peril policy that includes hazard insurance, theft, injury to others, and damages to another's property.

- **Prepaid interest.** Lenders often require the first month's interest to be prepaid at the time of closing.

- **Incidental recording, delivery, wire fees, etc.** These miscellaneous fees are paid by the borrower. Generally, they are the shipping and handling costs for the transport of documents from one entity to another, etc.

Many online lenders charge fewer points, have different interest rates, or charge lower origination fees for online borrowers. How much you save on these three costs varies from lender to lender. Often borrowers can save 1 percent of the loan amount by applying online. For example, if the loan amount is $350,000, you can save $3,500—a significant amount of money for individuals of all income levels. Here are a few examples of the different ways online lenders pass on cost savings to borrowers:

> At *Countrywide* (www.countrywide.com), if you use the Gold Credit Program, you'll save .75 to 1.25 of the loan points.

> *E-LOAN* (www.eloan.com) claims it can save you 80 percent of your loan fees.

> *Mortgage.com* (www.mortgage.com), shown below, claims that if interest rates maintain an all-time low, consumers can save as much as $1,500 in application and closing fees by shopping for mortgages online.

Mortgage.com includes online tutorials, information about current interest rates, and a mortgage wizard to help you with every step of the mortgage process.

Finding the best interest rate

It's important to shop around for the lowest interest rate possible. Let's say that when you use one of the following online calculators, you discover that you could afford a monthly interest and principal payment of $1,300, and online lenders are making 30-year loans at 10 percent. How large a loan can you afford? Using an online calculator, enter the appropriate data. You'll soon see that you can afford a $148,062 loan. Next, let's say that interest rates drop to 7½ percent. Again using one of the online calculators, enter the appropriate data. You'll discover that you can now afford an $185,714 loan. The following sites offer more information on interest rates:

> *Equity Direct Mortgage Corporation* (www.equitydirect.com/mortgage-amortization-calculator.html) offers a handy mortgage amortization calculator. Enter the number of months, interest rate, and loan amount. Then click on the amortization schedule.

> *Citizens Bank of Mukowongo* (www.citizenbank.com/calculators.cfm) provides a mortgage amortization calculator that offers a full amortization table.

> *The Mortgage Mart* (www.mortgagemart.com/amortize_calc.html) has an online calculator that displays an amortization schedule based on the given loan amount, interest rate, and loan term.

Getting the best deal by comparing mortgage loans

When searching for the lowest mortgage rates, don't forget to compare loans by APR. But be careful: Different lenders have different ways of calculating the costs included in the APR. This means that a loan for the same dollar amount and number of points may have a different APR with a different lender.

Overall, the APR can be misleading. The method of calculating the cost of a loan as a yearly rate assumes that the loan will not be paid off until the end of the loan term. Most loans are for 30 years, but many people pay off their loans within the first five to eight years because they move or refinance. One way to compare the real cost of different loans is to use the online mortgage and financial calculators at Fannie Mae's HomePath (www.homepath.com).

Another way to shop for the lowest mortgage interest rates is to check out the following companies. Each firm offers up-to-the-minute regional or national interest rate quotes. However, none of these firms are mortgage lenders:

> *HSH Associates* (www.hsh.com/mtgrates.html) lists the current mortgage rates offered by hundreds of mortgage lenders around the country. The firm is an independent source of mortgage information and does not originate loans.

> *MortgageQuotes* (www.mortgagequotes.com) includes more than 64 loan programs for every state, hundreds of lenders, and has thousands of mortgage rates that are constantly updated.

> *Mortgage Link* (www.sjmercury.com/svlife/ realestate/mortgage/), sponsored by the *San Jose Mercury News,* allows you to search for the rates by loan type, lender name, and amount. Additional information includes the latest rate averages and current adjustable-rate mortgage (ARM) index readings.

Mortgage-net (www.mortgage-net.com/ trends) has links to articles, data on current and historical interest rates, bond rates, the Shirmery Report on interest rate movements, and the U.S. Department of Commerce, Bureau of Economic Analysis reports. Find out if you should buy now or wait for a lower interest rate.

Types of mortgages

There are three primary kinds of loans, each of which has several varieties:

1. Conventional loans

2. HUD/FHA loans

3. Veterans Administration (VA) loans

Each of these loans has different requirements, the most important of which is usually the required minimum down payment. These types of mortgages and their variations are discussed in the following sections.

Conventional loans

Many would-be homeowners believe that all lenders require a 20 percent down payment. In other words, if you want a $100,000 home, the required down payment is $20,000. (The rules are different for homes valued at over $1 million.) This requirement is due to the lender's concern about loan default. If the borrower is paying a 20 percent down payment, the lender often feels secure about making the loan. In fact, the default rate of loans with a 20 percent down payment is frequently less than one half of 1 percent. However, some conventional mortgages are available with as little as a 5 percent down payment, in which case you would need a $5,000 down payment for a $100,000 house. These low down payment conventional loans are usually insured by the government and are described in the next two sections of this chapter. (For additional information, see Chapter 8, "Avoiding the Down Payment Cash Crunch.")

What makes low down payment mortgages possible is private mortgage insurance (PMI). PMI generally costs 1 to 5 percent of the monthly principal and interest payment amount, and its purpose is to protect the lender in case of borrower default. If the borrower defaults, the mortgage insurance company pays the mortgage payments.

Over time, homeowners build equity in their homes in two ways. First, the value of the house can appreciate. Second, the monthly house payment will pay down the principal of the loan and the equity position of the homeowner increases. Once you have reached a 20 percent equity position in your home (where you own 20 percent of the current equity in the house, not 20 percent of the purchase price), you can cancel your mortgage payment insurance. (Your bank likely won't tell you when you reach this point. You have to keep track of it yourself. For more on PMI, see Chapter 8, "Avoiding the Down Payment Cash Crunch.")

There are many varieties of conventional home loans. The following is a list of the most popular kinds:

- **Fixed-rate mortgages.** These loans have a fixed interest rate and loan term (15- and 30-year mortgages are the most popular). You'll always know what you're paying because the interest rate and monthly payments are fixed for the term of the loan.

Unofficially...
Studies show that up to 25 percent of ARMs are calculated incorrectly. You can audit your ARM to make certain it's calculated correctly with the help of Loantech Finance Central (www.loantech. com).

- **ARMs.** These loans change periodically (if the market index of the interest rates they are tied to increases or decreases). The monthly payment may stay the same, but the "shortfall" is added to the principal to create negative amortization. That is, the principal balance increases, not decreases, as payments are made. Most ARMs have a fixed ceiling and/or floor interest rate on the mortgage. It can go up or down, depending on market conditions, but only within stated limits that you agreed to when you received the loan.

- **Graduated-payment mortgages.** These loans have periodic payments that increase one or more times during the term of the mortgage. The loan may start with interest rates that are below market rate, and then increase over time.

- **Renegotiable mortgages.** The interest rate is fixed but renegotiated at specific periods to adjust the interest rate closer to the market rate.

- **Price-level-adjusted mortgages (PLAMs).** These loans provide for periodic increases or decreases in the loan amount on the basis of a predetermined price index. The interest rate and term remain fixed.

For more information on the different types of home loans, see Fannie Mae's HomePath (www. homepath.com) or the HUD Home Buying Guide (www.pueblo.gsa.gov/cic_text/housing/hudhome/ hudhome.txt).

HUD/FHA loans

In an effort to increase home ownership, the FHA, an agency of HUD, insures loans made by lenders to all U.S. citizens and aliens who are permanent residents and who meet its financial requirement rules. FHA insures the total amount of the lender's loan and lets qualified individuals buy affordable homes.

The minimum down payment for HUD/FHA loans can be less than 5 percent for single-family homes that cost between $67,500 and $151,725 in certain high-cost areas (maximum home loan amounts vary by region). For more information, see www.hud.gov/mortprog.html (shown below) or contact an online mortgage lender. (The FHA loan Web site [www.hud.gov] also provides state-by-state FHA maximum mortgage limits.)

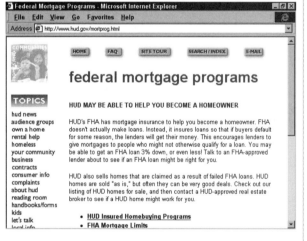

Visit the HUD Web site to find out if you qualify for a low down payment mortgage.

VA loans

The Veterans Administration has a home loan program for eligible veterans and selected reservists. Veterans are defined as individuals who served on active duty and were not dishonorably discharged. The department does not make mortgage loans, but it does guarantee part of the home loan you get from your online mortgage lender. VA loans require a 5 percent down payment, a maximum loan term of 30 years, and have low interest rates (the rate is generally about 1 percent less than the market rate). For more information, see the Veterans Administration Web site (www.vba.va.gov/bln/loan/index.htm).

Choosing a program that's right for you

Lenders Interactive Online Network (www.lioninc.com) is a Web-based company that posts lender interest rates, products, guidelines, and more. This allows you to compare hundreds of banks from one Web site. The Internet has additional advice on different types of loan programs. The following is a sample of what's available:

> *Mortgage.com* (mortgage.com) has a seven-step wizard that helps you choose the loan program that meets your financial profile.

> *AppOnline.com* (www.apponline.com) has a mortgage loan advisor that can assist you in finding the loan program that's right for you.

> *Mortgage101.com* (www.mortgage101.com) is sponsored by America Mortgage Online and includes a vast amount of information about loan programs.

> *iOwn.com* (www.iown.com/buy/) provides three types of assistance: defining mortgage types, calculating monthly payments, and suggesting a mortgage based on your personal needs.

Finding a mortgage online

Many organizations, including banks, credit unions, savings and loan institutions, insurance companies, and mortgage bankers, offer home loans. These organizations merge, change names, and get bigger or smaller as market conditions change. At the time of this writing, there are approximately 3,000 online mortgage lenders. Some are full-service online mortgage lenders; others offer just a few services online. Some of these organizations have "brick and mortar" branch offices and others are entirely Web-based. As a matter of fact, one of the top 10 home loan originators in the U.S. is a Web-based bank: HomeSide Lending, Inc. (www.homeside.com).

The cost of building a full-service online mortgage lending Web business starts at about $2 million. Development costs are ongoing due to the rapid change in online technology. This means that online mortgage lenders tend to be the large mortgage banks because they have the technical clout that has enabled them to build full-service online mortgage lending Web sites. The biggest players include Norwest Mortgage and Countrywide Credit Industries.

In the not-so-distant past, wholesale lenders like Norwest (www.norwest.com) provided their 6,000 brokers with daily interest rate sheets. This amounted to about 42,000 faxed pages per day! Now this information is transmitted using the Internet. Brokers enter their passwords and download the latest rates. Additionally, these rate sheets can be viewed on the broker's Internet browser. This assists mortgage brokers in being more effective and efficient in finding the rate parameters their customers want.

How Norwest provides interest rates to brokers illustrates how important up-to-the-minute information is in the real estate industry. Real-time interest rates and terms change every day. The online applications are matched to premier mortgage lenders like Countrywide, HomeSide Lending, the North American Mortgage Company, PNC Mortgage, LaSalle, Principal Residential Mortgage, and other similar mortgage banks.

Real estate has changed dramatically in the past several years. What you don't know could get you into trouble. The Web can assist you in protecting your wallet and finding the home of your dreams. Much of this information is provided at supersites sponsored by the government, industry professionals, trade associations, and businesses.

The following is a sample listing of these compilation supersites:

> *American Mortgage Listings* (www.loanlist.com) is a *Wall Street Journal* listing of real estate and mortgage loans.

> *General Services Administration* (gsa.gov/staff/pa/cic/housing.htm) is a federal government-sponsored site that has a Consumer Information Catalog for Housing. This Web site includes over 10 pamphlets on home buying issues. Some of the downloadable articles are free; others cost between $.50 and $1.00.

> Microsoft's *HomeAdvisor* (homeadvisor.msn.com/ns/) provides personal financial profile questionnaires to recommend specific loan programs and lenders. In addition to personalized mortgage rates, you'll find homebuyer guidance and online loan applications.

> *Homefair* (www.homefair.com) says you can keep more of your own money when you buy a home, sell a home, or relocate by using the

information at this popular Web site. The homepage is divided into two sections. Power Tools are interactive tools (online calculators, mortgage qualification calculation, relocation wizard, etc.). Instant Info includes many informative articles, as well as links to mortgage rates and real estate shopping sites.

HomePath (www.homepath.com/hpp2.html) provides a chart that you can print out and use to help keep track of the different terms and programs that mortgage bankers offer. You can compare three lenders on one checklist. The checklist can reduce mortgage loan confusion and help you remember those extra costs so you won't be surprised later on.

HSH Associates (www.hsh.com) is a financial reporting service. It provides a showcase of lenders by geographic region.

The Mortgage Company Search Engine (www. loanpage.com) is a mortgage loan database.

Mortgage Mag (www.mortgagemag.com) provides links to hundreds of mortgage banking sites and has listings of mortgage lenders, events, advisors, and more.

The Mortgage Mart (www.mortgage-mart.com) is a residential mortgage lending resource center designed to assist individuals in navigating the home purchasing process. The Web site includes a mortgage lending library, mortgage market information, mortgage professional locators, a standard mortgage loan application (with instructions), mortgage news, and good links to similar sites.

Intuit's *QuickenMortgage* (www. quickenmortgage.com) is a one-stop home loan shopping Web site that offers free real-time interest rate information. Additionally, you'll find mortgage quotes, advice, and online loan applications.

Getting ahead of the game with prequalification or preapproval

The Fannie Mae 1999 Housing Survey states that about one-third of those going through the mortgage process had some difficulty. This doesn't mean they were denied a loan—just that it wasn't smooth sailing. Getting prequalified or preapproved for your mortgage can save you future headaches.

Prequalification is a process in which you speak with a loan officer (either online, face-to-face, or by telephone) and indicate the type and size of the loan you are seeking. You can get help at the Chase Mortgage Web site (mortgage02.chase.com/noframes/frameset3.html). In this case, just complete the form and print your prequalification letter. If you contact a traditional mortgage lender and are prequalified, you'll receive a similar letter in the mail after several days.

To get prequalified, you usually need to provide information about your salary, any other income, your assets, and your debts. A prequalification letter is valuable when dealing with real estate agents and sellers because it illustrates that you are financially stable and likely to qualify for the necessary loan.

With online preapproval, loan underwriters examine the applicant's financial resources, income, and debt to determine if the mortgage is a good investment. A credit check is considered the foundation of this process. Before being preapproved for an online home loan, you may need to supply your loan consultant with the following information:

- W-2 forms from the last two years and profit and loss statements (if you are self-employed)
- One to two months' worth of pay stubs
- Bank, brokerage, and related financial institution statements for the last three months
- Copies of tax returns for the last two years

Some lenders use the originals of these statements to verify your financial situation before they issue your online preapproval letter. This doesn't mean that the online preapproval process is lengthy. You can get online mortgage preapproval within 48 hours at many online mortgage lending Web sites. One example is PNC Mortgage (www.pncs.com.au/managing_your_money/first_home/home_loans/48_hour_loan_approval.html).

The online prequalification process

More than 3,000 mortgage lenders are on the Internet. Many of their Web sites have online preapproval and prequalification features for prospective borrowers. A preapproval or prequalification letter provides real estate agents and sellers with an estimate of how much you can borrow. To get a home loan preapproval or prequalification, keep in mind the following points:

- The amount of cash you have available for a down payment. Also, gather at least three months' worth of bank statements (checking, savings, brokerage accounts, etc.).

- The amount of cash you'll need for closing
  costs (see Chapter 11, "Costs and Tax Benefits
  Associated with Buying a Home").

- Your current household income (wages,
  royalties, irregular income, etc.). Collect all
  your W-2 forms (at least two years' worth) and
  one month's worth of pay stubs. Self-employed
  individuals will need profit and loss statements
  for the last two years.

- Your job status (how many years you've been
  with your employer, your employer's address,
  and your job description).

- Your net worth (the amount of your assets and
  liabilities). You may want to include whole life
  insurance policies, the appraised value of col-
  lectibles, and other assets. See Chapter 2,
  "Creating a Financial Game Plan," for tips on
  how the Internet can help you with this task.

- Copies of tax returns for the last two years.
  (Tax returns often provide lenders with a
  wealth of financial information and may reveal
  unforeseen debt.)

The prequalification process is different from
the preapproval process. Online prequalification is
usually a calculator function that provides a ballpark
loan amount. Lenders often require current credit
reports that are "pulled" electronically. These credit
reports usually cost $15 to $30 and are paid via
credit card to the lender or broker. (If you are not
approved for the loan, the fee is not refunded.)
You can find a good example of an online loan prequalification tool at Accel (www.interest.com/accel/
pq-accel.html). The online prequalification form is
easy to complete.

The online preapproval process

Preapproval goes a step further than prequalification. With preapproval, your lender's underwriter has completed all the necessary checks on your financial background and approved your application; thus you will receive a loan, but it is contingent on the ability of the property you are purchasing to provide sufficient collateral for the loan. Preapproval means that the lender has pulled the borrower's credit report and contacted the borrower's employer, bank, and other places to verify all claims of earnings and assets. In return, the borrower receives a letter stating that he or she has mortgage approval for a certain amount.

Most online mortgage lenders provide preapproval. Generally, this is only credit approval and subject to an acceptable certified appraisal, clear title, and other issues for the specific house you select. Preapproval has the following advantages:

- You know exactly the maximum you can spend on a house before you shop.

- It gives you more "buying" power with a seller.

- It speeds up the loan process.

A preapproval letter has a lot more weight than a prequalification letter. However, it's not a final loan approval. It demonstrates that you are "credit-approved" for a certain amount of money subject to an acceptable appraisal of the property you select and verification of the documentation you submit.

Preapproval works especially well for first-time homebuyers who have no equity and self-employed individuals who often look bad on paper due to having irregular income.

The disadvantage of preapprovals is that they disclose to the seller the maximum loan amount you are approved for. If your preapproval amount is significantly higher than the amount of the house you are purchasing, the seller may counter your offer with a higher offer. One way to avoid this trap is to request a preapproval letter with a specific loan amount when you make your offer. Lenders can often act quickly when you need this type of letter; many lenders will fax the new letter to you within 20 minutes.

Comparing online preapproval and loan application forms

Usually, online mortgage preapproval forms are the "short form" of the lender's "long application form." If you find all the paperwork of getting a mortgage overwhelming, try completing the streamlined preapproval form and forget about hassling with the lengthier online application form.

See for yourself by matching up online preapproval forms to online application forms. Check out the following Web sites that offer loan application forms:

E-LOAN (www.e-loan.com) provides a program that includes a loan application (shown below).

Fair Oaks Financial Services (www.fofs.com) is an online mortgage agency.

Keystroke.com (www.keystrokenet.com/mortgage/apply4loan.html) provides free prequalification evaluation of your loan application.

Mortgage Mart (www.mortgagemart.com) provides step-by-step instructions on how to

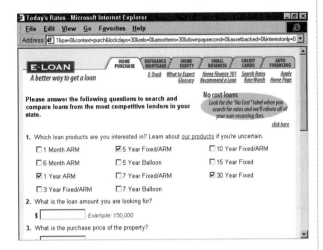

Check out an online loan application at E-LOAN.

complete the standardized form (it takes about 30 minutes).

eMortgages (www.emortgages.com) is a helpful discount mortgage supersite.

Just the facts

- The Web provides vast amounts of information on financing your dream home.
- The Internet provides all the information you need about the mortgage process to be a knowledgeable consumer.
- Today, you don't need to leave your computer to find the right type of home financing at the lowest rate; the Internet can assist you in pre-qualification evaluations, comparing mortgage loans, and mortgage types.
- Getting prequalified or preapproved for a home loan can give you a needed edge when dealing with agents and home sellers.

GET THE SCOOP ON...
Getting the money for a down payment ▪ Low
(and no) down payment loans ▪ Creative
financing options ▪ Special online programs
for first-time homebuyers

Chapter 8

Avoiding the Down Payment Cash Crunch

If you're feeling the pinch of not having the cash for a down payment, you're not alone. About 80 percent of all families have little or no cash savings. In general, buyers tend to fall into one of three categories: folks who will never be able to save the minimum amount for a down payment (the required minimum percentage of the house's price), individuals who can save between 5 and 10 percent for a down payment but can't save a 20 percent down payment, and people who have 20 percent or more for a down payment.

The down payment is the cash portion of the purchase price paid by a buyer from his or her own funds. In the past, you needed a down payment of at least 20 percent of the home's purchase price. These days there are many loan programs with no or low down payment options and below-market interest rates. There are also special programs for first-time homebuyers and individuals who earn low to moderate incomes. Due to these innovative loan programs, more individuals own homes than ever before.

With the wide assortment of loans available, prospective homebuyers can choose the type of loan that best fits their personal needs and financial objectives. In this chapter, you'll discover how you can get a variety of no or lowdown payment mortgages, using traditional and more unconventional ways to acquire a home loan. The chapter includes a discussion of the pros and cons of making a large down payment. Real estate offers the potential of high-leverage deals. This chapter includes a discussion of how the investment in your home may provide a better return if you make a lower down payment.

Coming up with a down payment

As I mentioned in Chapter 7, "Online Mortgage Advice and Lending," many online calculators can give you a good idea of what you can afford. Each of these calculators asks you about your down payment amount.

Lenders consider a 20 percent down payment an indispensable cushion against the risk (and costs) of foreclosure. For example, if the buyer loses his or her job and can't afford the house payments and the house has declined in value, the 20 percent down payment will protect the lender. In this situation, the sales value of the house is likely to pay off the mortgage and still provide the borrower with a small amount of cash. Additionally, mortgage lenders have to follow internal and regulatory guidelines about the required down payment and its size.

The actual money for your home loan often comes from a secondary source that has strict requirements. A few examples of these secondary sources are financial institutions such as Fannie Mae, Freddie Mac, or banks from other parts of the United States or other countries. It is these organizations that take the risk and often require a healthy down payment. After all, studies show the higher the down payment, the less likely the borrower will walk away or default on the loan.

For more online information on your down payment options, see Mortgage University (www. amo-mortgage.com/library/downpayment.html), shown below.

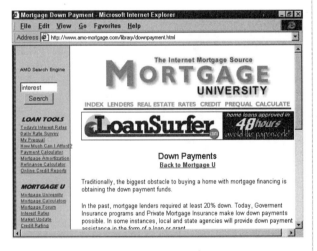

Mortgage University provides help with mortgage financing and understanding down payment requirements. (Information provided by LIONChoice.com.)

Often one of the biggest hurdles to home ownership is saving enough money for the down payment and paying for the closing costs for purchasing a home. Closing costs can range from 3 to 6 percent of the mortgage amount. If you're borrowing $100,000 for your new home, the closing costs can add between $3,000 and $6,000 to the cost of the home, in addition to the down payment. There also may be some prepaid items, such as property taxes and property insurance.

This means that even if you find a no or low down payment loan, you'll still need some cash. Bankrate (www.bankrate.com), a great source for current lender interest rates, has the following suggestions:

- Once you have your financial house in order (see Chapter 2, "Creating a Financial Game Plan"), start saving as soon as possible, and save as much as you can. If buying a home is your top priority, you may have to settle for a less expensive car or forego that luxurious vacation.

- You might be able to borrow enough for a down payment from your 401(k) retirement plan. You can generally withdraw funds, without any penalties, for your down payment. You pay back the funds to your employer over a specific time period. The downside is that your 401(k) account will not grow as fast as usual.

- For many individuals, the only way to get the required down payment is to get a gift from or borrow the money from family members. You can pay the loan back monthly over a specific time period (say, three to five years). In this situation, some lenders will require a letter that states the amount of the payments. This will be factored into your monthly debt amount, unless you and your relatives consider the down payment amount a gift.

How much should you put down?

In determining how much you should pay for a down payment, you need to first decide which of the following three categories fits your financial situation:

Bright Idea
First-time homebuyers can withdraw up to $10,000 from their individual retirement accounts (IRAs) without a penalty. This law also helps homebuyers who aren't making a first-time home purchase. If you haven't owned a home in the last two years, the IRS will still consider you a first-time homebuyer.

- **The no or low down payment category:** Within the time you have until you want to buy a house, can you save the required amount—up to 5 percent of the purchase price of a home?

- **The low down payment category:** Can you save between 5 and 10 percent of the home price, but not meet the 20 percent hurdle needed to avoid paying private mortgage insurance (PMI)?

- **The standard 20 percent or greater down payment category:** Have you saved 20 percent or more to cover the required down payment amount for a conventional loan? Do you want to make a small down payment and invest the rest of your funds, or make a larger down payment?

For additional information on down payments, see Real Estate Library's Mortgage 101 (www.realibrary.com).

The lowdown on private mortgage insurance

PMI makes low down payments possible by offering lenders the protection they'd normally have if the borrower makes a 20 percent down payment. Lenders often require PMI if you make less than a 20 percent down payment. Once the equity in your home increases to 20 percent (due to your payment on the principal from your monthly house payments or an increase in the properties value), you can discontinue paying the additional insurance fee. However, you'll have to remind your lender that the insurance is no longer necessary. (For more information, see Chapter 7, "Online Mortgage Advice and Lending.")

Moneysaver
Lower interest rates also help homebuyers. For example, payments for a $150,000 home with a 10 percent down payment and a fixed 30-year loan at 8 percent are $990 a month. With a 7 percent interest rate, the monthly payments drop to $898, a savings of almost $100 per month.

The advantage of PMI is that first-time home-buyers who can't afford a 20 percent down payment aren't prevented from purchasing a home. However, this benefit is not free. Private mortgage insurers look at a variety of factors (including your personal credit history) when evaluating your monthly premium, so it's impossible to determine in advance exactly what your monthly premium will be. However, some general rules apply. Let's say that you purchase a $100,000 home and put down 10 percent ($10,000). In the first year of your mortgage, your PMI will cost between $400 and $500 for a loan with a fixed rate. After the first year, your annual payments will likely drop to $340 to $440. Usually, you'll pay your PMI premium monthly, with your house payment.

For more information about private mortgage insurance, see:

> *Excite Money & Investing* (www.quicken.excite.com/mortgage/articles) includes 100 questions that every first-time homebuyer should ask. The answers are accurate and to the point.

> The *Mortgage Insurance Companies of America* (www.privatemi.com/main.html) provides educational information about PMI.

Buying a home with little or no money down

For many people, especially first-time homebuyers, down payments are often difficult to come by—in fact, they're the biggest hurdles to home ownership. Others might have the cash to make a sizable down payment, but they still have a choice about how much to pay. There are two schools of thought about making a small down payment versus making a large down payment:

- Making a small down payment often means that you'll have cash for emergencies, landscaping, and home improvements. Additionally, you may want to invest the extra cash if appreciation of your home is less than the return on your investment portfolio. A big plus to this approach is you will receive a larger mortgage interest deduction for your income taxes.

- Individuals who make large down payments often earn a lower interest rate with their lenders. The monthly house payments are less and they don't have to pay PMI costs.

The following table shows how much you'll pay for each $1,000 you borrow. For example, say you want to borrow $100,000 at 8 percent for 30 years. The interest rate for $1,000 is $7.34. If you want to borrow $100,000, you can estimate your payment by multiplying 100 × $7.34, which equals $734 per month. The lower the amount borrowed, the lower the monthly payment.

MONTHLY PAYMENT PER $1,000 BORROWED OVER THE MORTGAGE TERM

Interest Rate	15 Years	20 Years	30 Years
4.0%	$7.40	$6.60	$4.77
4.5%	$7.65	$6.33	$5.07
5.0%	$7.91	$6.60	$5.37
5.5%	$8.17	$6.88	$5.68
6.0%	$8.44	$7.16	$6.00
6.5%	$8.71	$7.46	$6.32
7.0%	$8.99	$7.75	$6.65
7.5%	$9.27	$8.06	$6.99
8.0%	$9.56	$8.36	$7.34
8.5%	$9.85	$8.68	$7.69

continues

continued

Interest Rate	15 Years	20 Years	30 Years
9.0%	$10.14	$9.00	$8.05
9.5%	$10.44	$9.32	$8.41
10.0%	$19.75	$9.65	$8.78

To be considered for a no or low down payment loan, you need to meet a few guidelines:

- Enough monthly income to pay the monthly house payment

- Enough cash to cover the low down payment amount, as well as closing costs, which vary from 3 to 6 percent of the mortgage amount

- A good credit history that indicates a willingness to pay creditors

- A certified appraisal that supports the mortgage amount

- In some cases, cash reserves that cover two months of house payments

Government-sponsored no and low down payment plans

In the past, home ownership was often difficult because lenders required a 20 percent down payment and interest rates were often high. Today, new and revised government-backed mortgage programs make home ownership more affordable than ever.

VA loans

The Veterans Administration (VA) has a program for eligible veterans and reservists that allows them to purchase a house valued up to $203,000 with no down payment. Additionally, the qualification guidelines are more flexible than those for Federal

Housing Administration (FHA) or other conventional loans. To determine your eligibility, check the nearest VA regional office. For more information, see the VA Web site (www.va.gov/publ/vbab/vbahome1).

RHS loans

The Department of Agriculture, Rural Housing Services (RHS) provides loans to farmers and other individuals buying property in rural areas and small towns. RHS offers low-interest loans with no down payments to folks with low or moderate incomes. For more information, see the Department of Agriculture's Web site (www.rurdev.usda.gov/rhs/index.html).

FHA loans

Housing and Urban Development (HUD) and FHA loans have no eligibility restrictions. Private lenders make HUD-insured FHA residential mortgage loans. With FHA insurance, you can purchase a house with as little as 3 to 5 percent of the home's price. FHA loans have a maximum loan limit that varies by geographic location. To discover what the limits are in your area, see Mortgage-X (mortgage-x.com/library/fha_loans.htm), shown below.

One of the benefits of the FHA low down payment program is that down payments can be 100 percent gift funds. (This strategy can't be used for all low down payment programs.) Verification of the source of the gift money is required and the funds need to be deposited in the borrower's bank or savings account before the lender will begin underwriting the loan. There are some restrictions on donors: They must be relatives or certain organizations, such as labor unions or charitable organizations. Of course, some items may be paid for by the

Bright Idea
The FHA's Bridal Registry is a savings account with an FHA-approved lender that allows friends and relatives to deposit their cash wedding gifts directly into an interest-bearing account. More than 30 mortgage companies nationwide have agreed to participate in the initiative. For more information, see www.hud.org/fwsf/fwbride.htm or call 800-CALL-FHA.

Mortgage–X has a handy search engine for discovering the FHA mortgage limits for high-cost areas.

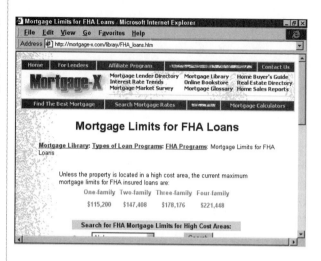

seller, depending on your (or your agent's) negotiating skills.

State and local government loan programs

Many state and local governments offer special loan programs that offer below-market interest rates with low down payments to qualified individuals with low or moderate incomes. Some programs even help with the closing costs.

You might be surprised at the high level of income that is acceptable in these programs, especially if you have children or dependents. Most agencies have purchase limits, but they are adjusted to the income qualification level. Additionally, if you can obtain down payment assistance, you may also receive a below-market interest rate. These programs involve a lot of paperwork, are time-consuming, and often include taking homeowner education classes, but the result—owning your own home—makes the time and effort worthwhile. Check with your state or local housing authority.

Other no and low down payment programs

When it comes to conventional mortgages, there are two formulas generally used to calculate how much you can afford. Home loan qualifying ratios are a lender-based requirement that your monthly debts (car payments, student loan payments, and other debts that require more than 11 months to pay off) do not exceed 26 to 28 percent of your gross monthly income. (The qualifying ratio for FHA loans is 29 percent of your gross monthly income.) Your second qualifying ratio concerns your total debt. This includes house payments and private mortgage insurance (if applicable). This ratio can't be greater than 33 to 36 percent of your gross monthly income. (The qualifying ratio for FHA loans is 41 percent of your gross monthly income.)

Fannie Mae's Community Home Buyer's Program (CHBP) includes Fannie Mae '97. Freddie Mac's Affordable Gold is a loan program that allows lenders to permit the borrower to pay as low as 3 to 5 percent down payment on loans up to $240,000. Participants must complete a pre-purchase education program that focuses on the responsibilities of home ownership.

The home must be the borrower's primary residence, and the combined income of the borrowers can't exceed the median income for the area. Under both programs, borrowers have two options:

- **Option 1:** First-time homebuyers can select a 25- or 30-year loan with a 5 percent down payment. Borrowers need a good credit history and must be able to meet debt guidelines. Usually, monthly debts can't exceed 28 percent of the borrower's gross monthly income, and

Unofficially...
With the Fannie Mae and Freddie Mac plans, you can even borrow your 3 percent down payment on a credit card!

all debt (monthly mortgage payments, taxes, and other debt) can't exceed 36 percent of the borrower's gross monthly income.

- **Option 2:** Gifts from parents or friends. In this plan, the borrower pays a 3 percent down payment and parents or others pay the remaining 2 percent. This can be a gift or personal loan. This 3/2 option allows for higher debt ratios of 33 percent for housing and 38 percent for all monthly debt.

After the closing, the lender keeps in contact with the borrower to prevent delinquencies and provide counseling.

For more information, see Fannie Mae's (www.homepath.com/hsp3.html) special low down payment plans for conventional mortgages.

When none of the traditional options work: creative financing

One way or another, it is possible to purchase your next home with nothing down or a low down payment. The Multiple Listing Service (MLS) doesn't indicate that a home is available with nothing down, but many individuals have purchased homes with no down payment. It's up to the homebuyer to structure the purchase so that he or she can walk away having spent little or no down payment cash. The following sections describe some of the structures that can make this possible.

Assuming someone else's mortgage

Hundreds of properties in every area of the nation can be purchased through assumable mortgages. If you aren't looking forward to having to qualify for a home loan, assuming someone else's mortgage is an attractive alternative. When you purchase the property, the mortgage is transferred to your name.

Another advantage of an assumable mortgage is that the new owner receives the previous owner's interest rate. Many older FHA, VA, and private-party mortgages are assumable.

Most fixed-rate mortgages are non-assumable. In some cases, lenders can call for full payment of the loan as a result of the transfer of the title. This makes the loan non-assumable.

When interest rates are high, lenders are reluctant to offer assumable mortgages. As a result, lenders are adding "due-on-sale" clauses to their mortgages, making their loans non-assumable. There are a few exceptions:

- Some due-on-sale clauses may not be enforceable. For example, FHA loans created after December 1, 1986, may be assumable with lender approval. VA mortgages issued before March 1, 1988, are assumable without lender approval.

- If the loan is non-assumable, you can always ask the lender to allow you to assume the existing mortgage. If the loan is in default, the lender may be motivated to accept your request to avoid foreclosure. (Mortgage lenders loan money, they don't want to own and manage property.)

Doing a seller-take-back

Vacant houses or condominiums are often clues that the seller is anxious to sell. Find out exactly why the seller has put the home on the market. Sometimes you won't get a truthful answer, but often you'll learn that the seller has to quickly

Watch Out!
You should go beyond asking the lender if the loan is assumable. Get a copy of the promissory note, deed or deed-of-trust, and some legal advice to make certain that there aren't any hidden due-on-sale clauses or other problems.

relocate, is falling behind on his or her mortgage payments, or has purchased a home somewhere else and wants to start his or her retirement. In any of these situations, the seller is motivated and you may be able to structure a seller-take-back deal, which could mean that you pay nothing down.

Seller-take-back is a type of seller financing in which a buyer assumes the seller's current mortgage and acquires a second mortgage from the seller for the balance of the purchase price. For example, suppose you want to purchase a $100,000 home. The seller owes the lender $70,000 at 8 percent. You, as the buyer, assume the mortgage (or assume the mortgage with a novation). With a mortgage assumption, you now owe $70,000 to the lender and $30,000 to the seller. The seller gives you a second mortgage, called a "seller-take-back," for, say, five years at 6 percent (or some other figure below the market rate).

Sometimes the lender may also require the buyer's assuming the mortgage to put some money down on the deal and/or pay closing costs. In addition, the seller may finance much of their equity, but need some cash from the new buyer to pay for some costs they have incurred. This will be part of the negotiation for seller financing with the buyer.

If you assume the loan, who is responsible if you default on it? Here are the general guidelines:

- With a mortgage assumption, the buyer promises in writing to pay the loan. In case of default, the lender will first look to the buyer for payment, then look to the seller because his or her name is still on the promissory note.

- With a mortgage assumption with novation, the lender substitutes the seller's liability for the buyers. This releases the seller from the personal obligation created by his or her promissory note. The lender can now require the buyer to prove financial capability and often has the option of adjusting the interest rate on the loan to reflect the current market rate.

The advantage of this type of deal is that it eliminates any hitches that could slow down closing the deal. Other advantages of seller-take-backs can include the following:

- Sometimes the seller can sell the house at a price slightly higher than the market value.

- In a soft real estate market, a seller-take-back makes a home more attractive to buyers.

- The seller can sell the property more quickly than using conventional methods. This technique is more likely to be used in a weak housing market with few buyers. In a strong housing market, it will not be used very often because most buyers will be able to get a regular mortgage.

- What if the seller wants money out of their seller-take-back financing? In many cases, they can sell the note to an investor or finance company and get cash for the note.

Renting with the option to buy

In some instances, you might be able to rent a property with the option to buy. In this plan, you rent the property and pay a premium for the right to purchase it within a limited time period, at an agreed-upon price. In some arrangements, all or some of your rent is applied to the purchase price. This option might help you save money if the current interest rates are very volatile.

This approach allows individuals to lock in a purchase price. You can also buy time, with the hope that lender interest rates will decrease in the future, making the house more affordable. If your credit history needs times to heal, this allows time for any problems to be remedied so you can find financing. Additionally, while living in the house, you may discover major structural problems or other issues that might make you realize that you don't want to purchase the home after all.

You will want to pay careful attention to the contract you sign on a lease purchase. Often you will be paying slightly higher rent than market rent, with part of your rent going toward the down payment on the house. If you decide not to buy the house, you may lose the amount you have accrued toward the down payment. You usually have a limited period of time in which to decide to buy the house. If you need to move in the meantime, or cannot meet the requirements for a mortgage, you may lose the amount you have accrued on this lease purchase, depending on the terms of your agreement.

Using equity sharing

Equity sharing, sometimes called a shared appreciation mortgage (SAM), is where you make monthly payments at a relatively low interest rate, and you agree to share with the lender a portion (usually 30 to 50 percent) of the appreciation in your home's value when you sell or transfer the home, or after a certain number of years. Usually, during times of falling house prices, these types of plans are not available.

A benefit of a SAM is a lower-than-market interest rate. A limitation is that you may be forced to sell your property (on the mutually agreed-upon date) before you're ready to move. Equity sharing plans come in a number of varieties:

- Some lenders offer one type of SAM, and individual sellers may offer SAMs with different terms. For example, a parent could enter into a SAM with a son or daughter who doesn't have enough money for a down payment. In this situation, an adult son or daughter is helped, but he or she may not qualify for a mortgage on his or her own because of a spotty employment record or marginal credit.

- Some SAMs are for tax purposes. In this partnership, the first individual puts up the down payment, and the second individual pays the house payments. In return, the first individual gets all the tax advantages. In this situation, the second individual may not need the tax advantages—perhaps she or he is a student going to school full-time or an elderly parent living on a pension.

Special programs for first-time homebuyers

Many down payment programs are designed to help first-time homebuyers. These programs can be divided into three categories:

1. **Down payment assistance programs.** These programs provide first-time homebuyers with the funds needed for a down payment and closing costs. They can be outright grants that don't require a down payment. Some programs require repayment when the home is sold or if the borrower moves before a specified time period. Other programs have deferred payments that are second mortgages

or loans at below-market interest rates.
Sometimes, down payment assistance programs
are combinations of these formats.

2. **Mortgage credit certificates.** Mortgage credit
certificates (MCCs) are offered by any lender
in partnership with the Internal Revenue
Service (IRS). Mortgage interest is tax-
deductible. Therefore the IRS does not deduct
funds from the homeowner's paycheck. This
allows the homeowner to make a larger house
payment.

Here's an example of how a mortgage credit
certificate can make buying a home affordable
for you: Say you obtain a mortgage loan of
$50,000 at 9 percent for 30 years with monthly
payments of $403 and an MCC credit rate of 20
percent. In the first year, you pay a total of
$4,486 of interest on your mortgage loan.
Because you have an MCC, you could receive a
federal income tax credit of $897 (20 percent,
or $4,486). If your income tax liability is $897
or greater, you will receive the full benefit of
the MCC tax credit. If the amount of your tax
credit exceeds the amount of your tax liability,
the unused portion can be carried forward (up
to three years) to offset future income tax liability. The remaining 80 percent of mortgage
interest, or $3,589, qualifies as an itemized
income tax deduction. By applying the
increase in your take-home pay of $75 toward
your monthly mortgage payment of $403, your
effective monthly payment would be $328
($403 − $75). Based on the effective monthly
payment of $328, your first year's interest cost

would be effectively reduced from 9 to 6.85 percent.

3. **Subsidized interest rate loans.** Many cities, localities, and states offer low interest rates that are subsidized by municipal bonds. The municipal bonds are exempt from some taxation, so the funds used for interest rates can be lower than the market rate. This increases the purchasing power of first-time homebuyers and often reduces monthly house payments.

Online resources that describe specific local down payment programs include the following:

Homeward Bound in Texas (www.amcity.com/ austin/stories/1997/10/27/focus5.html) is a site maintained by the *Austin Business Journal* that describes a down payment program for first-time homebuyers in the Austin, Texas, area.

Affordable Home Ownership in King County, Washington (www.metrokc.gov/exec/news/ 7698nr1.htm), provides a news release about its Housing Finance Commission, which, in partnership with Fannie Mae, makes down payment loans to first-time homebuyers.

First-Time Homebuyer Mortgage Programs for Iowa (www.ifahome.com/partner_home_ buyer.htm) help borrowers in Iowa obtain below-market interest rate home loans. This organization has helped more than 21,000 Iowa families and individuals purchase their first homes.

The *California Housing Financing Authority* (www.chfa.ca.gov) is a government agency that offers loans to low- to moderate-income first-time homebuyers with no money down.

For additional housing information on these special first-time homebuyer programs and other government-assisted programs, see the FHA Web site (www.hud.gov), shown below.

Get additional information about local and regional housing assistance programs at the HUD Web site.

Just the facts

- The Internet can introduce you to a variety of loan programs that require no down payment, a low down payment, and below-market interest rates.

- Real estate listings do not advertise no down payment or low down payment homes, but you can often fashion no and low down payment offers that are advantageous to the seller and the buyer.

- The Internet lists many city, local, and state entities that offer first-time homebuyers special programs that pay for the down payment and offer lower than usual interest rates.

Closing In on Your New Home

GET THE SCOOP ON...
Using the Internet to hire a top-notch
appraiser ▪ Home inspections ▪ Shopping for
homeowners insurance online ▪ Finding title
insurance online

Online Help with Appraisals, Inspections, and Insurance

Chapter 9

This chapter covers selecting and managing many of the professionals and services you'll need to hire after you have selected the home you want to purchase. You'll require a certified appraisal to determine the value of the property you have selected. The Internet can help you understand what an appraisal is, why it's needed for your mortgage loan, and how you can select a top-notch appraiser.

In this chapter, you'll discover how to select a professional home inspector and how to read the inspection report. You'll have to shell out money for the physical inspection, but the cost is minimal compared to the steep repair costs you may have to pay if you don't get the home inspection.

This chapter will show you how to shop online for homeowners insurance and how to select the policy that meets your needs. Finally, you'll discover information about online title search services and title insurance. Find out what you can do online and what is being done online in the industry. Overall, this chapter shows how you can manage a number of real estate professional services by going online. It provides the information you need to select the best of the lot and get the best price for services rendered.

Getting a property appraisal

Virtually all government-related loans require certified appraisals. Since most mortgage lenders are tied into the government in one way or another, this means that all mortgage loans need a certified appraisal. Property appraisers determine how much real estate is worth. All states require appraisers to be licensed or certified after completing coursework and field experience. Specific requirements for appraiser licenses vary by state.

Appraisals usually cost between $150 and $400. Fees vary, depending on the size and complexity of the structures involved. There are independent appraisers and appraisers who work for the bank but charge their fees to you directly, either prior to or at closing. Not all lenders approve all appraisers, so make certain the bank approves your appraiser before you hire him or her.

Property appraisers use the Uniform Standards of Professional Appraisal Practices, as established by the Appraisal Standards Board of the Appraisal Foundation. The appraiser collects data about regional and national economic conditions, focusing on interest rates, employment trends, and population demographics. This resale value is often used to determine the general market demand for the given property.

Appraisers take into consideration the condition of the house, number of bedrooms and bathrooms, amenities, and the home's interior and exterior dimensions. Appraisers research the supply and demand of similar homes. This analysis includes the availability, building costs (including the cost of the land and wages), absorption, and rental rates. Other research includes defining leasing trends to gauge short-term price movements that may affect the property's value. Finally, the appraiser makes an assessment of the neighborhood. This includes traffic patterns and neighborhood amenities (for which homebuyers may pay a premium), such as nearby schools, shopping, historical landmarks, and religious facilities.

The majority of appraisals are requested by mortgage lenders to validate a property's purchase price. If the mortgage lender orders the appraisal, the appraiser is responsible to the mortgage company. Mortgage lenders may use appraisals for:

- Verifying loan repayment (loan repayment is based on the borrower's income and the value of the property)

- Loans guaranteed by the Federal Housing Administration (FHA), the Veterans Administration (VA), Rural Housing Services (RHS), and other government agencies

- Situations where the loan is greater than 80 percent of the debt and a private mortgage insurance (PMI) company may insure the remaining 20 percent

Appraisals in rural areas are more difficult than in urban areas. In rural areas homes are usually sparse, older, and sometimes historic or

Moneysaver
It's a good idea to get a certified, independent appraisal— separate from the one the mortgage company requires— to ensure that you're not over-paying for the house. Sources for appraisal bias include the availability of data, behavioral factors, and appraisal methodologies. An alternate appraisal may find information your first appraiser did not, which may help in obtaining more financing, or a defect, which may result in either a repair by the current homeowner or a reduction in the selling price.

custom-built. Therefore, there are few comparable homes, or if the area is newly developed, comparable home values may not exist.

Additionally, the appraised value of the property can often be different than the market valuation of your real estate. Sometimes homebuyers fall in love with a new home and are willing to pay more than the appraised value. Their lender's primary concern is the certified appraised value or probable selling price of the property. In this situation, if the buyer wants the house, he or she will have to pay the difference between the selling price and the appraised value out-of-pocket.

Using the most probable selling price is one way of stating market value because it reflects current market conditions. Lenders have different goals than homebuyers (borrowers). They are concerned with default and must focus on the most probable market price (the highest price a homebuyer is willing to pay and the lowest price a seller is willing to accept). For more information about how appraisals are completed, see the following sites:

> *Mortgage 101* is provided by the Real Estate Library (www.relibrary.com). Click on Mortgage 101, then click on Appraisals. There is a six-page tutorial that covers appraisal basics, appraisal methods, reasons for an appraisal, a home's market value, appraisals to obtain a loan, and how you can help the appraiser.

> *Home Purchasing Guide* (www.homeowners.com/new135.html) has a great article about appraisals and what appraisers do to develop their reports.

Lenders generally have a list of local pre-screened, preapproved, certified appraisers they use for certain types of properties. Homebuyers can check with their lenders to see if the appraiser they selected is on the bank's recommendation list or approved by the lender. Additionally, homebuyers can investigate the background of the lender's appraiser at the following online sources:

National Association of Real Estate Appraisers (www.iami.org/narea.html) is a professional association founded in 1966 that provides information, real estate news, publications, links to related Web sites, and toll-free telephone numbers for its membership.

Federal Financial Institution Examination Council Appraisal Subcommittee (www.asc.gov) is a national registry of professional appraisers, searchable by name, location, type, or revoked or suspended appraisers by state. Internet users can download a list of all appraisers in any of the 50 states. The site also contains a list of all state licensing agencies.

Appraisal Network (www.appraisal-network.com) estimates real estate values in southwest Ohio and northern Kentucky. They have a list of available appraisers that can assist you in valuating a home.

Appraisal Institute (www.appraisalinstitute.org), shown below, is a nonprofit appraisal organization with member contact information and helpful advice.

The Appraisal Institute is a professional association that provides online information about appraisals.

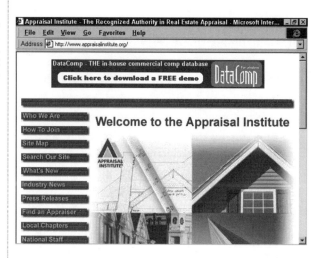

How property is appraised

Appraisal reports can be as long as 14 pages and take up to six hours to prepare, due to the appraisal verification process and the collection of pertinent data. Appraisers typically use three methodologies to determine the value of the property:

- The *cost approach* is the analysis of comparable improved properties. This assists in the determination of whether the property should be held, rehabilitated, or demolished. The land value estimate is used as a separate valuation and can be established through comparable land sales.

- The *market approach* is often referred to as the direct sales approach. Recent data about similar properties are collected and analyzed. Since each property is unique, adjustments are made to equalize the selected properties. The final adjusted value is the market value of the property.

- The *income capitalization approach* is the determination of the value of the improvements based on future cash flow. Some homes don't have a cash flow history; that is, the property was never rented. In this situation, appraisers look at factors such as the income and expense histories of comparable properties, recently signed leases, and vacancy levels of the comparable properties. Appraisers use specific data sources for different property types.

To arrive at a final valuation, the appraiser uses all three approaches. The conventional wisdom is that this threefold approach is an internal check that shows how various properties compare with each other. Generally, appraisers use their expert judgment to assign subjective weights to each of the three approaches. Approaches with less reliable data require more adjustments and are likely to be given less weight than methods that require little adjustment. The appraiser then reconciles all the information into a single-value estimate, or in situations that are uncertain, a range of values.

Online comparable sales reports

Often in the mortgage lending process, the appraisal is the bottleneck that stops the process from being quickly completed. Online automated valuation models (also called comparable sales reports), such as those listed at the Appraisal Network (www.appraisal-network.com), are now available online.

Online comparable sales reports attempt to match similar properties to give homebuyers an idea of the range of sales prices in a certain area. The information is limited to factual data, such as the age of the house and number of bedrooms and bathrooms. Most of the information is from county records and some appraisal reports. The quality of the information varies from provider to provider. Costs range from free to $50 per report. Examples of online automated valuation models include:

CSWOnline (www.cswonline.com/index.shtml) can show you how much a home is worth. The automated valuation systems provide an objective estimate of the value of your home in a matter of minutes. Each report is about $35, payable by credit card or by faxing them your credit card number, if you do not want to pay online. Reports usually take 5 to 10 minutes to be processed. The results are automatically sent via e-mail and may also be viewed at the CSWOnline Web site.

HomeValueCheck (www.homevaluecheck.com) is designed to allow you to compute the value of your home, calculate the value of your home improvements, and check your homeowners insurance. The cost is approximately $15. Each report includes:

- Computed current market value of your home

- Details on 30 comparable sales

- Complete property data (number of bedrooms, bathrooms, the square footage of the property, etc.)

- Property tax information

- Comparison of your property with neighborhood statistics

RealEstate.com (www.realestate.com/ evaluating_property/home.asp) is probably the best deal on the Internet. This analysis includes a residential property report with area map, market overview, and average rate of appreciation, equity analysis, and area demographics. The report is comprehensive and free of charge.

Getting a home inspection

Although inspections are optional, it's generally a good idea to hire a professional to inspect a property before you purchase it. Sellers also benefit from home inspection reports. The home inspection report protects them from the liability of future nondisclosure claims. Sellers can also use the inspection report to get a house ready for sale. Knowing what a house needs in advance allows the seller to shop for bids and set the sales prices.

Home inspection costs range from $150 to $500 depending on the size, location, and condition of the home. For a very large home, the cost may be a thousand dollars or more. Considering how steep home repairs can be, the cost of a professional inspection can be minor in the long-term.

Specialized inspections, such as the following, may be necessary:

- In many areas, a pest inspection may be necessary. The inspector will check for evidence of termites and other pests, and make sure there is no existing damage from pests.

- In many areas, a radon inspection may be necessary, or it may be part of the physical inspection of the house.

If there is pest damage or radon at an unacceptable level, it may be necessary for the seller to remedy the situation prior to settlement.

Doing your own home inspection

To get an initial idea of a home's quality, you can do an informal inspection of your own. Start out by asking the seller a few questions. Next go through the house and evaluate its condition, based on the defects you find, such as those suggested in the following checklist):

Note! →
Adapted from eHow (www.ehow.com/ehows/ehow00003235.asp), October 11, 1999 .

HOME DEFECT FINDER CHECKLIST

Satisfactory?	Description
☐	What is the home's general layout? Do you have to carry groceries up two flights of stairs? Where is the laundry room located? Can you get to it easily?
☐	Does the home have enough space and room for expansion if needed?
☐	Does the house have enough closets and storage space?
☐	What about parking? Is there enough for two cars? Where will visitors park?
☐	Are there cracks in the driveway? They may indicate a drainage problem in the backyard.
☐	Is there water damage on the walls and ceilings?
☐	Are the windows in good condition? Do they open and close easily, and are the bedroom windows large enough for escape in case of fire?
☐	Do all the doors open and close easily and include weatherization? Sliding glass doors should also open easily and include insulated glass so they are energy-efficient.
☐	Do the floors and carpeting show wear or damage due to moisture?
☐	Do the walls, floors, or ceilings contain any asbestos or slate? Asbestos is considered a health hazard. Slate often emits radon gas that can be a health hazard.

Before you make your offer or during the contingency period (that is, after you make a deposit on the property), you'll want to hire a professional home inspector to check out the major systems (roof, plumbing, electrical and heating systems, drainage, and so on). Home inspections take between three and five hours to complete. Make certain you accompany the home inspector so he or she can show you specific defects. If the home inspector is reluctant to have you join him or her for the inspection, immediately be suspicious.

The benefits of professional home inspections

The home inspector can teach you a lot about the home you want to purchase, so plan to accompany the home inspector when he or she evaluates the house. The home inspector will point out which problems are major and which are minor. This way, you'll have a better idea what you're paying for. The property can have patent defects (problems that everyone can see) and latent defects (hidden problems that can cause big trouble). To ensure the most thorough inspection, make certain all utilities are turned on when the house is inspected. Inspectors can only inspect "visible" parts of the structure, and generally will not look behind walls or remove ceiling tiles to check those areas.

The standard home purchase contract includes a long list of areas that an inspector should check for problems, such as a bad roof, dangerous wiring, septic tank drainage problems, and dry rot. The following are a few examples of online resources for more information about home inspections:

Home Inspection Kit (www.freddiemac.com/ sell/consumerkit/english/index.html)

Unofficially... Sometimes real estate agents recommend home inspectors who are not nitpickers so the home sale can be quickly completed. Therefore, it may be a good idea to select your own home inspector instead. Usually agents will just give you a list of three inspectors and have you pick one.

provides a useful home inspection kit for homebuyers, helpful home inspection hints, and information about what you can expect.

Home Inspection and You (www.pueblo.gsa.gov/ cic_text/housing/inspect/inspect.txt) is a booklet published online by the federal government and written as a public service by the American Society of Home Inspectors.

How to select a home inspector

A good inspection report should be more than a checklist; on the other hand, there's no reason to get verbose and have a 20-page report. To avoid a conflict of interest, certified home inspectors are not allowed to do repairs or recommend others to do them.

Be careful whom you select. Home inspectors in Missouri and Illinois don't need any type of certification or licensing (the profession is unregulated in those states). To become certified, home inspectors must generally complete 250 inspections and pass six hours of written tests. For more online information about how to hire a home inspector, see:

Insight Professional Home Inspections (www. inspectit.com/insight/questions.html) provides a list of questions you should ask when selecting a home inspector.

American Society of Home Inspectors (www.ashi. com), shown below, provides a list of home inspectors, tips for homebuyers and home sellers, breaking news, and other information.

The American Society of Home Inspectors Web Site is a great place to find certified home inspectors.

Real Estate Library (www.realtimes.com/ rtnews/repages/19990820_inspector.htm) has a helpful article on how to hire a home inspector.

How to read a home inspection report

There are several types of home inspection reports. Inspection reports can be checklists or computer-generated reports that use a narrative style. The report can be delivered on-site or within a few days of the inspection.

While reading the home inspection report, keep in mind that you want to make sure the condition of the home meets your needs. Sellers are not responsible for the needed repairs detailed in the home inspection report, unless you have signed a contract with the seller making the sale contingent upon the seller's repairing items above a certain dollar amount. If the repairs are costly, you'll likely want to negotiate with the seller.

The home inspection report may indicate that the heating system needs some repairs and is near the end of its useful life. Repair costs could be steep. Don't be afraid to ask the home inspector questions. For example, if there are cracks in the concrete, ask why. The answer may be that when the concrete dries, it's normal to have some cracks or shrinkage. When reading the report, look for:

- The general condition of the home. Homes are generally ranked as being in good, fair, or poor condition.

- Information about defects and recommendations about repairs. For example, a problem with the kitchen sink may be cosmetic, or it may require extensive repairs.

- Keywords, symbols, or icons that make the report difficult to read. Check the report's legend so you understand what each symbol means. You don't want to overlook a problem because you didn't know what a symbol on your home inspection report meant.

The following is a list of items that a professional home inspection should include:

- **Foundation.** Are there any cracks, shifting, or moisture problems?

- **General construction.** When was the house built? How does that compare to today's building codes?

- **Exterior.** Are any repairs needed?

- **Plumbing.** Are there any leaks or water pressure problems? What is the general condition of the plumbing?

- **Electrical.** Are there any dangerous electrical situations? What is the general condition of the wiring? Would it pass today's building codes?

- **Heating and cooling systems.** How old are the systems and do they need any repairs?

- **Interior.** Do all the doors and windows work? Are the floors level?

- **Kitchen.** Do all the appliances function properly? How old is the dishwasher and is it in good repair?

- **Baths.** Is the floor beneath the bathtubs or shower stalls solid? How is the plumbing?

- **Attached structures.** Are there any porches, garages, sheds, decks, etc.? Are they in good repair?

- **Roof.** How old is the roof and what condition is it in? What is the estimated remaining life of the roof?

If your home inspection report does not include this information, talk to the company (or ask for a refund and find another professional inspection company).

If the property needs repairs, or appliance or system replacements, make your sales offer contingent upon the home improvements or offer a lower sales price with the understanding that you will complete the needed repairs or replacements. For more on this topic, see Chapter 10, "Negotiating and Closing the Deal."

Finding homeowners insurance

Before closing your loan, you'll have to show the mortgage lender your homeowners policy for the subject property. Many lenders require homeowners and hazard insurance. Check with your lender to verify that the policy you select meets its requirements.

The basics of homeowners insurance policies

There are many kinds of "standard" homeowners policies. Usually your lender will specify the type and amount of insurance coverage your home should have. Selecting either a high or low deductible depends on individual preference. The average deductible is $250, but you can save money if you go with a higher deductible. Basic liability protection is generally sufficient for anyone, and the amount of money needed to replace your home should not include the value of the land. Here's a quick summary of the primary types of homeowners insurance:

- The Basic Form (HO-1) provides coverage for 11 types of potential losses to the home and its contents.

- The Broad Form (HO-2) covers the 11 types of potential losses in HO-1, plus insurance for six more areas.

- The Special Form (HO-3) provides the maximum amount of protection for the home, but is not as complete as some other policies. In general, HO-3 covers everything but damage from floods, earthquakes, war, nuclear accidents, and similar catastrophes.

Table 9.1 provides an example of the coverage included in the three most popular types of insurance policies. These three types of policies are categorized by insurers as HO-1, HO-2, and HO-3. Each has different features and costs. An × indicates if an item is covered by the insurance policy.

Look over the options and decide which homeowner's policy (HO-1, HO-2, or HO-3) meets your
needs. Keep in mind that policies can sometimes be
customized to meet your individual requirements.
Pay close attention to the exclusions. You may want
to purchase a rider that covers those excluded
items, such as earthquake insurance.

TABLE 9.1: WHAT DIFFERENT HOMEOWNERS POLICIES COVER

Losses Covered	HO-1	HO-2	HO-3
Fire or lightning	×	×	×
Windstorm or hail	×	×	×
Explosion	×	×	×
Riot or civil disturbance	×	×	×
Aircraft	×	×	×
Vehicles	×	×	×
Smoke	×	×	×
Vandalism	×	×	×
Breakage of the glass part of a building	×	×	×
Falling objects		×	×
Weight of ice, snow, or sleet		×	×
Accidental discharge, leakage, or overflow of water or steam from heating and air-conditioning or appliances		×	×
Sudden and accidental tearing apart, cracking, or burning of the building's heating and air-conditioning or appliances for heating water		×	×
Freezing of plumbing, heating and air-conditioning, and appliances		×	×
Sudden and accidental injury from artificially generated currents		×	×
Volcanic eruption		×	×
Other perils, except flood, earthquake, nuclear accident, and those specified in the policy exclusion list			×

← Note!
Adapted from
Ralph Nader and
Wesley J. Smith,
*Winning the
Insurance Game*
(1993).

If you have a mortgage, you'll need homeowners insurance, and even if you don't have a mortgage, you'll still probably want it. The Internet can assist you in your search for a quality policy and can broaden your understanding of residential insurance. After all, your home is the largest asset you have, and you should protect it. The following are a few examples of sites that provide information on homeowners insurance:

> *General Services Administration* (www.pueblo. gsa.gov/cic_text/housing/12ways/12ways.txt) has an informative online booklet, "Twelve Ways to Lower Your Homeowners Insurance Costs." This helpful guide was developed by industry professionals and provides quality information and good advice.

> *Insweb* (www.insweb.com) provides information about homeowners insurance and can give you a quote over the Internet. Simply enter information about yourself and your home. Use Insweb's Quotepad to review the quoting companies. Insweb uses a secured questionnaire to help you insure your home for the correct amount.

> *The Insurance News Network* (www.insure.com) provides industry news, state-by-state residential insurance rates, information about six basic homeowner's polices, and more.

> *Insurance Information Institute* (www.iii.org) is a nonprofit organization designed to educate consumers about insurance. For tips on reducing your homeowners insurance, see the Insurance Information Institute's helpful articles atwww.saftek.com/insurance/1/lower.htm.

Keeping your insurance costs low

Residential insurance policies are relatively stable but exist in a competitive market. This means that prices vary. The annual premium for a $300,000 residential insurance policy ($200,000 for the house and $100,000 for the contents) can range from $500 to $700 per year. Experts suggest that you get as many as 10 quotes before you buy. (These online quotes are subject to an insurance appraisal, so you won't have 10 insurance appraisers marching through your home.) Keep in mind that you only need insurance for the value of the improvements on the property, not the land. If you purchased your house and land for $200,000 and the land costs $50,000, then you only need insurance for $150,000 (for the structure itself).

There are many discounts that you might want to take advantage of. The following are a few examples:

- **Multiple-policy discount.** You get a price break if you use the same company for your auto insurance and liability policies.

- **Safety-device discount.** If you have smoke detectors and a burglar alarm system, you may save money.

- **Nonsmoker's discount.** Some insurance companies offer discounts to nonsmokers. (They're not likely to go to sleep with a lighted cigarette.)

- **Fire-resistant material discount.** Houses that are constructed using fire-resistant materials (cement block, brick, and related materials) often qualify for a discount.

> **❝**
> Life is full of uncertainty, but three things are constant: death, taxes, and insurance.
> —Ralph Nader and Wesley J. Smith, *Winning the Insurance Game* (1993)
> **❞**

- **Mature homeowner discount.** Some companies award longevity and maturity with a discount.

- **Loyal customer discount.** Certain companies reward long-term customers.

Getting title insurance

Making sure you have the title to real property is important to lenders. The lender's mortgage is a lien on the real estate. If there's a "cloud" on the title, the lender can't follow foreclosure procedures. That is, if the borrower doesn't make payments on the mortgage or fails to meet the other requirements of the mortgage and the loan goes into default, the lender must be able to foreclose on the property and sell it to settle the debt.

To verify ownership of the property, a title search is completed. The title search can disclose unpaid real estate taxes, special assignments, judgments, federal tax liens, other government liens, mechanic lien claims, decedents, court proceedings, covenants, conditions and restrictions, and easements. However, title searches can overlook secret spouses, undisclosed heirs, minors or the elderly who may have questionable competency, forgery, and fraud. This is why lenders also require title insurance.

All that title searches can do is state that the property has a valid title. Title insurance protects against undisclosed title defects that can't be discovered from public records—for example, forged signatures, impersonation, homestead rights of a spouse, or recording errors.

The title attorney, your lender, or the title company of your choice usually orders title searches. In some states, it may be customary for the seller or the real estate agent to select the title company. When the title search is complete, you or the closing attorney will provide a mortgage title insurance policy that protects the lender against losses due to a faulty title. Prices vary and may be based on a percentage of the home's value. The title search and insurance are usually paid by whatever the local custom demands—the seller, the buyer, the lender, or the fee may be split 50-50. This will be a one-time purchase for the buyer.

Online title companies can perform title searches and asset searches, as well as filing of ownership and encumbrance reports and buying title insurance. One such company is Computitle Limited (www.computitle.com), a firm that provides online searching for deeds and documents and cause lists. The database can be accessed by entering a person's name, company name, subdivision, or condominium. Available information includes document type, document date, lodging date, recorded reference, grantee, other referenced documents, consideration (since 1987), grantor and property description, and chattels. Digital copies of documents are available for downloading. Other title companies also use the Internet in the following ways:

> *Stewart Title* (www.stewart.com) enables online customers to exchange orders and documents, then view or print out title and closing documents, flood certifications, and automated property valuations.

> *Lender's Service, Inc.* (www.lenderservice.com) provides a broad spectrum of collateral assessment, flood, title, and closing products, and services for every stage of the mortgage

cycle. The company uses the Internet to reduce expenses, better manage capacity, mitigate risk, and significantly decrease the home loan processing time.

Just the facts

- Use the Internet to find a certified appraiser and to check his or her background.

- Home inspections are necessary to point out both the patent (easily recognizable) and latent (hidden) defects in a property.

- A good home inspection will cost you a few dollars now but can save the cost of major repairs in the long run.

- The Internet is the perfect place to shop for home insurance and to discover what type of policy is best for your financial situation.

- Some title companies send the results of their title searches to you via e-mail, or you can view the report using your Internet browser.

GET THE SCOOP ON...
Negotiating to get the best deal possible
■ Making an offer they can't refuse ■ The final
walk-through ■ The closing and taking
possession of your new home

Negotiating and Closing the Deal

When you go to the grocery store, you don't dicker at the counter about the price of fruit. If you purchase stock on the New York Stock Exchange, you don't barter with your broker. Things are different in real estate. Here, almost everything is negotiable. That's because it's difficult to place a specific value on a property. It's not unusual for two certified, professional appraisals to be thousands of dollars apart when valuating the same property. This uncertainty over price is based on the fact that each piece of real estate is unique as an economic good.

This means that homebuyers have to negotiate if they want to pay the least a seller will accept and the most they are willing to pay. Unfortunately, most individuals are not experienced negotiators. They are not familiar with the rules of the game. This chapter shows how the Internet can assist you in becoming a savvy negotiator, including how to make an offer they can't refuse, how to determine the right price for your special home, how to determine how large a deposit to make, and what sort of contingencies you should include in your offer.

In this chapter, you'll learn how to determine what sort of counteroffers the seller will likely make, get negotiating tips and strategies, and discover when to stay and when to walk away from negotiations.

Finally, you'll find out what to expect at the closing meeting. This chapter shows how the Internet can assist you in reducing the stress associated with home buying, and points the way to mastering the paperwork involved in closing the deal.

Everything is negotiable

Your negotiations with the seller begin long before you submit your offer. There are many steps in the course of negotiating, but the entire process centers on three things: information, preparation, and realism.

Gathering information

It's important that you gather as much information about comparable house prices as possible. One site that can help you do this is Experian (www. experian.com/ecommerce/realestate.html), which provides Property Profile Reports (approximately $8 per report) to assist homebuyers in determining how much a home is worth. You can also order its Recent Homes Sales Report (approximately $10 per report), which has five matching properties. In addition, Experian offers a Home Portfolio Report (approximately $18), which includes the Property Profile Report, Recent Home Sales Report, and statistical information about homes and homeowners in the selected zip code. For more information

Watch Out!
Environmental issues are more important than ever. Neighborhoods that are near manufacturing areas are particularly vulnerable to underground water pollution due to the improper disposal of manufacturing waste. This means that you need to consider the condition of the land, as well as that of the home. Land can have a negative value because the cost to clean it up is higher than the land's sales price.

about online automated valuation models like Experian, see Chapter 9, "Online Help with Appraisals, Inspections, and Insurance."

Good real estate negotiators have comparable sales information, know the history of sales prices in the neighborhood, and have forecasts of how quickly neighborhood housing prices are expected to increase. All this information is available on the Internet, and most of it is free. After you have gathered your online comparable sales and valuation reports, drive by the homes that have recently been sold. Compare the sales price and condition of these homes to the home you plan to purchase. If these homes are in better condition and recently sold for the same price as the home you have selected, you should probably lower your offering price.

Knowing why the seller wants to sell can help your negotiations. Does the seller *have* to sell or *want* to sell? For a list of questions for you (or your agent) to ask the seller, go to HomeAdvisor (homeadvisor.msn.com), shown below.

HomeAdvisor suggests that you work these questions into your conversations with the seller or listing agent.

You may want to talk with a neighbor about the history of the house you selected or have your Realtor inquire for you. Additionally, you may want to ask your real estate agent (who has access to such information) about the marketing history of the property. For example, how long has the home been on the market? What was the original asking price? Has the selling price been reduced? In this situation, the type of real estate agent you hired plays a big role:

- A buyer's agent represents you and will seek this information.

- If you are working with the seller's agent, you are not likely to get the information you want.

- If you are working with a dual agent, he or she can disclose this information only with the seller's consent.

For more about types of agents, see Chapter 5, "Using a Real Estate Agent."

Being prepared

Next, you need to make sure you use the information you gathered to your maximum advantage. One way to make an offer the seller can't refuse is to make certain you are preapproved for a mortgage (see Chapter 7, "Online Mortgage Advice and Lending," for more information). Sellers often prefer preapproved buyers because they can usually close the deal faster.

Your frame of mind is also important. Be prepared to walk away from the deal if the price is too high for your budget or not at the fair market value. Organize the data you have gathered so you can quickly access it when needed. (How to organize your offer and prepare for negotiating are discussed in detail a little later in this chapter, in the section "Making an offer they can't refuse.")

Being realistic

The final key to being a good negotiator is to know how to play the negotiation game. For example, a low-ball offer on a home that is priced at the fair market value may be unproductive because the seller might shut down negotiations. If you manage to get the seller to reopen negotiations, it's likely that the seller will stick to the original listing price more closely than before.

Using the Internet to be a better negotiator

Real estate and automobiles are among the few things in America for which you can negotiate a sales price. Because we don't barter in the normal course of business, many people don't understand the rules of negotiating a sales price. Being a good negotiator and making a well-prepared offer can save you lots of money over the long term. To assist you, the Internet provides many online tutorials and guides to help you negotiate the best sales price for your special home. The following are a few examples:

> *Real Estate Home Buying FAQ* (www.suntimes. com/realestate/homebuyingfaq3.html) provides good advice on the best way to negotiate a sales price.

> The *HomeAdvisor Guide to Negotiating the Deal* (homeadvisor.msn.com/ns/offerclosing/ finalsteps.asp) includes a guide that shows the dynamics of negotiating so you can stay focused and unemotional during what can be a nerve-wracking process. To find the guide at HomeAdvisor, click on Offer & Closing, then click on Advisor in the left margin. Find the category titled Guides in the next page and click on Negotiating the

Deal. The bargaining strategies detailed in the tutorial can greatly assist you in your negotiations.

The Eight Rules of Negotiating (www.homespot. com/r4main3a.htm), by Robert J. Bruss of Tribune Media Services, shows the basics of negotiating.

Making an offer they can't refuse

Once you find your special home, you'll want to move on it as fast as possible. Regardless of how long a property has been on the market, others may have just discovered the property at roughly the same time you did. Writing up the offer usually takes about an hour to an hour and a half, with or without a real estate agent. If you write the offer yourself, make certain your attorney reviews it before presenting it to the seller. If you have a real estate agent, your agent will present your offer to the seller.

Making an offer is serious business. You sign a contract (that includes all the details of your offer) to purchase a home, and if the seller accepts your offer, you are legally bound to follow through. Before you put your offer in writing, you'll have to make several important decisions. Your offer will become a legally binding sales contract if the seller accepts it. If you don't have an agent, you may wish to have an attorney review the contract before signing. For an example of a sales contact, go to the Real Estate Center (recenter.tamu.edu/hguide/ hboffer.html) and select Click Here to see a copy of a sales contract used in Texas. Preprinted sales contract forms are available from real estate associations, title companies, and stationery stores.

Sales contracts vary, but they generally cover the same basics. When making an offer, at a minimum, you'll need to include the following information:

- The sales price.

- Any seller concessions. For example, the seller may pay some or all closing costs.

- The amount of deposit, or earnest money, you'll provide.

- Whether and how the sale is contingent upon your securing financing.

- Whether and how the sale is contingent upon an acceptable appraisal and home inspection report.

- Time and date of the closing meeting.

- All exclusions or inclusions in the property (appliances, chandeliers, etc.), including whether any of the appliances are under a warranty agreement, and copies of those warranties.

- The specific time period for which the offer is good.

Paragon Decision Resources (www.pdr.com/beforeoffer.htm), a relocation firm, offers three online buyer worksheets. These worksheets are designed to assist you in gathering information and developing strategies to determine the best offering price that will be acceptable to the seller. After all, careful planning and strategizing at this point can save you thousands of dollars as you negotiate with the seller. The three worksheets include information on the following:

- **Evaluating the property's features.** This worksheet is a good reference tool for noting the property's fundamental good and negative features.

- **Comparable and competitive property analyses.** This handy worksheet is great for listing comparable properties sold and competitive properties listed.
- **Negotiating with the seller.** This worksheet lets you identify seller concessions (discounts, repair allowances, closing costs, and other items). Additionally, you can list your counteroffers.

Determining your offer price

To determine an offer price, you should use information from the automated valuation reports and the other data you collected from the Internet. Compare sales to the home you have selected. Note any amenities that similar homes don't have, such as a swimming pool, hot tub, landscaping, remodeled kitchen, or added rooms. Keep in mind that the addition of a hot tub should not make a substantial difference in the sales price, but an extra bedroom can make a big difference.

It's a good idea to research the difference between the asking price and the selling price for homes in the area you have selected. For example, it may be typical for homes to sell for 5 percent less than the listed price. The discount amount in the area you selected may be more or less. In a hot market, it's not unusual for homes to sell above the listed price. This means that you may have to pay more than the asking price.

Determining how much the home is actually worth also involves some physical legwork. You should visit the home at least twice, during the day and in the evening. On these visits, don't forget to talk with the neighbors to get a sense of who's next door and what they think about the neighborhood and housing prices.

The reality of "low-ball" offers

There are two schools of thought about low-ball offers. The first school believes that sellers are often emotionally involved with their homes. Features they cherish may have no value to you. A low-ball offer will offend these sellers and force buyers to pay more than if they had begun by making a reasonable offer.

The second school of thought believes that buyers have nothing to lose if they make a low-ball offer. These individuals are gambling that the seller *has* to sell or is in a hurry to sell and just may go for the offer. They believe the risk of closing down negotiations is worth the possibility of saving thousands of dollars.

Many real estate professionals believe the best approach is to make a realistic offer. Realistic offers have a higher probability of being accepted by the seller. On the other hand, don't let your Realtor force you into making an offer you feel is too high just so he or she can quickly collect a sales commission.

How large a deposit?

The offer is submitted in writing to the seller and accompanied by a deposit, called *earnest money*. This shows the seller that you are a serious buyer; that is, you are earnest about purchasing the property. Generally, in earnest money is about 1 to 5 percent of the sales price, but the specific customary amount varies from region to region. Some listings state that offers without deposits of a certain amount won't be considered. If your offer is rejected, your earnest

Moneysaver
Make sure the contract specifies that the deposit will be added to your down payment. Without specific instructions, it may be interpreted as money in addition to the down payment, money in addition to the sales price, or even a signing bonus.

money will be returned. If your offer is accepted, it becomes part of the down payment.

Some of the advantages and limitations of making a large deposit are:

■ Some real estate agents encourage large deposits, but it's to your advantage to make as small a deposit as possible. This way, if there are any problems and you lose your deposit, you'll lose less money.

■ In a hot market, a seller with several offers may accept the buyer with the larger deposit.

■ If you pay a large deposit and the deal falls through, you may or may not be entitled to a refund of your deposit. If the deal is cancelled and it's not your fault, you'll likely get your deposit refunded. If the deal falls through because you changed your mind, you'll likely have to forfeit your deposit.

Adding contingencies to your offer

A *contingency* means that your offer is good only if certain conditions are met by the seller. Typically, sellers don't like offers with contingencies, but there are three things that *must* be included in any offer:

■ **Financing.** Including a contingency based on financing allows the buyer to back out of the contract if the home loan is not approved.

■ **Inspections.** You wouldn't buy a car without checking it out. The same is true for a residence. Make certain that you word the contingency in such a way that the seller pays for the inspection and the seller must fix problems uncovered in the inspection or the offer is canceled.

- **Title.** Make certain that if there is a "cloud" on the title you can back out of the contract. A cloud on the title can be a dispute of ownership, liens, or judgments against the property. Notice whether or not there are easement or utility rights on the property, as they could affect how you can use parts of the land.

Adding optional contingencies

Actually, you can add all sorts of contingencies to your offer—even a hot tub in the front yard! However, there are several common types of contingencies that you may want to consider adding to your offer:

- **Sale of current home.** If you can't sell your current home by a certain date, you can back out of the contract.

- **Insurance.** If you are unable to get a homeowners insurance policy for the property (generally a requirement for lender financing), you can back out of the contract. For example, if the survey indicates the house is in a flood plain, you may not be able to insure it.

- **Disclosures.** If the seller does not disclose environmental hazards or other material defects in the property, the contract is void.

- **Time limits.** Set a time limit for the seller to respond to your offer. What is customary varies from state to state. Generally, sellers have three days to respond, but if you are in a hurry, you may require a response in 24 or 48 hours.

- **Contract review.** The buyer has the right to have the sales contract reviewed by an attorney.

Online help with making an offer

Once you've found the house that meets your needs, you must decide how much to offer. The Internet can assist you in making an offer that is likely to be accepted. The following are several of the resources you'll find on the Web:

Real Estate Offers and Contracts (www.nolo. com/encyclopedia/articles/re/re17.html) provides the most frequently asked questions about making an offer to purchase a home.

Homebuyer's E-Guide (recenter.tamu.edu/ hguide/hboffer.html) by Jack Harris, Mark Bauman, and Charleen Knapp provides good advice for new and experienced homebuyers.

Homespot (www.homespot.com/homespot/ r4main3e.htm) focuses on making an offer. It includes hyperlinks to the essential terms in a real estate contract and suggests potential counteroffer clauses.

Inman News Features (www.inman.com/ inmanstories.asp?ID=10005&cattype=) provides a helpful article titled "Your Home Purchase Offer: How to Make Sure It's Accepted," by Robert Bruss of Tribune Media Services; it can help you write a knockout offer.

Counteroffers

After you have signed the sales contract, your agent will deliver it to the seller. The seller usually has about three days to contemplate your offer. The standard time to consider offers may differ depending on the locality; ask an agent about this. The seller can reject, accept, or counter your offer. This

is where those negotiating skills you've been working on enter the picture.

Keep in mind that many sales contracts go
through several rounds of negotiations before being
accepted or rejected. Most sellers' objections relate
to the following:

- **Sales price**—your offer is too low.

- **Financing**—you want too much time to find
  financing.

- **Inspections**—you should buy the house as is.

- **Occupancy**—you want to move too soon or
  too late (the seller may want to move
  immediately).

Negotiating tips

You may want to include a few items in your offer
that will lower your costs. Some of the most common items are as follows:

- **Ask the seller to lower the sales price.** You are
  in a strong bargaining position if you're an
  all-cash buyer, preapproved for a home loan,
  or don't have to sell a home before you can
  purchase. These factors can help you negotiate
  a lower sales price.

- **Ask the seller to pay your closing costs.** This
  lowers the up-front costs for the homebuyer.
  Frequently, lenders will allow sellers to credit
  buyers up to 5 percent of the purchase price
  for nonrecurring closing costs. In return,
  you'll pay a little more for the house to offset
  the seller's paying the closing costs.

- **Ask the seller to pay for a home warranty or
  home inspection to move things along.** If the
  seller won't pay for these items, ask the seller
  to split the cost with you.

Watch Out!
This is an anx-
ious time for
even the most
experienced
homebuyer. Try
to keep your
emotions in
check if you talk
directly with the
seller and be
careful what you
say. Comments
like "we just love
the house" or
"we have to find
a home within
the week" can
give the seller
extra leverage.

Bright Idea
As part of your
negotiations, ask
the lender to pay
your closing
costs. You'll pay
a little higher
interest rate, but
in return, you'll
walk away from
the closing with
more cash in
your pocket
for moving
expenses, furni-
ture, and so on.

Typical seller counteroffers

Most sellers realize they won't receive initial offers they consider satisfactory for their properties. Making a counteroffer can indicate that the seller is not willing to accept the offer as written, motivated to sell the home, willing to negotiate, or desires different terms for the contract.

A seller counteroffer must be in writing and state the length of time a buyer has to accept the counteroffer, generally from several hours to several days. Then you have to decide if you want to accept the changes, revise the changes, or withdraw your offer. Counteroffers frequently include:

- A counteroffer for the sales price stated in your offer.

- A counteroffer that requires additional payment for the appliances, fixtures, and other amenities.

- Contingency release clauses that specify deadlines for the contingencies you have in your offer (for example, the home inspection must be completed within 5 to 10 days).

- An "as is" clause. This means you're responsible for all repairs. However, the seller must disclose any known defects to the buyer.

The offer and counteroffer process can continue as many times as needed to reach an agreement, or it can stop if one of the two parties decides to call it quits. This process does have some risk to the buyer:

- When a seller provides a counteroffer, he or she can revoke it (in writing) anytime before the buyer accepts.

■ The seller is free to accept another offer while you are contemplating his or her counteroffer.

Once you and the seller agree upon the terms of the sale, you must communicate in writing to the seller that you accept the counteroffer. This acceptance must be within the limits stated in the counteroffer and before the seller revokes the counteroffer.

Sold!

When you and the seller have finalized a contract, you sign the revised sales agreement and make a deposit (or increase your deposit, if required). The deposit is placed in an escrow account held by an independent trustee such as the closing agent, the real estate agent, or a title company. In this situation, an escrow account is a bank account maintained by a real estate broker to hold funds for others. State real estate laws require that the money, such as the deposit funds, held in the escrow account cannot be mixed with the broker's personal or company bank account. For more information, see Chapter 11, "Costs and Tax Benefits Associated with Buying a Home."

Based on the negotiations, the seller needs to finish any necessary repairs before the transaction can be completed. You have the right to hire an independent inspector to make certain that the completed repairs are as stated in your negotiated agreement.

Read the revised contract carefully. You may want your attorney to review it to make certain that you actually receive what you are buying. If you discover something in the contract that you don't like, get it changed. After all, in real estate just about everything is negotiable.

The final walk-through

To protect yourself and the seller, you should conduct a final walk-through prior to the closing meeting. Take your sales contract with you. This way, you can ascertain that the seller has moved, no damage has occurred, all repairs are complete, and all the appliances or other negotiated items are on the premises.

Take your time and check the house from basement to attic. Turn on the appliances to make certain they're in working order, test the plumbing, verify that the water heater works, and so on. Remember when you settle, the agreements you negotiated will not survive the closing unless there is a "survival clause" in the sales contract. If you settle without the needed work completed, you accept the property "as is."

You can use the Internet to find a variety of checklists that will help you with the final walk-through. The following are two sites that you may find helpful:

You can use Star Home Inspection Group's checklist as a baseline of your current home's condition and as a status report of any agreed-upon repairs or modifications.

Buyer's Walk Through Inspection Form - Microsoft Internet Explorer

File Edit View Go Favorites Help

Address: http://www.stargroup.com/walkthru.html

BUYERS WALK-THROUGH INSPECTION FORM

Many buyers choose to perform a walk-through or pre-settlement inspection prior to the settlement date to review the property's condition. A systematic review of the building's components prior to settlement or as soon thereafter as possible will help you develop a baseline of the building's condition and will provide a status report on any agreed upon repairs or modifications.

General	N/A	YES	NO	OTHER
Any major changes to the property?				
Agreed upon modifications or repairs completed?				
Receipts/warranties/guarantees provided by repair contractors?				
Pest control clearance provided?				

Roofing	N/A	YES	NO	OTHER
Indications of roof leakage?				
Gutters and downspouts secure?				
Signs of roof surface, flashings, vent or chimney				

Our Family Place (www.ourfamilyplace.com/ homebuyer/walkthru.html) has a home-buyer's information center that includes a final walk-through checklist.

Star Home Inspection Group (www.stargroup. com/walkthru.html) offers a useful form, shown below, for a systematic review of a building's components for your final walk-through.

Closing the deal

The closing meeting is where you complete the transaction. For many people who use online mortgage lenders, this is the only time they have to leave their computers. The day of your closing meeting is called the *closing date*. Some states don't have formal closing meetings, however. In this situation, the escrow agent processes all the paperwork, arranges for all documents to be signed, and collects and disburses the required funds.

The meeting takes approximately an hour. Attendees usually include the buyer and the seller, or their representatives; attorneys representing various parties; representatives of the lending institution; and some representative of the real estate broker of record.

The closing meeting

The *closing meeting,* sometimes called the settlement meeting, is where ownership of the home is officially transferred from the seller to you. Your closing agent coordinates the signing of documents and the collection and disbursement of funds. Your main role at the closing is to review and sign all the documents related to the mortgage loan and to pay the closing costs.

Unofficially...
This is not the time for the buyer to make an initial inspection of the property. You should have a professional inspect the property as a contingency on the contract. If the property does not pass inspection, or repairs are not made as necessary, you may decide not to complete the sale without penalty, if you included the property inspection clause in the contract to purchase the house.

The primary documents used to close the deal are the settlement statement, the sales contract, the loan papers, title insurance, homeowners insurance, the title or deed to the property, and the down payment and closing costs. Before the closing, you'll probably need to deliver the following documents to the closing agent:

- A copy of the signed sales contract (your offer) and any contingencies that were added

- A copy of a homeowners insurance policy for the property you are purchasing

- The money necessary to cover the balance of your down payment and closing costs

For more information on the closing, see Chapter 11, "Costs and Tax Benefits Associated with Buying a Home."

If you are moving to the country, you may need to obtain well and septic certifications. If the property is not connected to a local water and sewage system, you'll need a certification of a private water source and sanitary sewer facilities before closing. (Usually you have to contact the county government for this certification.)

Many new homes need a certificate of occupancy. This certification is required before you can move into a newly constructed home. The builder obtains the certificate, usually from the city or county, and provides the form for the closing. For a recently renovated home or a home of a certain age, an inspection may also be required to determine if the property meets local building codes. For more about a certificate of occupancy, see Realtor.com (www.realtor.com/closing/closing.asp).

The meeting is usually held at the closing agent's office. The exact procedure for closings varies from

Bright Idea
Before closing and taking possession of your new home, arrange for utilities such as electricity, water, and telephone to be turned on in your own name at the new address.

state to state. The following explains, in general, what you can expect:

1. All unresolved walk-through deficiencies are resolved.

2. With the buyer, the closing agent explains the deed of trust, the note, the truth-in-lending statement, and the settlement statement. There should be no surprises at the settlement meeting, but problems can arise.

    Make sure the date on the settlement statement is correct, as all allocated costs (real estate taxes, insurance, mortgage interest, etc.) are calculated based on this date. You don't want to pay more than required.

    The settlement statement reflects all the applicable details of the transaction and details the amount of money due to and from various parties. Many of the fees are called closing costs (closing costs are discussed in detail in Chapter 11, "Costs and Tax Benefits Associated with Buying a Home").

    Review the settlement statement carefully. Bring a calculator and ask questions if anything seems unexpected. If everything is correct, you sign all the appropriate documents.

3. With the seller, the closing agent explains the deed and settlement statements and gets the home seller's signature on them. (The closing agent will review any negotiated closing costs the seller has agreed to pay.)

4. If you and the seller decide that everything is correct, you and the seller submit certified or cashier's checks to cover the closing costs and any balance of funds due. (Title companies do

Timesaver
The Home Buyer's Information Center (www. ourfamilyplace. com/homebuyer/ closing.html) shows an example of a settlement statement. Read the categories to gain an understanding of what closing costs you'll be expected to pay. Being familiar with the paperwork will save time at the closing meeting.

not accept personal checks for real estate closings.) The check from the lender covering the
mortgage amount is submitted to the closing
agent.

5. In some cases, the lender pays your annual
property taxes and homeowners insurance for
you, and a new escrow account (or reserve) is
established at this point.

6. At the end of the meeting, you receive keys to
your new home and can tell the movers to get
rolling.

After the closing

After the meeting, the closing agent officially
records the mortgage and deed. The legal transfer
of the property may take a few days after the closing.
The closing agent usually will disburse the funds to
everyone who is owed money from the sale (including the seller, real estate agents, and the lender) at
the closing. Any adjustments to payments that arise
at the settlement will be paid a few days later. In
some areas, disbursements take place after the deed
is recorded. Check with a local title company as to
the custom in your area. When the deed is actually
recorded, you become the official owner of the
home.

You should keep a copy of each document you
sign at the closing in a file folder that is dedicated to
the house purchase. Many of the fees you're paying
now are tax-deductible.

Online resources to help you prepare for the closing

The days before your closing are likely to be stressful. You may have second thoughts or fears that the
deal will fall through. Remember that an informed

consumer is less likely to be taken advantage of or defrauded than an uninformed one. The Internet provides a variety of resources to help you increase your understanding of the closing process and how to close the deal. The following are a few online sources that you may find useful:

Fannie Mae's *HomePath* (www.homepath.com/hpp51.html) helps you discover what your role and responsibilities are before the closing.

MSN *HomeAdvisor* (homeadvisor.msn.com) offers information and checklists for creating a closing plan. You'll discover what to do in advance, during the week of your closing, and how to be prepared for the closing meeting.

iRichmond (irichmond.com/escrow.htm) provides a lengthy checklist that shows what happens when you process your sale through escrow. This is helpful, and right on target.

Realtor.com (www.realtor.com/closing/closing.asp) is sponsored by the National Association of Realtors. This Web site includes definitions of closing terms and documents, high-quality data on what a closing is, and other relevant information.

Owners.com (www.owners.com/tools/library/mainlisting.asp?lib=1) has helpful information at its Owners.com Reference Library. Uncover information about what happens at the closing, and find out exactly what documents the buyer and seller each sign.

Just the facts

- Don't assume that the point of all negotiations is to lower the purchase price.

- If the seller accepts your offer, it immediately becomes a legally binding sales contract.

- Don't hesitate to add contingencies to your offer.

- Counteroffers between the buyer and seller can go on until one party accepts an offer or decides to walk away from the deal.

- When the seller accepts your offer, you'll go to a closing to finalize the transaction and take possession of your new home.

- Keep your closing documents in a file so that you can easily access them later.

GET THE SCOOP ON...
Closing costs ▪ Lender errors and overcharges
▪ Lowering your closing fees ▪ Escrow accounts
▪ Tax deductions related to buying a home

Costs and Tax Benefits Associated with Buying a Home

Chapter 11

What you don't know about closing costs can cost you thousands of dollars. High closing costs surprise most homebuyers. At the closing, you'll need money not only for the down payment, but also for the closing costs. Become an educated consumer to avoid overpaying or making a mistake at the closing table. Closing costs, sometimes called settlement costs, are the fees and taxes associated with buying a home, borrowing money, and preparing the necessary paperwork to finalize the sale. Closing costs for government-backed loans (such as VA, FHA, and RHS) are usually less than 2.5 percent of the mortgage loan. The closing costs for conventional loans can range from 3 to 6 percent of the mortgage amount. The total of your closing costs can vary due to geographic location, type of property, price of the home, and complexity of the transaction.

Often homebuyers discover that closing costs are more than they anticipated. Knowing what fees you'll be charged and how they are presented can speed up your closing, reduce the probability of your overpaying, and lower the possibility of fraud. Either the agent or the title company handling the closing should provide you with a list of all expected closing costs. This will be an estimate, but it is important in terms of estimating the amount of cash you will need in the qualifying process.

This chapter shows how the Internet can help you make certain you don't overpay or make mistakes at the closing table. You'll discover how the Internet can assist you in comparing your settlement statement with the lender's to ferret out errors. You'll get an understanding of what settlement costs are all about and learn how to estimate closing costs by using an online calculator. Finally, you'll discover how the Internet can provide the information you need for lowering closing costs and discovering which closing fees you can deduct from your income taxes.

Understanding closing costs

The more familiar you are with the closing paperwork and fees, the better your chances of lowering settlement costs and ensuring a smooth closing. For example, any funds that are due will have to be paid by a certified or cashier's check. If you are not prepared and have to run to the bank during the closing, the settlement may be postponed to another day. Changing the closing date means changing the settlement statement. This can add to the settlement costs.

Who pays what closing costs varies from one geographic region to another and is often open to negotiation between the buyer and seller. For example, a motivated seller may pay all the closing costs if the buyer purchases the house at the asking price. This allows the buyer to pay less money upfront, and the seller gets a slightly higher-than-usual selling price.

The following online sources offer helpful information on closing costs:

> The federal government's *Consumer Information Center* (www.pueblo.gsa.gov/ cic_text/housing/settlement/sfhrestc.html) provides a helpful online manual titled "Buying Your Home: Settlement Costs and Helpful Information." Section III of the manual includes specific information about settlement costs, shows how to calculate the amount you'll need at the closing, and details the cost adjustments frequently shared by buyers and sellers.

> Another way to calculate your closing costs is to use *Financenter* (www.financenter.com), shown below. Financenter provides a useful online calculator for determining your closing costs. At the Financenter homepage, click on the House icon. Next, in the ClickCalcs text box, select What Will My Closing Costs Be? Enter the amounts you expect to pay at closing using the information listed above. The online calculator will do all the math for you.

Don't get sur-
prised by high
closing costs. Be
in the know by
calculating your
closing costs
online.

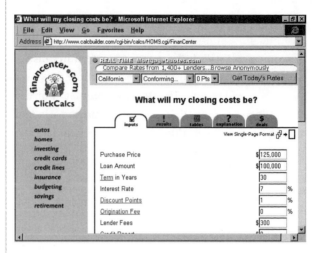

Many lenders provide borrowers with a copy of "Settlement Costs: A HUD Guide" to help them understand closing costs. You can see a similar guide at HUD's Web site (www.hud.gov/fha/sfh/res/ sfhrestc.html).

Documents related to closing costs

The closing revolves around four documents: the settlement statement, the truth-in-lending form, the mortgage promissory note, and the mortgage. These documents describe your loan terms, respon-sibilities, and the closing costs you are expected to pay at settlement. If you're familiar with these docu-ments, you can quickly complete the closing or catch potential errors.

The HUD-1 settlement statement and the truth-in-lending form include important information about your closing costs:

- **Settlement statement.** The settlement state-ment is usually delivered or mailed to you at or before the settlement. (By law, you have the right to inspect the HUD-1 settlement statement one business day before the closing.)

The HUD-1 settlement statement itemizes each service provided to you and the fees charged to you. This form is completed by the closing agent. This is the same person who will oversee the closing, so make sure you have the name, address, and telephone number of this individual. In cases where there is no settlement meeting, the escrow agent will mail you the HUD-1 settlement statement after the closing.

You can locate a copy of the HUD-1 settlement statement form at the HUD Web site (www.hud.gov/fha/sfh/res/stcosts.pdf), shown below.

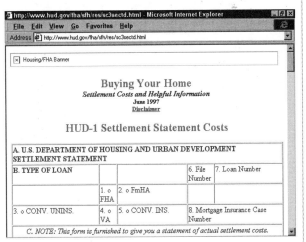

Your settlement statement shows how much you'll have to bring to the closing table.

■ **Truth-in-lending form.** This form details all the major financial terms of the home loan. There are two types of disclosures made in this form: the numerical disclosure, so consumers can

Bright Idea
If you don't already have Adobe's Acrobat Reader for PDF-formatted documents, you can download a free copy from the Adobe Web site (www.adobe.com/products/acrobat/readstep.html).

compare the cost of one loan to another, and the disclosure of the terms of the mortgage agreement.

For example, numerical disclosures include the annual percentage rate, finance charges, amount financed, total payments, amount of payments, number of payments, security interest, assumption policy, variable rate, filing fees, late charges, payment due date, prepayment policy, hazard insurance, and mortgage insurance.

- **The mortgage promissory note.** This legal document obligates a borrower to repay a mortgage loan at a stated interest rate during a specified period of time. This is your I.O.U. to the lender and a promise to meet the requirements of your home loan. Depending upon when you close (settle), this document will outline the prepaid interest you will have to pay at the closing.

- **The mortgage.** This legal document pledges a property to the lender as security for payment of a debt, giving the lender a legal claim on your property if you don't fulfill the terms of the promissory note. In some states a "deed of trust" is used instead of a mortgage. In other words, you receive title to the property but convey it to a neutral third party until the mortgage promissory note is paid in full. The mortgage is not related to certain closing costs, but central to the closing process. Without the mortgage, you can't close the deal, unless you are paying all cash for the property.

Comparing actual closing costs with estimates

To make certain you are paying the correct amount for these fees, the day before your closing, you should compare the lender's original good faith estimate of the closing costs to your completed HUD-1 settlement statement. (Lenders are required to provide borrowers with this good faith estimate no later than three business days after receipt of your application.)

The estimated closing costs are likely to change during the time between your application and closing. Some costs may be higher than expected, while others may be lower, due to changes in appraisal fees, interest rates, and so on. However, there are four costs that should be *exactly* the same on your settlement statement as on your good faith estimate:

- **Title search.** A check of the title records to ensure that the seller is the legal owner of the property and there are no liens or other claims outstanding.

- **Title insurance.** Protects the lender (if it's the lender's policy) or the buyer (if it's the owner's policy) against losses arising from disputes over ownership of a property.

- **Loan origination fee.** A fee paid to a lender for processing a loan application, stated in the form of points. (Remember that 1 point is 1 percent of the mortgage amount.)

- **Mortgage insurance premiums.** A private mortgage insurance (PMI) company policy protects lenders against losses if a borrower defaults.

Bright Idea
To help understand your closing costs, become familiar with the words and terms used in real estate transactions. Go to the federal government's Consumer Information Web site (www. public.gsa.gov/ cic_text/ housing/ home-vocab. hmvocab.txt) and print out a copy of the Home Buyer's Vocabulary.

Moneysaver
If you close on your home during the last week of the month, you can reduce the amount you are paying for prepaid interest on a monthly loan payment.

The types of closing costs

Both recurring and non-recurring costs are associated with home loans. Recurring costs are payments you'll make periodically throughout the life of the loan (such as interest, property taxes, and hazard insurance). Some of the closing costs are one-time expenses, or non-recurring costs.

Non-recurring costs are usually miscellaneous fees and government-related expenses. In most parts of the United States, homebuyers are expected to pay a variety of miscellaneous charges and fees to local and state governments for services related to the purchase of real property. Government-related closing costs vary from state to state. For example, Maryland has some of the highest government-related closing costs in the nation. For some homebuyers, government-related fees can be the largest expense paid at closing.

Another non-recurring cost may be a prepayment penalty on the loan, if this is permitted by law in the area you are buying the house. Check with your lender as to whether there is a prepayment penalty, and if so, does it apply for a limited number of years or for the life of the loan.

Closing costs can be divided into three main categories:

1. **Lender-based fees,** which are often not charged to borrowers until the closing. Typical costs in this category are the loan origination fee, loan discount points, appraisal fee, credit report fee, assumption fee (if applicable), prepaid interest, and escrow accounts (for insurance premiums, private mortgage insurance, and property taxes).

2. **The amounts paid to government entities.**
   These costs usually include recordation fees
   and transfer charges.

3. **Miscellaneous charges,** which generally include
   closing agent costs, property survey fees, termite inspection charges, well and septic certification, homeowners association or condominium fees, and so on.

The following sections describe these three categories in more detail.

The following table lists many of the individual
costs involved in closing, and provides examples of
what they generally cost. (You'll learn more about
the individual costs later in this chapter.)

If your closing costs are much higher than those
listed, you should find out why the charges are so
high. Use an online calculator and determine your
costs in advance of the closing. You might discover
that you are being charged twice for the same service or that the closing agent made an error.

AVERAGE CLOSING COSTS

Description of Closing Fee	Average Cost
Mortgage Fees	
Loan application fee	$0 to $500
Credit report fee	$40 to $150
Lender's processing fee	$75 to $150 (sometimes negotiable)
Lender's document preparation fee	$50 to $200
Appraisal fee	$200 to $450 or more
Survey fee	$50 to $175
Prepaid interest on loan	The daily cost of your loan from the day you close the loan through the end of the month in which it occurs.

← Note!
Adapted from
RealEstate.com
(www.realestate.
com), October
25, 1999.

continues

continued

Description of Closing Fee	Average Cost
Title-Related Fees	
Title search	$25 to $75
Title insurance	Based on the dollar amount of your mortgage
Recording fees	$25 to $75
Additional State and Local Fees	Based on the value of your home and the local and state tax rate. Property taxes can range from $0 to $5 per $1,000 of the purchase price. Some areas have a flat fee of $25 to $50 per transaction.
Other Professional Fees	
Escrow company fees	$150 to $600
Homeowners insurance and hazard policy	Based on the value of your home, from $2 to $6 per $10,000 of the purchase price
Closing company or closing attorney fees	$150 to $1,000, depending on geographic location
Home inspection fees	$200 to $400
Termite infestation report	$50 to $100

Lender-based closing costs

Lenders are required to tell you in advance how much they charge for various services, but most borrowers don't pay these fees upfront. Examples of the types of fees you can expect are:

■ **Loan origination fee and discount points.** Mortgage lenders earn their money by charging points. One point is equal to 1 percent of the loan amount. Points can be divided into two categories. First, the loan origination fee is expressed in points. This is the lender's charge for evaluating the borrower, reimbursement of the lender's administration expenses, and the fee for creating the loan package and the home loan. Second, points can be used as

prepaid finance charges and are a way of
increasing the yield to the lender beyond the
stated interest rate. As a general rule, the
higher the points you pay, the lower your interest rate, and vice versa. (In some situations,
part of the points may be financed as part of
the loan amount.)

- **Appraisal fee.** The fee for a lender-approved,
certified appraisal of the property to determine the market value of the property. (For
more information, see Chapter 9, "Online
Help with Appraisals, Inspections, and
Insurance.")

- **Credit report fee.** A detailed financial history
of the borrower used by the lender to determine whether to approve the home loan application. (For more information, see Chapter 2,
"Creating a Financial Game Plan.")

- **Assumption fee.** The fee paid to the lender for
the assumption of an existing mortgage (if
applicable). In this situation, the new borrower
takes the title to the property, which has an
existing mortgage, and agrees to be personally
liable for all payments due for the existing
mortgage. Non-qualifying borrowers are often
charged a flat fee of between $100 and $200.
For qualifying borrowers, the assumption fee is
1 percent of the loan amount or less. (For
more information, see Chapter 8, "Avoiding
the Down Payment Cash Crunch.")

- **Prepaid interest.** Prepaid interest is a one-time
interest paid at loan closing to pay for the cost
of borrowing for a partial month. For example,
if a loan closes on the 15th of the month and

the first payment is due 45 days later, the
lender will charge 15 days of prepaid interest.

- **Escrow reserves (sometimes called impounds).**
  Payments to the lender to be held in reserve to
  ensure payment of property taxes, hazard
  insurance, and private mortgage insurance
  (PMI) as they become due.

- **Mortgage insurance.** If your down payment is
  less than 20 percent of the value of the home,
  your lender (and the law in some states) will
  require that you pay for PMI. This insurance
  policy covers the risk of borrower default, that
  is, not making monthly payments or failing to
  meet loan requirements. (For more information, see Chapter 7, "Online Mortgage Advice
  and Lending.")

- **Homeowners and hazard insurance.** Must be
  equal to the replacement value of the property.
  This is insurance against physical damage by
  fire, wind, vandalism, and other similar problems. The lender may also require flood insurance. Mortgage lenders expect borrowers to
  pay the insurance premium for the first year of
  homeowners and hazard insurance and have
  the policy in effect at the time at closing. (For
  more information, see Chapter 9, "Online
  Help with Appraisals, Inspections, and
  Insurance.")

Government-based closing costs

Local (or county) government often requires fees
and transfer taxes for the recording and transfer of
ownership, and local and state governments frequently require payment of property taxes. The following is a summary of these costs:

■ **Property taxes.** Property taxes are often prorated for the year of purchase. This adjustment
can be negotiated between you and the seller,
and is shown on the settlement statement. The
amount of prorating depends on when the
property taxes are due, what portion has
already been paid, and what period of time
they cover.

Let's say you purchase a home on April 1
and the seller has paid school taxes in
September and local taxes in January. For
school taxes, the homebuyer would pay six
months, or $6/12$ (one half) of the total amount.
For local taxes the homebuyer will pay nine
months, or $9/12$ of the total amount. (See
"Using an escrow account" later in this chapter
for more information about prorating.)

■ **Recording fees and transfer taxes.** Recording
fees and transfer taxes are charged by most
states and many local governments for recording the purchase documents and transferring
ownership of your new home. In some states,
these charges are called *documentation stamps.*
The costs are calculated by your closing agent
and are usually a percentage of the home's
selling price. In some areas of the country, the
seller pays one fee and the buyer pays another.
Your real estate agent can tell you what's customary for your area.

Other costs for establishing ownership

Each real estate property is unique, and each real
estate transaction is unique. Depending on where
you are in the nation and what extra services you or
your lender requires, you may have to pay these
additional closing costs:

Moneysaver
First-time buyers
and individuals
with low to
moderate
incomes can
often qualify
for special
community,
employer,
charity, state,
and federal
programs that
pay all or some
of the closing
costs. One
example is in
Austin, Texas,
called the HOME
Down Payment
Assistance
Program
(www.ci.austin.
tx.us/housing/
hshnhmdp.htm).

- **Survey.** The survey verifies that the boundaries are as stated in the sales contract. That is, a survey is an independent verification that the lot has not been encroached upon by any structures since the last survey of the property. Conversely, the lender may require a survey to ensure that the house and any other structures are where you say they are (and not on someone else's property).

- **Home and termite inspection fees.** These inspections are for the homebuyer's protection. For more information on home inspections, see Chapter 9, "Online Help with Appraisals, Inspections, and Insurance."

- **Prorated homeowners association or condominium fees.** Many residences are in planned areas where residents are charged a monthly fee by an association for landscaping, security, or other amenities. These fees may be paid annually, so the expense will be prorated at closing.

- **Other lump-sum professional service charges.** Other professional expenses, such as those for an attorney, an escrow and a closing agent, or company fees, might also be required.

Reducing your closing costs

Now that you're more familiar with the types of closing costs you'll have to pay, you may wonder what you can do to reduce your costs. The following are five suggestions provided by Inman Real Estate News (www.inman.com/index.asp) to help you lower your closing costs:

1. **Get a no-points loan.** In this situation, the borrower pays closing costs but doesn't pay for

points. No-points loans have a higher interest rate. However, if you're short on cash and can qualify for a no-point loan, you can substantially reduce your mortgage-related closing costs.

2. **Get a no-cost loan.** Here, the lender includes the points and the closing costs in the home loan. No-cost loans usually have a higher interest rate but lower the amount of cash you need upfront to purchase your home. One alternative to this approach is getting seller financing. (See Chapter 12, "The Internet and Do-It-Yourself Real Estate," for more information.)

3. **Negotiate.** One way for new homeowners to lessen the burden of these settlement costs is to shift some of these government-related expenses and miscellaneous fees to the owner. However, this suggestion should be included in the original offer and negotiated with the seller before the closing. Fees you should consider negotiating include the following:

   ▪ Government-based closing costs, such as transfer, recording fees, property taxes, etc.

   ▪ Fees such as termite and home inspection, mortgage broker, and real estate agent fees.

   ▪ Discount points that you may pay a lender at the time of closing to reduce your interest rate.

4. **Lease with an option to buy.** This gives you more time to save the cash you'll need for the down payment and closing costs.

Watch Out!
Some fees are prohibited by law. It's illegal for anyone to pay a fee, kickback, or anything of value because they refer you to a certain service, organization, or individual. For example, your mortgage lender cannot add a referral fee in addition to your charge for an independent appraisal.

5. **Shop around for the best loan available.**
Each direct lender (like AppOnline, at
www.apponline.com, or Countrywide, at
www.countrywide.com) has its own fee
structure. Check out several online
mortgage lenders before you submit your
loan application.

Using an escrow account

Unofficially...
There are three
ways to avoid
using an escrow
account. First, if
you make a 20
percent down
payment on your
home, you'll
likely avoid hav-
ing to pay into a
lender escrow
account. Second,
if you've paid off
20 percent of
your mortgage
and have never
been late on a
payment, you
likely can stop
having to pay
into a lender
escrow account.
Third, you can
make a 10 per-
cent down pay-
ment and have a
first mortgage of
80 percent and a
second mortgage
of 10 percent.
This enables the
borrower to
avoid paying
PMI.

An *escrow account* is money, documents, or an item of
value that is deposited with a third party to be delivered upon the fulfillment of a predetermined condition. For example, when you close, you may have
to deposit funds with your lender so the lender can
pay taxes and insurance premiums when they
become due. Another example is the deposit of
funds or documents with an attorney or escrow
agent to be disbursed upon the closing of the sale of
real property.

Your lender may require monthly payments to
an escrow account for homeowners insurance, mortgage insurance, and property taxes. (These are
recurring closing costs.) The cost of these items is
included in your monthly house payment. When the
lender receives your check, the portion that doesn't
apply to your mortgage goes into an escrow account.
Next, when property taxes or similar recurring closing costs are due, the lender pays from your escrow
account.

Some lenders don't require an escrow account
for homeowners insurance, mortgage insurance,
and property taxes. Other lenders charge homeowners a fee for not escrowing these funds. Still
other lenders may require you to keep an extra two
months of payments in your escrow account at all
times for future payments.

The tax implications of buying a home

Over the past several years, the tax code has changed. Most deductions for middle-class taxpayers have disappeared, and the only remaining deductions are for expenses related to home ownership. The major federal tax benefits of owning a home are:

- You can deduct interest costs on getting the financing for a home with a principal balance of up to $1 million.

- You can deduct the interest costs on a second mortgage or home equity loan with a principal balance of up to $100,000.

- You can deduct all property taxes on your primary residence.

What can you write off?

Some of the closing costs you pay are deductible in the tax year in which you purchase your home. You should check your settlement statement for the exact amounts you can deduct for the following expenses:

- Prepaid mortgage interest paid at the closing can be deducted in that year's income tax return.

- Points paid at the time of closing are treated like mortgage interest and can be deducted from your income taxes.

- Any property taxes you pay at closing and during the year can be deducted from that year's income tax return.

For more online information about the tax benefits of home ownership, see Publication 530 from the Department of the Treasury, Internal Revenue

Service (www.irs.ustreas.gov/prod/forms_pubs/ pubs/p530toc.htm). This Web site provides an online booklet titled, "Tax Information for First-Time Homeowners," shown below. Get high-quality information from the source about how to handle deductions for closing costs, property taxes, and mortgage interest.

Owning a home has other tax benefits as well. When you begin owning a home, you pay more interest than principal. You can deduct the interest paid on your mortgage on each annual tax return. However, there are a few restrictions:

- The interest deduction is limited to a million dollars. If your borrowing exceeds that amount, see a tax consultant or estate planner.

- Certain itemized deductions (including home mortgage interest) are limited if your adjusted gross income is more than $124,500 ($62,250 if you are a married couple filing separately). For more information, see IRS Publication 936 (www.irs.ustreas.gov/prod/forms_pubs/pubs/ p936toc.htm).

Online tax help

The Internet provides many resources that deal with the tax implications of home ownership. The following is a short list of Internet tips, recommendations, articles, and other sources of information on the tax benefits of home ownership:

Century 21 Real Estate Tips: Tax Considerations (db.inman.com/inman/qa/c21/invest.htm) provides answers to frequently asked questions about property tax deductions, federal tax deductions, and other tax-related issues.

Lycos Real Estate (www.lycos.com/realestate) includes snappy articles, downloadable software, and other resources to assist you with your taxes and closing costs.

The IRS Problem Solver (www.taxhelponline. com/solp5.htm) solves 29 of the most common IRS problems. Visit this Web site and get answers before tax time.

Just the facts

- To avoid making costly mistakes at the closing table, become familiar with the closing documents and fees you'll be expected to pay.

- Avoid surprises—use an online calculator to determine your closing costs.

- Check for errors by comparing your settlement statement with your lender's good faith estimate of closing costs.

- Compare your settlement statement with the average costs listed in this chapter.

- Many of your closing costs are tax-deductible; find out which ones you can write off by using information provided by online IRS publications.

The Real Estate Road
Less Traveled

PART V

GET THE SCOOP ON...
Going FSBO and avoiding FSBO risks ▪ Finding
FSBO listings online ▪ FSBO financing that can
save you money ▪ Closing your FSBO deal

The Internet and Do-It-Yourself Real Estate

A property that is for sale by owner, sometimes called a FSBO (pronounced "fizz-bo"), is a commission-free real estate property that can save sellers and buyers thousands of dollars. Currently, FSBOs represent about 20 to 30 percent of all home sales. Note that this figure does not necessarily mean the property was advertised for sale to the general public. It means the property transferred from one owner to another without an agent involved in it. Thus, family transfers or an employee's selling his or her house to a corporation prior to moving would be included here.

The number of FSBO sales remained stable for around a decade, and then the Internet revolutionized the FSBO market. FSBO Web sites are growing at a phenomenal rate. Today, there are well over 100 FSBO Web sites on the Internet. The quick expansion of FSBO Web sites and their related entrepreneurial real estate services has led to an

Chapter 12

increase in the advertising and marketing options of FSBO sellers.

Many large FSBO Web sites have teamed up with well-known online entities. For example, Owners. com (www.owners.com) and AOL (www.aol.com) sponsor a FSBO listing at AOL's ClassifiedPlus Directory. (If you are not an AOL subscriber, go to the AOL homepage at www.aol.com and click on Classifieds. Click on Real Estate, and then click on Owners.com.) HomeGain.com (www.homegain. com) has linked up with RE/MAX in California and Hawaii. HomeGain matches FSBO sellers with real estate agents to facilitate quicker sales.

Many experts believe that in the future, FSBO Web sites will put pressure on traditional real estate agents. This in turn will create a more competitive atmosphere for agents. The impact of the Internet can be seen today in the reduction in the number of real estate licenses. For example, in the state of Wisconsin, according to the Department of Regulations and Licensing, the number of licensed real estate brokers and sales agents has fallen by more than 6 percent over a two-year period. In January 1997, there were 28,719 real estate licenses; two years later there were 27,010. This may indicate that as online competition heats up, real estate agents are seeking opportunities in other areas.

Why go FSBO?

On the Internet, you'll discover heaps of literature to support the notion that you should use a real estate agent when buying a home. After all, purchasing a home may be the biggest financial decision you make in your lifetime, and you'll want all the help you can get.

However, some real estate agents aren't as helpful as they could be. For example, let's say you visit a home that you think is wonderful. The agent tells you the sales price, and you think the asking price is too high. Your agent may or may not agree with you, but you have to keep in mind that unless you are using a buyer's agent, the agent is obligated to represent the interests of the seller. If you think the price is too high, make an offer that is lower, and see if it is accepted. Remember, property is only worth what the next person will pay for it.

If the broker represents the seller, he or she can't indicate anything that may lead you to make an offer at a lower price. This means that you're on your own for finding comparable homes and recent sales prices. Other areas where an agent may be less than helpful include the following:

- The real estate agent may not mention (or may make certain he or she doesn't know) that the neighbor's dog barks all night or the couple living next door has loud arguments at all hours.

- The real estate agent may not mention (or may make certain he or she doesn't know) that your magnificent view will be gone in several years due to new construction that's currently in the works. The agent is obligated to inform you of any issues which would affect the value of the property, if he or she is aware of them. You should check out these things for yourself, if it is important to you.

Although these situations don't happen all the time, on occasion they do occur. This is why some individuals want to work directly with the seller.

Bright Idea
If you like a certain neighborhood, you or your agent can send a letter to every home in the neighborhood, saying you are looking to buy in the area. You might discover that someone is planning to sell but hasn't put his or her home on the market yet, and both you and the seller could save some time and money.

They want to be in control of the situation and save the thousands of dollars normally paid in real estate commissions. However, FSBO property buyers often find themselves needing to hire an attorney. Your lawyer can assist you with the paperwork and can possibly negotiate for you. Often attorneys charge a flat fee of around $1,000 for this service. Hiring an attorney is not that unusual; in most traditional real estate transactions, homebuyers hire attorneys at hefty hourly rates to review sales contracts and mortgage loan documents.

The benefits of FSBOs

The residential real estate market, which accounts for $1 trillion in annual business, is changing. As homeowners become more sophisticated, they are less wary of selling their own homes. After all, each real estate transaction comes down to just two people: the buyer and the seller.

Both first-time and experienced homebuyers can succeed and be rewarded by *not* using an agent. Purchasing a FSBO home can allow you to share in the benefits of a no-commission sale. Sellers generally pay the real estate commission, which will be negotiable, but this cost is built into the home's sales price. This means that you, the buyer, are really paying the real estate commission. Additionally, buying direct is quick. Not having to go through a third party frequently saves you time. You can accomplish more because you deal directly with the FSBO seller.

The problems of FSBOs

Buying your home directly from the seller may provide you with a home at a bargain price. On the other hand, you may encounter a few problems. The following is a short list of what you may find:

- The seller doesn't want to pass any cost savings on to you, so the home is not the bargain you expected.

- The seller is very sentimental about the house and has set an unrealistic asking price.

- You discover you don't have the time or the required knowledge about real estate financing to close the deal.

- You don't realize any savings due to the cost of hiring an attorney to negotiate for you, review the sales contract, and assist you with the closing.

Fair housing and FSBOs

Fair housing laws are federal and state regulations that prohibit discrimination in the selling of real estate. Under the fair housing laws, it's illegal for a real estate agent or a FSBO seller to deny equal treatment on the basis of the other party's race, color, religion, national original, gender, handicap, or presence of children in the family.

One way to check out the regulations and be sure you're being treated fairly is to go to the National Housing Fair Housing Advocate Online (www.fairhousing.com/legal_research/fha/index. htm) and read the U.S. fair housing code. If you still have questions, check with an attorney.

FSBO financing options

You can finance a FSBO with all of the methods detailed in Chapter 7, "Online Mortgage Advice and Lending." Lenders don't care if you hire a real estate agent or not. They have their own in-house experts who will go over the documentation with a fine-tooth comb. Keep in mind that they are looking out for the mortgage bank's interest, not yours.

FSBOs offer several interesting financing options. The most popular are assuming the current home loan, having the seller finance a portion of the sale, or asking the seller to finance the entire sale if he or she owns the property. (Again, for more about financing options, see Chapter 7, "Online Mortgage Advice and Lending.")

Finding FSBO listings online

Online listings provide an effective, low-cost alternative to traditional real estate marketing methods. Today, there are well over 100 FSBO Web sites. Some Web sites are regional, others are national, and a few are global (these are usually for luxury and vacation homes). Advantages of online FSBOs listings include:

- The cost to the FSBO seller for listing his or her home online varies from free to a few dollars per month.

- Potential buyers can view the home online and read a detailed description of its features and benefits 24 hours a day, 7 days a week.

- Out-of-town homebuyers can view the property from across the country and enjoy a pictorial walkthrough of the home.

- Multiple pictures show the interior, exterior, garage, neighborhood, and key features of the property.

- Prospective buyers can contact FSBO sellers via e-mail to ask questions, make offers, and negotiate the sale.

To reap the rewards of buying a FSBO property, buyers have to do a little more work. At the top of this list is locating the FSBO property you desire.

This is where the Internet plays a large role. Finding a FSBO property online is easier than ever before, with national and regional FSBO listings and personal search agents that will send you e-mail when new listings match your search criteria.

Nationwide online FSBO listings

FSBO Web sites are terrific places to start your house hunting, and visiting is well worth your time. Many of these sites provide buyers with property evaluation checklists, neighborhood fact sheets, and information on how to conduct comparative market evaluations. Many also provide hyperlinks to lawyers, mortgage lenders, online calculators, and real estate support professionals. The following are a few examples of FSBO sites:

Moneysaver
Working with a FSBO seller is often harder than working with an agent, but don't get discouraged. Getting the right house, often at a below-market price, can far outweigh the inconvenience.

> *4SaleByOwner.com* (www.4salebyowner.com) is a national site that includes FSBO listings, a search engine, photos of homes for sale by owner, a bookstore, a mortgage calculator, and other resources.

> *Advanced Real Estate Listing Service* (www.homeportfoliojunction.com/home/index.htm) offers nationwide FSBO listings, a search engine, suggestions for homebuyers and home sellers, virtual home tours, links to appraisers, mortgages, a mortgage calculator, current interest rates, free real estate forms, and more.

> *BuyOwner.com* (www.buyowner.com) includes free listings of properties, a search engine, loan information, and suggestions for buying or selling a home.

For Sale By Owner Network (www. forsalebyownernetwork.com) includes a national FSBO listing, a search engine, and FAQs about their services.

iOwn.com (homescout.iown.com/realtor/ rc_online_listings.htm) provides listings that include the seller's contact information, a photo, and description of the property. These listings will include listings from realtors also.

Private For Sale.com (www.privateforsale.com) includes a national FSBO listing, a search engine, online help, a homebuyer checklist, and links to real estate professionals such as appraisers, mortgage lenders, and Realtors. FSBO sellers can list their homes for about $40 per month. All services are free to homebuyers.

Owners.com (www.owners.com), shown below, includes nationwide FSBO listings, a search engine, a buyer handbook and resources, tools, and services. FSBO sellers can list their

Owners.com is a classy way to shop online for house bargains.

homes for a limited time for free, standard rates are $90, and premier rates are around $140. All services are free to homebuyers.

RealScout.com (www.realscout.com) provides nationwide FSBO listings, a search engine, information center, news, articles, and more. Cost is approximately $50 for four months.

Virtual For Sale By Owner (www.virtualfsbo. com) includes nationwide FSBO listings, a search engine, and a homebuyer notification service. The buyer's workshop includes current interest rates, mortgage calculators, online mortgage loan prequalification, credit rating information, home insurance links, and data about loan programs. Prices vary from $20 for one month to $80 for six months.

Regional online FSBO listings

Many regional FSBO Web sites are available. These sites list anywhere from one to several hundred properties at a time. Don't let this possible lack of variety discourage you. You only need one house that meets all your needs. The following are a few examples of what you'll find on the Internet:

> Arizona: *Tucson FSBO* (tucson-fsbo.com) includes property listings, helpful tips, online calculators, links to services, advertising data, and information about Tucson.

> Wisconsin: *FSBO Properties* (www. fsbomadison.com) includes property listings, purchasing information, local links, and a company profile.

Bright Idea
You can find real estate and personal property auctions at Yahoo! Auctions (www.yahoo. com). At the homepage, click on the hyperlink to Auctions. Next, click on Other Goods & Services. Click on Real Estate, then select Residential Properties. You'll find residential lots, primary homes, and vacation homes in all price ranges. Buying real estate in an online auction is such a novel idea, it's worth checking out.

Michigan: *MichiganFsbo.com* (www.michiganfsbo.com) includes property listings, a bulletin board, link exchange, mortgage rates, an online loan calculator, and maps.

Ohio: *Cleveland Classified* (www.clevelandclassified.net) includes FSBO property listings for Cleveland and the surrounding area.

Oregon: *Bringing You Home* (www.byhome.com) includes FSBO listings, complete home seller packages, and an à la carte menu of services.

Tennessee: *Tri-Cities TN/VA* (johnson-city.com) includes property listings, a map of the area, and links to local business Web sites.

New York: *For Sale By Owner Properties* (wnyfsbo.com), shown below, includes property listings, marketing help, and advice for buyers and sellers in the Rochester, New York, area.

For Sale By Owner Properties includes a search engine, seminars, and links to real estate support professionals.

FSBO notification services

Many sites let you search for newly listed FSBO
homes by country, state, maximum price, minimum
price, and type. Some sites even let you sign up for
a notification service that sends you e-mail messages
about properties that meet your criteria until the
specified expiration date. Private For Sale (www.
privateforsale.com), shown below, is a good example of a buyer notification service.

Private For Sale
searches ads for
your home selec-
tion criteria and
automatically
notifies you of a
new FSBO listing.

If you're looking for more information about
how to purchase a home without an agent, the
Internet is a great research source. Online
resources include information from state real estate
departments, online mortgage lenders, FSBO Web
sites, and other sources. One timely article on this
topic is "How to Buy a House for Sale by Owner."
You can find this short guide at eHow (www.ehow.
com/ehows/ehow00004377.asp). This article gives
you the required steps to purchase a FSBO home,
along with savvy buyer tips.

Watch Out!
Your FSBO offer
becomes a
legally binding
sales contract
when the seller
accepts it. It's
always wise to
check with your
attorney before
submitting your
offer. Since your
offer can quickly
become a sales
contract, you
want to make
certain you have
included all
the necessary
contingencies to
back out of the
contract if
necessary.

Closing the FSBO deal

The FSBO offer is similar to any offer you would create. In fact, the offer and counter-offer process are the same. If the seller has hired a discount brokerage to handle the negotiations, you'll submit your offer to the representative. If you have a real estate agent, submit your offer to your agent. Then he or she will present your offer to the FSBO seller.

If you don't have an agent, you can purchase a sales contract at a stationery store or download and print one from the Internet. For example, see Offer for Purchase at the Home Buyer's Information Center, Making Real Estate Offers (www.ourfamilyplace.com/homebuyer/offer.html). For a generic agreement of purchase and sale, waiver, and amendment forms, see Private For Sale (www.privateforsale.com/contracts2.html). It's wise to have your attorney look over the offer before it's presented to the seller. (For more on preparing an offer, making counter offers, and accepting a sales contract, see Chapter 10, "Negotiating and Closing the Deal.")

One of the biggest benefits of using an agent is that he or she acts as a go-between during the negotiation phase of purchasing a home. The Internet offers a similar benefit. You can contact the FSBO seller via the Internet, and you can also negotiate electronically if there are no agents involved in the transaction.

Potential FSBO negotiating difficulties

Online and offline, each FSBO transaction is unique. Consequently, you may find yourself dealing with issues that you didn't expect. Here are some common problems, along with their remedies:

■ **Unrealistic sales prices.** The FSBO seller may
not use an agent because the agent valued the
home at a market price that was below what
the owner felt the house is worth. Negotiating
with a seller who is expecting too much may be
next to impossible.

Remedy: Provide the FSBO seller with
copies of your automated valuation model
reports and online reports of recent sales. (See
Chapter 10, "Negotiating and Closing the
Deal," for details.)

■ **No bargains for you.** The FSBO seller may list
the property to save commissions but none of
the savings are passed on to you. In this case,
the FSBO seller may want to negotiate directly
with you. You don't get a share of the savings
and may get the headache of dealing with a
difficult seller.

Remedy: Point out to the FSBO seller how
much money he or she will lose if they keep
the house on the market and don't close the
deal as soon as possible. For example, let's say
the market is slow and it will take another
three months to find another buyer. The seller
will lose the opportunity of moving to the
home he or she wants and will have to pay for
more advertising. If the house is empty, the
FSBO seller will have to pay additional monies
for utilities and property taxes.

■ **Improper disclosures.** The FSBO seller may
not know what needs to be disclosed to the
buyer. Material defects may not be disclosed
and the FSBO seller may insist that the property be sold "as is." In this situation, the FSBO
seller may be ignorant or sly. Either way, this

Unofficially...
It's easy to say
things you don't
mean or create a
miscommunica-
tion when talk-
ing on the tele-
phone with the
seller. Try not to
negotiate over
the telephone.
That's where
most deals are
lost.

makes closing the transaction more difficult for you.

Remedy: Contact your State Real Estate Department and get a copy of the proper disclosure form. Often you'll find FSBO advice online and the standard form at a local stationery store. For example, California has stringent disclosure requirements. California sellers must give buyers a mandatory disclosure form. For more information about when seller disclosure forms are required, see the Pennsylvania Association of Realtors (www.parealtor.org/sf/disclos.htm).

- **Not mastering the paperwork.** You may have to educate the FSBO seller about the paperwork involved in a real estate transaction (sales contract, title searches, insurance, escrow account, and other documentation). In today's world, it takes more than a handshake to legally transfer ownership of property. The FSBO seller may not know what's needed.

  Remedy: Provide the FSBO seller with government pamphlets, online help from mortgage lenders, and Internet addresses for online FSBO resources.

- **FSBO sellers who are emotionally attached to the home.** The FSBO seller may not want to hear anything negative about the property. Your home inspection report may indicate that major work needs to be done. You want a discount on the price of the home, or the seller to pay for the repairs. The FSBO seller thinks everything is wonderful (and has been for the past 20 years) and just can't understand your concerns. This can make your negotiations very difficult.

Remedy: Use your best negotiation skills. If nothing works, be prepared to walk away from the deal.

Congratulations! You've struck a deal!

When you and the seller have completed your negotiations and the financing is arranged, the FSBO seller will likely need to hire a closing agent (attorney) to complete the transaction. The closing is the final step in purchasing your home. For many FSBO transactions, the closing is the trickiest part of the deal. Complying with all the legal requirements takes some experience. Attorneys who specialize in this type of work get a flat fee and may charge $1,000 or less.

At the closing meeting, the closing attorney will hold all monies, explain the settlement sheet based on your sales contract, and complete the actual transfer of ownership. The paperwork involved includes the deed, title report, mortgage, mortgage note, property tax statements, survey, and so on. (For details about closing the deal, see Chapter 10, "Negotiating and Closing the Deal.") The meeting will take an hour or less. At the end of the meeting, you can take possession of the property.

Just the facts

- Buying a FSBO property has some disadvantages, but the potential costs savings can be worth it.

- You can take control and save money and time by going it alone and using the Internet to find a FSBO.

- In the past, FSBO properties were expensive to advertise and received little exposure, but today, there are well over a hundred FSBO Web sites.

- Some FSBO Web sites have search engines and automatic notification programs.

- You may know more about buying a house then the FSBO seller knows about selling it, enabling you to negotiate a better deal.

GET THE SCOOP ON...
Building your own home ▪ Using the Internet to
find a residential lot ▪ Selecting house plans
▪ Finding the best contractors and
subcontractors ▪ Sticking to the budget
and schedule

Getting Online Help with Becoming an Owner-Builder

Chapter 13

The U.S. Commerce Department's Bureau of the Census estimates that in 1999, more than 1.6 million privately owned new homes were built. About two-thirds of the new homes built are single-family residences, and the remaining one-third are residences of two or more units. (For more online information from the Census Bureau, see www.census.gov/indicator/www/housing.html.) These statistics indicate that there's a lot of building going on. If you plan to build your own home, the Internet can assist you in realizing your dream.

Besides the personal pride involved in building your own home, there can be financial advantages. Overall, the cost savings of being your own general contractor are about 10 to 20 percent of the home's value. That is, if the home you're building is valued at $250,000, you will save $50,000 if you build it yourself. However, keep in mind that actual cost savings will vary due to the complexity of the home design you select, the land you build on, and the fees you'll have to pay to government's entities (school taxes, water and sewer connection fees, and building permit fees).

Building your own home can be a terrific or a frustrating experience. Generally, the advantages of building your own home are all the new housing components, customization, and the personal satisfaction of managing the home building process. In contrast, the disadvantages of building your own home include construction delays that can play havoc with your family life, new house problems that are time-consuming to isolate and fix, the complications of finding a residential lot, and getting a construction loan.

Deciding to build your own home

The Internet can assist you in building your dream home and realizing a sizable cost savings. The more you know about home building, the better your home building experience. You should not try to build your own home without some prior research and preparation. Luckily, the Internet can assist you every step of the way. For example, professionally built homes generally take between three and six months to build. Depending on how much you want to be involved in building your own home, it can take some or all of your spare time. The completion time can vary between several months to several years and depends on how much time and money you have.

A good way to start planning your new home and researching the construction process is to go online and check out all the owner-builder sites. However, your research should not stop there. For example, you can:

- **Read about what's involved in becoming an owner-builder.** The Internet suggests many books and online sources that can help you decide if you want to be an owner-builder.

- **Attend weekend owner-builder construction courses.** The Internet provides contact information for many owner-builder seminars and weekend courses.

- **Hire a contractor who will assist you as much as you like.** You'll find many general contractors online with special owner-builder programs. With these contractors, the more work you do yourself, the less you have to pay the contractor.

- **Build a kit home.** You can uncover many online sources for modular and prefabricated homes. In this situation, much of the work is already done. All you have to do is put the pieces together on your residential lot.

The following sections detail some of the resources you'll find online that can assist you in becoming an owner-builder.

Reading all about it

For a good overview of the owner-builder construction process, see B4UBuild.com (www.b4ubuild. com). This Web site covers all the construction phases and provides a plethora of hyperlinks to related Web sites. The Internet provides information about a number of owner-builder guides and house plans. The Home Buyer's Information Center has a good list of books (www.ourfamilyplace. com/homebuyer/buildresource.html). For sample chapters, checklists, and general information, see the online write-ups of these and other owner-builder books:

You Can Build It is a comprehensive book on building your own home. You can read the author's description at www.icanbuildit.com.

Contracting Details is a do-it-yourself construction schedule and homebuilding handbook. It includes general contractor checklists, cost breakdown sheets, material specification forms, planning worksheets, cost-estimate guidelines, construction timetables, and more. Get all the details at www.househowto.com.

Built Online is designed to show owner-builders how they can save thousands of dollars. The guide includes easy-to-understand, step-by-step instructions on building your own home. See www.builtonline.com.

Your New House is a consumer's guide to buying and building a quality home. To check out the table of contents, see www.windsorpeak.com/newhouse/toc.html.

Getting smart with owner-builder seminars and classes

In addition to reading about building your own home, you can attend classes or seminars designed to assist owner-builders. This way, you can ask the instructor specific questions about the areas that concern you. A few examples are:

The Owner Builder School of Oregon (www.ownerbuilderschool.com), located in Portland, Oregon, has provided high-quality courses for the past 17 years. The two-day classes cost around $400 and include the text, workbook, and a computerized cost-estimating program. The course covers foundations, framing, roofing, siding, doors, windows, plumbing, electrical, heating, cooling and ventilation, energy efficiency, home design, estimating, contracts and contractors, scheduling, and working with government entities and regulations.

Oakland Builders Institute (www. buildersinstitute.com), located in Oakland, Michigan, provides classes on how to build your own home, home remodeling and additions, basement remodeling, builder's pre-license seminars, and buying and remodeling a home for profit.

Skip Morgan's Construction Seminars (www. goodpeople.com/right.html) teaches week-end construction seminars in Albuquerque, New Mexico, Austin, Texas, Raleigh, North Carolina, and cities across the nation.

Yestermorrow Design Build School (www. yestermorrow.org), located in Warren, Vermont, provides hands-on home design courses for the owner-builder with no previous experience.

Bright Idea
The Internet offers owner-builders access to many resources. A good example is You Build Owner-Builder Center (www.youbuild. com/home.htm). This Web site is a one-stop-shopping site for owner-builders, offering classes and seminars, construction loans, and help-ful advice. Located in Fair Oaks, California, Owner-Builder has contractor seminars for two weekend days. These cost about $300 and include a course work-book. Check the Web site for details.

Contractor-assisted programs

One of the limitations of books and classes is that they don't explain how to be an expert plumber or electrician. Professionals in these areas have years of experience. Building your own home may not look complicated, but it can be dangerous to your finan-cial health. After all, if anything goes wrong, you're the one who has to fix it. With this in mind, you may be interested in working with an experienced contractor in an owner-involved program.

An alternative to hiring a full-time general contractor is to participate in a reduced-price general contractor program designed for owner-builders. In a contractor-assisted program, the owner-builder pays for specific services provided by the general contractor. The more work the owner-builder does, the less cost. However, if the owner-builder encounters a problem, he or she can rely on the expertise of the general contractor. The following are a few online examples of contractor-assisted programs:

> *Creative Home Services, Inc.* (www. creativehomeservices.com/howit.htm) is a program for motivated owner-builders who have the time to manage their own home's construction. Creative Homes Services (CHS) assists individuals in selecting the home design and obtaining bids from subcontractors. The program also shows how to stay on schedule and on budget, coordinates work projects, and helps owner-builders understand each work phase.

> *Owner Builder Construction Loans* (www. degeorgeinc.com) offers an owner-involved building program that can assist you in getting construction financing and acts as project manager to oversee the building of your new home.

> *The Owner Builder School of Oregon* (www. ownerbuilderschool.com). Normally homeowners pay 20 to 30 percent of a home's value for the services of a general contractor. However, there are now contractor/owner-builder–involved programs that only cost

homeowners 5 to 6 percent. The homeowner assumes the responsibilities of the general contractor, but the organization assists the homeowner in getting a construction loan, reviews the designs, cost estimates, subcontractors, and so on. For their services, there is a fee of 15 percent of construction costs or an hourly rate, depending on how much assistance the homeowner requires.

Texas Help-U-Build (www.ushub.com) has created an environment where owner-builders can act as their own general contractors. Texas Help-U-Build assists with planning, regulatory agency inspections, subcontractor inter-phasing, discounts on materials and supplies, and ongoing daily help.

Estimating the cost of a building project

There are many software products you can use for your material and labor estimates. Some of these products can be directly downloaded from the Internet. Others have downloadable trial versions that are just like the real thing. The following are a few construction-estimating software products you'll find online:

Craftsman Book Company (www.craftsmanbook.com/downloads/index.htm) provides National Estimator, shown below, an estimating program that works like a book. National Estimator is an easy-to-use program that exports to QuickBooks, Excel, and Word. You can change just about anything you want, from materials to wage rates. Try it for free, and buy it for around $70.

If you're tired of working out your budgets by hand, download the free trial version of National Estimator.

Construct Software (www.constructsoftware.com/demos/demos.html) provides WinEst LT—a powerful, yet simple-to-use estimating program that includes the Craftsman Light construction database, an estimator program, a two-hour multimedia tutorial, a 400-page user manual, and 90 days of free technical support.

NorthWest BuildNet (www.nwbuildnet.com/nwbn/esti_books.html) offers a 616-page book, *National Construction Estimator—2000,* with a companion CD-ROM. Information includes current building costs for residential construction and the estimated price for common building materials. The book provides man-hours, recommended crew, and labor costs for installation. The CD-ROM is the electronic version of the book, a stand-alone Windows estimating program, plus an interactive multimedia video.

UDA Construction Office 99 (www.uniteddesign. com/excel_spread.html) provides a Home Estimating Guide and Excel spreadsheet template on disk for estimating construction costs in your geographical area.

Location, location, location

After you decide to build your home, you need to decide where to build it. All the rules of finding the perfect neighborhood still apply, as discussed in Chapter 4, "Finding a Neighborhood Next Door or Across the Country." However, this time you're buying a building lot and not a finished home.

In addition to online information, you can find offline information in free real estate magazines and Sunday newspaper ads. You'll quickly learn the names of the real estate agencies that specialize in building lots. Even the Yellow Pages can help you narrow your search. Of course, you should drive around the area you want to live in. Write the addresses of vacant lots and look up the owners in the county recorder's office. Talk with neighbors to see if the owners are interested in selling. Tell your family, friends, co-workers that you're looking for a residential lot. They may talk to someone and provide you with a hot lead.

It's important to get your priorities in order when you build your own home. You'll need to select the land you plan to build on before you select your house plan. After you select your house plan, it's time to develop your materials and labor budget.

There are many items to take into consideration when selecting a building lot:

Bright Idea
For a handy land acquisition checklist, see Creative Homes (www. creativehomeservices.com/ land_selection. htm). Building lot characteristics are divided into three categories: critical items, important items, and personal preference.

- Is the property served by public utilities, or will you need to have a "perc test" performed for a septic tank and a well drilled for water?

- Is there an architectural review committee that has to approve your house plans? For example, does the architectural committee have restrictions on building a home with an aluminum roof?

- What about zoning restrictions, setbacks, and future development in the area? For example, say all the homes on your block must be built at least 20 feet from the street. Or there may be plans to build a three-story building on either side of your residential lot. When these buildings are complete, they may loom over your planned two-story building. You should also check out area flood zone, planned changes to traffic patterns near the site, plans for schools in your area, and any moratorium issues.

- Can contractors easily access the site? Check for easements and other regulations about the property.

- What does the lot look like in bad weather? Talk with the neighbors and local authorities.

- Are there wetland or other features on the property that may prevent it from being developed? This may include streams, steep slopes, or other pre-existing environmental issues in the area.

Determining how much to pay for your lot

Keep in mind two general rules when selecting a residential lot:

- As a rule of thumb, the price of the land should be no more than two-thirds of your annual income. If your annual income is $60,000, you should spend $40,000 on a lot. (Note that when discussing residential properties, most people don't include rural or country properties with vast tracts of land.)

- A home's value is generally one-fourth in the land and three-fourths in the structure of the home. If you spend $40,000 on the lot, you should spend approximately $120,000 building the house. If you don't build a house using these proportions, you'll likely regret it later when you decide to sell. In areas where land is expensive, the ratio may be one-third for the land and two-thirds for the house.

Using the Internet to find the perfect residential lot

You might be surprised at how much information you can find online about lots for sale. The following are some sources to try for finding properties throughout the United States and in individual states:

> Throughout the United States: MSN *Home-Advisor* (homeadvisor.msn.com) lets you enter a desired location and price range, and then it searches for properties listed in the Multiple Listing Service (MLS).
>
> Colorado: *Westcliffe Land & Investment Company* (www.csd.net/~west;amd/vac.html) provides photos of building lots, short property descriptions, and contact information.
>
> Colorado: *Century 21 American Real Estate* (www.c21amre.com/bh_206s.html) offers

Moneysaver
If you purchase a residential lot that includes municipal water and sewage services, you'll save money on drilling a well and installing a septic tank, which can cost up to $20,000. Of course, there may be connection charges to pay. Sometimes this can be paid out over time to the local government.

building sites in wooded locations and information on other residential lots in nearby states.

Florida: *Prudential Geisinger Realty* (www.hschneider.com/homes.html) covers vacant land on the waterfront, in established communities, and in the wide-open spaces.

New Mexico: *Alberto Candelaria* (www.premiersystems.com/candelaria/index.html) is a Realtor that includes descriptions of vacant land and finished lots.

North Carolina: *Realty One Services, Inc.* (www.realtyoneservice.com/land1.htm) includes descriptions and contact information for a variety of residential lots.

Tennessee: Old Hickory *Real Estate and Auction Co., Inc.* (www.ohrea.com/buildinglosts/page3.htm) provides descriptions of many kinds of lots and includes contact information.

Wyoming: *Matt Brown Real Estate* (www.realestate-wy.com/resilots.htm) offers a wide variety of residential lots and contact information.

Using the Internet to find land for sale by owner

For individuals who like to purchase directly from owners, there are several online sites such as Yahoo! Auctions (www.yahoo.com) and occasional building lot listings on popular residential FSBO Internet sites (see Chapter 12, "The Internet and Do-It-Yourself Real Estate").

A good example of a FSBO residential lot Web site is LAND-fsbo.com (209.35.72.21). This Web site offers vacant land for sale by owners:

- At the search engine, enter the name of the state where you want to live and click on Search.

- Your search results include location, land description, and the availability of utilities, sewer, roads, and a way to contact the seller via e-mail.

Selecting your house plans

You can generally figure that the house plans you select will cost from a few hundred dollars to several thousand dollars, depending on the type and cost of home you want and who you choose to design it. There are a couple of ways to acquire a design for your home:

- **Hire an architect to get customized blueprints.** This is the costliest approach, but if you're looking for clever ways to use standardized windows, doors, etc. to reduce costs, architectural plans often offer construction cost savings not available in ready-made house plans.

- **Purchase ready-made designs from the many available online sources.** This is the most inexpensive approach. Additionally, standard plans can often be slightly modified by a structural engineer and draftsman to meet your individual needs.

Finding an architect online

If you're wondering how to select an architect, see the Home Buyer's Center at www.ourfamilyplace. com/homebuyer/build.html. Then check out pre-screened architects at ImproveNet (www. improvement.com/tools/form_36.asp). All the architects listed in the database of ImproveNet are

Moneysaver
A good architect can assist you in getting furniture discounts (up to 40 percent), additional functionality with small spaces, and other added-value features that increase your profits when you want to sell.

professionals with at least three years of business experience and no legal or credit problems. The database provides a hyperlink to the architect's corporate Web site. There you should take note of the architect's license (where required) and the testimonials of his or her customers. See Chapter 15, "Online Help for Making Your House a Home," for additional listings of architects.

Finding ready-made house plans on the Internet

Ready-made house plans are frequently offered in magazines, books, on CD-ROM, and on the Internet. Costs are in the hundreds of dollars, and some plans can be customized at little or no charge. The following are several of the online sources of ready-made house plans:

> *Alternative Home Plans* (www. alternativehomeplans.com) provides unique alternatives to traditional house plans. At the Web site, you can view home plans, see what's included, and check out the pricing options. One set of blueprints is in the range of $400 to $1,500, five sets of blueprints are $500 to $1,500, and one set of reproducible blueprints are $750 to $1,700.

> *Homes for Today* (www.homes4today.com) provides plans for Colonial, country, farmhouse, retirement, vacation, and Victorian homes. You can view price lists, order plans, and find answers to the most frequently asked questions. One set of architect construction blueprints is around $300, four sets are about $400, and seven sets are approximately $500.

> *Planhouse Home Plan Studio* (www.planhouse. com) provides online one-stop shopping for

blueprints, modifications, information gathering, custom designs, and drafting. Planhouse has over 25 years of experience and hundreds of house plans. The Web site provides product information and services, general information and articles, and views of plans. Prices vary from $325 to $625 for a five-set package, $300 to $400 for a one-set package, and $450 to $500 for a reproducible master.

Stephen Fuller (www.stephenfuller.com) offers plans for one-, two-, and three-story single-family dwellings, vacation homes, townhouses, country homes, Victorians, traditional homes, and more. There are a total of 3,600 house plans available on CD-ROM. Prices vary.

Archway Home Plans (www.archwaypress.com) can assist you if you're concerned about your budget. One approach to estimating materials and costs is to select one of more than 400 Archway Home Plans. Archway plans cost between $200 and $600, depending on the size of the house and the number of blueprints you select. If you're wondering what it would cost to build an Archway house in your region, you can use their estimating service. This customized service is available to U.S. or Canadian residents for about $10 (U.S.). The estimating service includes:

- A complete estimate of total construction costs (excluding land) in the general area you plan to build.

- Estimates of labor and materials are reflected in this single figure, which assumes average

Unofficially...
Generally, you can expect to pay between $65 and $80 per square foot for materials, labor, and fees. These costs will vary, depending on the area of the country and labor costs in your area. They also depend on how luxurious a house you plan to build. The land is a separate expense.

quality of materials and a moderate level of finish, and even includes appliance costs and an allowance for floor coverings.

Although this single figure is just an estimate, it can save you time by helping you get a better handle on your total cost outlay, plus serve as a useful benchmark figure when evaluating bids from local builders.

Selecting the right house plan for the lot

In the preconstruction stage, let's say you selected your lot and the house plan that meets your wants and desires (while keeping building costs within an affordable range). Ask yourself the following questions:

- **Is the lot large enough for the house you selected?** You'd be wise to check local regulations about house placement on lots to make sure you are following local regulations.

- **How does the house you plan to build compare to others in the neighborhood?** Don't overbuild for the neighborhood, or you'll be penalized when you try to sell and will likely not recoup your cash investment.

- **If you sell the house, will another family find the house easy to live in?** Keep in mind that what you like, others may not find attractive. For example, the next family may not want a three-bedroom house with only one bathroom.

Online help with selecting and evaluating contractors

After you select your lot and house plan and establish a construction budget, you'll need to select a contractor (or subcontractors). It's wise to get the best contractor your budget can afford. In home building, quality is worth more than quantity. The Internet can assist you in locating contractors and subcontractors.

When evaluating contractors and subcontractors, take into account how frequently they complete their projects on time and within budget. However, your evaluation should not stop there. Here are a few helpful suggestions:

- **Examine references thoroughly.** Run a credit check and see if the contractor or subcontractor has recently (or ever) filed for bankruptcy.

- **Visit jobs that are currently in progress.** If there are any problems, see how they're being resolved.

- **Get at least five estimates.** Throw out the high and low bids. Select the contractor who is nearest the average.

- **Avoid change orders.** That is, don't change your mind about a certain item after you begin construction.

- **Bring in outside inspectors to verify the quality of what you are paying for.**

For more suggestions about finding and evaluating contractors and architects, see "Finding Builders and Architects" at the Home Buyer's Information Center (www.ourfamilyplace.com/ homebuyer/buildfind.html).

The following are a few places to start your search for construction help:

> *Contractor.com* (www.contractor.com) provides a search engine that allows you to find builders, remodelers, subcontractors, and other construction help by state, company name, or alphabetically.

Timesaver
Don't lock in your moving date. You can always count on construction delays that can move your completion date to several weeks later than you expect.

American Builders Network (www.
americanbuilders.com) is a good place to
search for well-established homebuilders. All
the homebuilders listed are pre-screened.
Select the state and city you are interested in,
then click on the hyperlink for the Web site
of the contractor.

ContractorNet (www.contractornet.com) provides a large database of state-licensed contractors. ContractorNet has each contractor's
license and insurance paperwork on file.

NorthWest BuilderNet (www.nwbuildnet.com/
nwbn/barnsoutbuildings.html) includes a
directory of builders and contractors. Just
click on the type of contractor you need.
You'll see a listing of the appropriate contractors listed by state. The directory includes all
the contact information you'll need (even
e-mail addresses).

Finding owner-builder financing online

A construction loan is generally short-term interest-
only financing that is "rolled over" to permanent
financing when construction is complete. Although
construction loans are interest-only, they are usually
about 1 percent higher than conventional financing
and require a one-point upfront financing fee and
closing costs.

Some construction lenders require a permanent
loan from another financial institution before
they'll approve your construction loan. It sounds
backward, but this is a frequent lender requirement.
The permanent loan commitment from another
mortgage guarantees the construction lender that
the construction loan will be paid off.

The closing for a construction loan or a combination construction loan/permanent loan is similar to the closing of a home loan. However, it involves a lot more paperwork. Requirements vary from lender to lender, so check to make certain you have all the required documents before setting a closing date.

Shopping for a construction loan is like shopping for any other big-ticket item. You want to know what you are buying and pay the lowest price possible. When shopping for your construction loan, ask the following questions before you make any commitments:

- **What are the lender's requirements and exactly what is the lender's process for acquiring a construction loan?**

- **Will the lender provide information about the cost of the loan?** Ask for a truth-in-lending statement that details the lender's charges, closing fees, and other expenses.

- **Does the construction lender offer permanent financing?** This can cut down on your closing costs and the hassle of getting two separate loans from two different lenders.

- **What about deposit money?** The construction lender may require that you pledge the lot as collateral or place a sizable deposit (say, $25,000 for a $175,000 construction loan) into the construction account.

- **What are the procedures for draws on the construction loan?** Often lenders divide the construction process into six steps and hold 10 percent of the funds as "retainage." Retained funds are usually paid 30 days after the first payment. This ensures the lender that the work is satisfactory. If the work is not satisfactory, the retained funds are used to make repairs or correct subcontractor mistakes.

■ **What are the required tests for the lot?** Often lenders require soil tests, surveys, and plan appraisals. These reviews are not unusual, but they can be costly and time-consuming.

The following are a few examples of online lenders that offer construction financing:

SunChase Financial Corporation (www.sunchasegroup.com/o1.htm) provides owner-builder do-it-yourself construction loans. Check out this Web site to discover the benefits of the program, fee structure, a documentation needs list, and a preliminary loan application.

National Mortgage Enterprises, Inc. (www.nm4greatrates.com/lot.htm) provides an online application form as well as construction and permanent financing.

Pacific Rim Finance (www.pacificrimfinance.com/construction-hb.htm) offers construction loans as well as interim and permanent financing. There are no upfront financing fees, and you'll find an online application form for your convenience.

Tips for staying on schedule and within your budget

It's important to keep a close eye on your construction budget. A few dollars here and a few dollars there can quickly add up to thousands of dollars you didn't expect to pay. Some of the keys to affordable construction are:

- Use off-the-shelf components such as windows, doors, and so on.

- Rely on easy-to-assemble components (in construction, time really is money).

- Use common, low-cost materials. For example, commercial-grade carpet for the bedrooms may be acceptable. At $1 per square foot (including installation), it can't be beat.

- Know where to spend a little extra to save in the long run. For example, high-traffic areas may require hardwood floors.

Watch Out!
If you change any of the items on your approved construction budget, you have to tell the bank and provide support for the change. Bank verification of the changes can slow down payments to subcontractors.

Working with building regulations

Many state and local governments have rules and regulations about the development of the area they govern. Before you make a large investment of time and money, you may want to check out these regulations and determine if they will interfere with your building plans. If you are not sure where to look for the information, try the handy directory at B4UBuild.com (www.b4ubuid.com/links/codes.htm). This directory provides links to online information sources for building codes, construction standards, and building permits.

The following are a few areas to check out when you're sorting out the details of your construction project:

- **Getting into the zone.** Most areas in the country have a zoning board that determines what types of properties can be built in certain areas. There should be a zoning map for your area. See if you can purchase a copy of this map or if you can reproduce it in some way. Additionally, some areas have zoning code-books that describe the zones in a certain area.

It may be helpful to discover how strictly zoning codes are enforced—what direction zoning is taking and if zoning board members are for or against development. If you need to request a variance to a zoning code, find out how easy or difficult it is to get approval.

■ **Building permits and you.** What are the rules and regulations regarding building and improvements in the area where you plan to build? What are the hours of the building department? Will they answer questions over the telephone? What type of work requires a building permit? What types of construction work are you permitted to do yourself?

According to NewHomeNetwork (www.newhomenetwork.com), many local building departments will only issue a building permit to licensed contractors. Obtain a copy of the building codes or discover where you can get a reference copy.

■ **Breaking the code.** Monitor the construction of your home as much as possible. As you inspect, remember the building code. The following are several examples of online sources for information about building codes:

Check out building codes at *ICBO Code Central*—The International Conference of Building Officials (www.icbo.org). This association has an online product store, code chat sessions, links to building products, seminars, and more.

Code Check (www.codecheck.com) is a book published by Taunton Press. You can use Code Check to get a grip on your local building codes.

B4UBuild.com (www.b4ubuild.com/special/ articles/codefusion.shtml) includes an article titled "Code Fusion—Building Codes & the International Code Council," which discusses the latest building code issues.

- **Preparing for building inspections.** During construction, you'll need to schedule building inspections with the local building inspector before you can continue your construction. Contracting Details (www.househowto.com/ buildinginsp.htm) provides a useful building inspection schedule checklist. You may find this valuable when scheduling your project.

Acquiring building hazard insurance

Your lender will require a "builder's risk" insurance policy. This insurance policy covers the building site before construction and during all phases of the construction process.

Some residential insurance companies are unfamiliar with builder's risk insurance policies. A builder's risk policy protects lenders and owner-builders from hazards that the structure may encounter while half-finished. Like the construction loan, the builder's risk insurance often changes to a homeowners policy when construction is complete.

The Internet provides information about many online insurance companies. The following are a few construction insurance companies you may want to check out:

Copelan Insurance Agency, Inc. (www. copelaninsurance.com/construct1.html) provides residential contractor insurance that covers liability, property, tools, and

Moneysaver
Take special care in the framing stage. Not using the correct property building code at this point in the construction process can be costly if you have to correct errors later on.

Moneysaver
Some lenders recommend an additional "minimum premium" workers' compensation policy for your personal protection. This is important if one of your subcontractors lets his or her workers' compensation policy lapse and something happens on the work site. Be sure your subcontractors all have both workers' compensation and a liability policy, in case someone gets hurt on the job.

equity. For insurance tips and more information, see the Web site.

First Indemnity of America Insurance Company (www.fiagroup.com/public_html/builders. htm) provides builder's risk coverage on an "all-risk" basis for new construction, renovations, rehabilitation properties, and installation risks.

Insurance Resource (www.insuranceresource. com/irgcons1.htm) insures contractors with programs that include special coverage and pricing benefits.

Just the facts

- Many individuals build their own homes and use the cost savings as a down payment on their permanent home loan.

- Thousands of house plans are available on the Internet; your only difficulty may be choosing which one is right for you.

- If you're wondering how to prepare your materials and cost estimates, the Internet can assist you with free downloadable trial copies of job-costing software.

- The Web offers sources for acquiring a residential lot and construction financing.

- The Web has free directories of pre-screened contractors and subcontractors so you don't have to wonder if the company you hired is truly qualified for the job.

Wrapping It Up, Moving In, and Moving Out

PART VI

GET THE SCOOP ON...
Developing a moving plan ▪ Choosing a moving
company or moving yourself ▪ Using the
Internet to change your address ▪ Estimating
the cost of moving ▪ Deducting moving
expenses from your income taxes

Getting Moving Help Online

Chapter 14

Moving to your new home is the last step of the home buying process. Your sales contract should specify the day you'll get the keys and move in. Taking possession of your new home is exciting, but a rough move can dampen your joy.

The Internet can make your move easier than ever before. This chapter shows you how to plan a move that meets your financial and personal resources. You'll find out how the Internet can help you determine what type of move is right for you—whether it's a do-it-yourself move or a full-service move. You'll also discover how you can find movers you trust and save money by comparing moving company surveys to online moving cost estimates.

Whether you're moving next door or to the next state, preparing to move is essential. In this chapter, you'll find out how you can use the Internet to assist you in changing your address and arranging for utility connections. You can make certain you don't forget anything by using online moving schedule checklists and receiving e-mail messages about your individual moving schedule. You'll also learn how to handle special concerns and issues about moving your children, pets, and automobiles. The chapter concludes by showing you how to get online assistance for lowering your taxes by deducting your moving expenses.

Developing a moving plan

As you start preparing for your move, develop several moving scenarios and compare the moving plans. Do you want to move yourself? Will the professional movers handle the entire process? What are your alternatives? There is a variety of movers available at a variety of costs. The choices are listed below, with the most expensive approach listed first:

- **Relocation services.** These are generally for corporate-sponsored national and international moves. This is usually the most expensive approach to moving. Relocation services provide special programs for the challenges that occur in predeparture, during the assignment, and upon return to the original city (or repatriation to the home country) of individuals and families. One example of a relocation service is Windham International (www.windhamworld.com).

- **Full-service moving companies.** These moving organizations pack your household belongings, transport them to your new home, and unpack them. A good example of an interstate moving company is Bekins (www.bekins.com).

- **Trucking services.** These firms provide transportation for your household goods. They do not pack your belongings and only move the crates and cartons to the truck. Trucking services can be local, intrastate, or interstate. A good example of a trucking service is the Worldwide Cargo Express Company (www.wessco.com/trucking.htm).

- **Pack-and-stack services.** These companies do not actually move your belongings from one house to the next, but they professionally pack the goods you have designated into boxes or crates. A good example of a pack-and-stack service is Crown Van Lines International Movers (www.crownvan.com/servic1.htm).

You can find further moving assistance and guides on the Internet. The following are some examples of what you'll find:

SmartMoney.com (smartmoney.lycos.com/ac/ home/buying/index.cfm?story=moving) offers a helpful article titled "Ten Things Your Mover Won't Tell You" that describes how movers really work. For example, the Department of Transportation (DOT) oversees movers but is concerned only with their driving records. The DOT does not evaluate the records of moving companies.

RELO.com (www.relo.com/relo/publicgoodies/ faq.cfm) provides answers to the most frequently asked questions about moving to a new community.

Find-a-Mover (www.find-a-mover.com/rights. htm) provides helpful advice on how to get estimates, evaluate quotes, and what to expect from a mover.

American Moving and Storage Association (www. moving.org) is an association of more than 3,000 professional moving companies. Its Web site provides tips for finding professional movers, evaluating costs, information on moving, and more.

Establishing a timeline for moving

It's a good idea to start planning your move as soon as the seller has agreed to your offer. Drop in the Ocean Software has created a program called Move! that includes a flexible inventory database, a project management database to organize your move, and flexible auto-configuring of change-of-address letters to notify friends, relatives, and business associates of your new address. You can download a limited trial version at www.ditos.dynamite.com.au, or purchase the program at a retail store.

The key to a smooth move is to be well-prepared. The following is a short overview of the tasks that need to be completed and when they should be done:

- **Four to six weeks before you move:** Have an inventory session and decide what you're going to move. You may want to schedule a moving sale, arrange for a nonprofit organization to pick up your donations, or arrange for the disposal of unneeded items. Gather all your personal records and arrange for transcripts to be sent in advance to new schools. Close local department store and other charge accounts. Start changing your address (see "Using the Internet to change your address" later in this chapter). Open a checking account in your new town so that you have access to your money right away.

■ **Two to three weeks before you move:** Fill and transfer prescriptions for the family and pets. Pack them to travel with you. Arrange for the transport of your pets, plants, and automobiles if you can't take them with you. Dispose of any flammable goods and combustible items. Items like your outdoor barbecue grill's half-filled propane tank can't be transported in a moving van.

■ **One week before you move:** Defrost the refrigerator and freezer and let them air-dry to prevent mildew. Dispose of all frozen foods, clean the oven, transfer bank accounts, and drain fuel from lawn movers and other fuel-powered tools or recreational equipment. Drain garden hoses and pack items to be carried with you in the car or plane. Collect your valuables and carry them with your personal records. Send drapes, curtains, and rugs out for cleaning. Leave them in their wrappings for the new owner or for transport. Take down curtain rods, shelving, and the TV antenna. Have the car serviced for the trip (if applicable) and make sure your proof of car insurance is in the glove compartment. Finish all your local business, such as picking up photos and dry cleaning, and collecting any spare keys you gave the dog walker, neighbors, or friends.

To make your move as easy as possible, you can use online personalized moving schedules and checklists. Here are a few examples of what you'll find on the Internet:

Homefair.com (www.homefair.com/wizard/
wizard.html) offers a relocation wizard that
plans your move and creates a customized
timeline.

Atlas Van Lines (www.atlasvanlines.com) pre-
pares a personal moving schedule and sends
you e-mail reminders about the steps you
need to take each day.

Estimating the cost of moving

Moving companies are not required to provide you
with an estimate of moving costs, but most movers
provide estimates if requested. It's important to note
the type of estimate the mover submits. There are
two types:

- **Binding estimates.** Movers may charge you a
  fee for preparing a binding estimate. To be
  effective, the binding estimate must be in writing, and a copy given to you before the move.
  The estimate states the terms of the move,
  spells out the services the company will provide, and states exactly what it will cost.

- **Nonbinding estimates.** Movers may not charge
  for a nonbinding estimate. With a nonbinding
  estimate, the mover provides an approximate
  price and does not guarantee that the final
  cost will not exceed the estimate. However,
  movers cannot charge more than 10 percent
  over the original estimated cost. Additionally,
  you have at least 30 days after the delivery date
  to pay for the additional amount due.

Reputable online moving companies recommend an on-site estimate when possible. This
way, both the mover and you know exactly what
needs to be moved and how much it will cost. Most

companies do not charge for the estimate, but some may charge you if you do not use their service, as they have to travel to your location to do it.

It's a good idea to get at least three estimates from licensed full-service movers. Each estimator, sometimes called a moving counselor, will visit your home to complete a survey of what needs to be done. Reliable movers will often provide helpful tips about how you can reduce your moving costs. Ask about discounts, and make certain you get the quote in writing.

For a quick estimate, the Internet provides access to many free online move-estimating services. Here's a sampling of what you'll discover online:

> *MoverQuotes.com* (www.moverquotes.com), shown below, is unique because it offers real-time online quotes on your real-life move. The quotes are free, cover all the states, and the database is constantly updated. Quotes are for both full-service and self-service moving companies. (They will even give you a quote on moving your automobile.) Price

Unofficially...
Movers usually require at least two weeks' notice. Check in advance how they expect to be paid (cash, cashier's check, or credit card). Most moving companies will not accept a personal check.

MoverQuotes.com is an advertiser-funded Web site supported by prescreened participating moving companies.

quotes are estimates based on the size of the move. The Web site uses a weight calculator to help you estimate your moving weight (the total weight of your belongings) and thus the cost of your move.

Homefair.com (www.homefair.com/calc. movecalcin.html) is an online calculator that estimates interstate and local moving costs in the United States.

Moving.com (www.moving.com/guide/ selfestimate.asp) is an online cost-estimation calculator that can help you determine the total weight of your belongings in pounds. Compare this estimate with the survey from a moving counselor. For a quick estimate, click on the Average Moving Estimate link. The number of rooms, number of people, and cubic feet give you the average total weight.

Realtor.com (www.realtor.com) provides useful information on selecting a mover and what should be included in your estimate.

Avatar Moving (www.avatar-moving.com/kb/ doc_apples.html) provides a useful article titled "How to Make an Apples to Apples Comparison of Your Different Moving Estimates."

Allied Van Lines (www.alliedvan.net/02guide/ 04charg.html) describes how moving charges are determined and provides an online calculator to determine a "guesstimate" of your moving costs.

Moneysaver
You can lower your moving costs by having a garage sale, throwing out broken or worn-out items, or donating possessions you no longer want.

Deciding whether to move yourself or hire a moving company

There's no doubt that moving yourself is the least expensive way to go, but it usually involves lots of time, energy, and patient friends. However, hiring a professional mover doesn't necessarily mean a smooth move. You'll need to evaluate the mover and ask many questions. This way, extra charges for special handling or additional fees for the travel distance won't surprise you.

If you can't move into your new home right away, hiring a moving company that provides short-term storage for your personal property can be very beneficial. Make sure you check on warehouse security and storage conditions, and get a firm bid on rates.

Moving yourself

There are many advantages and disadvantages to do-it-yourself moving. The advantages are lower costs and more control over your belongings. The limitations include the challenge of driving a 24-foot truck if you have little experience, the hard labor involved, and the time you'll have to devote to moving. Additionally, if you break or damage something, you are responsible. This could wipe out any cost savings you were hoping to realize.

If you decide to try a do-it-yourself move, complete the following steps:

1. **Determine how far you're moving (in miles).** If you must travel over 35 miles to get to your destination, your move is not considered "local." If you plan to leave the truck in another city, there may be a charge for that service.

Bright Idea
The estimates of some moving companies include special services, such as helping you unpack your first-night needs, providing boxes, and setting up the television and beds.

Bright Idea
Keep in mind that the demand for do-it-yourself moving equipment is at its highest during the summer, at the end of each month, and at the times when college students are likely to be moving. If possible, try to avoid moving during these times.

2. **Determine what's going to the new house and what's staying.**

3. **Inventory your belongings room by room.** Consider the volume of your belongings in terms of cubic feet.

4. **Get estimates from do-it-yourself moving companies.** When calculating the expense, don't forget to include the cost of moving boxes, tape, marking pens, padding, and so on. Check out All Boxes Direct (www.allboxes.com) to get a general idea of costs. For example, the packing materials you'll need for three to four rooms are around $180 and the materials for five to six rooms are about $230.

5. **Consider your resources (your health, family, and friends).** You may want to hire some part-time help, which will add more cost to your do-it-yourself move.

For more online information about managing a do-it-yourself move, see the following sites:

AAA Move Services, Inc. (www.aaamove.com) provides moving and packing tips for the do-it-yourselfer, maps, and other recommendations.

ABF U-Pack Moving (www.upack.com) is a low-cost alternative that provides many of the conveniences of a full-service moving company with the option of packing yourself.

Hertz Truck & Van Rental (www.hertztrucks.com) provides rates and reservation information, a truck and van guide, moving tips, supplies, and the location of the Hertz Truck and Van Rental nearest you.

MoveCentral (new.movecentral.com/ planyourmove/default.asp) has three guides: "Before Your Move," "During Your Move," and "After Your Move."

Moving.com (www.moving.com/gmoving/ diy.asp) has an article titled "Do-It-Yourself Moving."

Penske (www.penske.com/ptl/index4.html) allows you to rent your truck online, provides rental information, discount storage coupons for public storage, and includes a moving kit.

Probe Consultants (www.go-probe.com/ beforeumove.shtml) provides "The Economical Do-it-Yourself Residential Moving Organization Guide."

Ryder Commercial Truck Rentals (www.ryder. com/rental/tr.shtml) provides information for truck rentals. According to Ryder, 25,000 trucks are just a telephone call away.

U-Haul (www.uhaul.com), shown below, is the granddaddy of all do-it-yourself moving

Moneysaver
Often you can get leftovers from full-service movers for much less than you'd pay at do-it-yourself places that provide paper, boxes, and other shipping materials.

Reserve your U-Haul moving van online and work with a company that has a long history of assisting do-it-yourself movers.

Unofficially...
You can often
get do-it-yourself
companies to
lower their prices
if you tell them
what other
companies
quoted you. For
example, Penske
(www.penske.
com/ptl/index4.
html) cut its
price in half for
a cross-country
move when
told the quotes
from other do-it-
yourself movers.

companies. It provides rates, reservations, and assistance in selecting a moving van and contact information for your local U-Haul company. You can even order U-Haul boxes online and have them delivered to your door.

Using a moving company

When selecting a mover, make certain it is licensed, insured, and has had an established place of business for at least three years. The Better Business Bureau (www.bbb.org) keeps track of business complaints and may provide you with some useful insights about the moving company you are planning to hire.

The Internet is a great place to start researching full-service moving companies. The following are some examples of what you'll find online:

Moving.com (www.moving.com) includes movers that meet strict state and federal standards. The appropriate state's DOT licenses each, and those who move interstate are also licensed by the U.S. Interstate Commerce Commission (ICC). Moving.com provides a search engine so you can easily find movers either by state or area code.

Moving-Guide (www.moving-guide.com), shown below, has a comprehensive listing of relocation services on the Internet. You'll discover lots of information, including supply and service data in this directory.

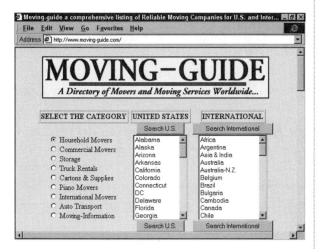

Moving-Guide provides a helpful listing of movers and moving services worldwide.

HandiLinks.com (www.handilinks.com/cat1/
m/m82.htm) includes a moving and storage
directory, a moving and storage guide, and
an index of links related to transportation.

Using a corporate relocation service

Corporations are becoming more sensitive to the
stress employees feel when they have to relocate.
According to a 1996 Atlas Van Lines survey, about
28 percent of all U.S. companies provide relocation
services. The costs of relocation services vary by the
services offered. However, according to the Atlas
Van Lines survey, the average relocation cost per
family is about $50,000.

Today, it's not unusual for corporate relocation
services to provide child care, schooling assistance,
and eldercare services. Many corporations even
have customizable relocation assistance programs so
employees can design a relocation package that
meets their specific needs. Many corporations "out-
source" their relocation needs. To locate the best

relocation service providers, see the Relocation Council (www.erc.org), a nonprofit organization based in Washington, D.C. The Web site includes a useful searchable database.

If you're purchasing a new home due to a corporate relocation, your company may be willing to pay for relocation services to make purchasing your new home and moving as easy as possible. If your corporation is relocating you and your family, it may also provide you with various types of relocation assistance. In fact, you may be entitled to some services that you are not aware of.

Watch Out!
Check the references of your movers. Recently, scam artists have posed as movers, collected the moving fee, and made off with the customers' possessions!

To determine the qualify of the service you are receiving and to check on the type of services offered by relocation companies, see Cross Country Relocation, Inc. (www.crosscountryreloc.com/guarante.html). Cross Country Relocation suggests that relocation companies provide the following services:

- The relocation company contacts the employee and begins the home guarantee program. In this program, if the employee can't sell his or her home through a real estate agent, the relocation company will act as an agent for the corporation and purchase the home from the employee.

- The relocation coordinator discusses what the employee can expect and offers assistance to the employee for finding a new home. (Be sure to mention any special needs you have that require extra attention or time.)

- The employee can list the home with any brokerage he or she selects. Wording in the listing contract must allow the relocation company to also offer the house for sale. If the relocation company sells the home, the brokerage does not receive a commission.

- To establish the value of the property, it must be appraised (for more on appraisals, see Chapter 9, "Online Help with Appraisals, Inspections, and Insurance"). The relocation company will suggest a short list of knowledgeable appraisers. The employee selects two appraisers.

- If the two appraisals are within 5 percent of each other, the relocation buyout price is the average of the two appraisals. If the difference is greater than 5 percent, a third appraiser is asked to value the property. If the third appraisal falls within 5 percent of one of the two previous appraisals, the average of those two prices is the buyout price. If the third appraisal is not within 5 percent of the previous appraisals, the relocation buyout price is the average of all three appraisals.

- The employee has 60 days to accept the relocation company's buyout price. During this time, the employee can hire an agent to sell the home at a price that is greater than that of the relocation company.

For more about corporate relocations, see Cross Country Relocation (www.crosscountryreloc.com), which provides information on taxes, relocation procedures, corporate rental programs, and helpful links.

Insuring the valuables you are moving

Some homeowner's policies cover possessions during a move. Are you insured for replacement value (called *liability insurance*) as well as the cash

Bright Idea
The American Community Network (www.acn.net) is designed to help individuals research, evaluate, and compare communities. The firm provides a detailed profile of every county and metro area in the United States and includes links to local community Web sites and professionals across the nation.

value of your possessions? A good online source for more information is Insurance Guidelines—The Insider's Guide to Relocation (www.insiders.com/relocation/13fins.htm).

When the moving company insures your personal property, it does so by the pound. The amount of insurance is usually 30 to 60 cents per pound, per article. In other words, if you have something that weighs 100 pounds and you have coverage of 30 cents per pound, the liability insurance for the item is no more than $30. The following arc a fcw tips to protect you:

- Find out if insurance is included in your moving costs.

- Have high-value items (antiques, jewelry, Oriental rugs, and so on) appraised before the move. The appraisal may be necessary to verify the value of your personal property.

- Take photographs of your antiques and make a video inventory of the contents of each room.

- Cross-country moves usually have a conditional inventory that lists all the items you are moving and the exact condition of each item. You'll sign this form at your old home and sign it again at your new home. Anything missing or damaged should be noted on the form.

- Local moves generally do not require a conditional inventory. You can use the bill of lading to document any damaged or missing items. Review this with the driver and have him or her sign the notations you've made on the form.

- If there are any missing or damaged items at your destination, contact the mover and file a claim. For your convenience, some moving companies have online claim forms that allow you to file your claim as soon as possible.

Other moving issues

Moving to the next town or state includes more than just transporting your physical belongings. If you are moving your household, you'll have to deal with the special issues of relocating your children, pets, or automobiles.

Moving children

Every move has some advantages and limitations. Synchronizing your move with the school year can be difficult. You may want to consider coordinating your move to mid-year, say, during the winter holiday season (December or January) or during the summer break. For other recommendations on moving with children, see:

> *Realty Times* (www.realtimes.com/rtnews/ rtcpages/19990513_children.htm) provides an article titled "When is the Best Time to Move Your Children?" Discover what the relocation specialists have to say.

> *Allied Van Lines* (www.alliedvan.net/02guide/ index.html) provides online guides that point the way to a good move, offer moving tools, and give suggestions for moving with kids.

Moving pets

Getting your children ready for a move may be easier than preparing your pet for a big environmental change. However, there are some things you can do to lessen the shock. Start by putting together a special "suitcase" to make the trip as comfortable as possible for both you and your pet. Include the following:

Watch Out!
If you do your own packing, the movers are not responsible for any damage unless there is evidence of exterior damage to the outside of any box you packed. The damage will be insured if the movers pack, regardless of the box's exterior condition.

Bright Idea
If your pet is in the cargo hold of a plane or is anxious about traveling by car, ask your veterinarian for a few tranquilizers. Test them on your pet to make certain there are no allergic reactions. On the day of your departure, give the prescribed dose to your pet to make the ride as stress-free as possible.

■ Water and food dishes, plastic utensils, and a can opener. Take enough bottled water and food for the entire trip. It may sound strange to suggest giving your pet bottled water, but in the long run it's well worth the extra effort. A sudden change in water may upset your pet's stomach.

■ The phone numbers of your current veterinarian and the recommended veterinarian at your new hometown. Include your pet's medical records, any medication, a flea comb, and shampoo.

■ Your pet's favorite toys, bed, or sleeping mat.

■ Your pet's collar, ID tags, and leash.

■ Plastic bags for picking up waste, sponges, and paper towels (for cleanups).

For more online suggestions about moving your pets, see Realty Times (www.realtimes.com), which provides articles such as "Moving Your Pet" and "Moving Your Pet: It's a Jungle Out There."

Moving automobiles

Relocating to another state or country often means moving your automobile. In this situation, the family often flies to its new location and a company that specializes in moving vehicles transports the automobile. However, there are many unscrupulous automobile transport companies around. The following red flags can help you determine if the automobile transportation company is a legit operation. Watch for the following signs of trouble:

■ **The company offers unusually low rates.**
Compare prices to determine what the going rate is. If the quote is extraordinarily low, ask the carrier why.

■ **Unusually short delivery times or a promise to pick up the car without a contract.** Get *everything* in writing. Some companies may give you a verbal agreement, but without a contract you don't have any legal recourse.

■ **Unconditional cancellation fees.** This might be a fee of up to $200. If you agree, you can be charged even if the company doesn't pick up your car.

■ **Insurance.** Don't assume you are fully insured. Make certain it's included in your written contract and carefully read the terms and conditions.

■ **Short time in business or uses several names.** Find out if the company uses a different name or changes ownership every few years. It's not a bad idea to check with the Better Business Bureau (www.bbb.org).

The following are a few online resources for car shippers:

Express Auto Transport (www.theexpressauto. com) provides shipping quotes and online forms for arranging the shipment of your vehicle.

Allen Auto Transport (www.allenauto.com) offers automobile transport and motorcycle shipping to and from anywhere in the United States. Get an online quote—it's free.

Using the Internet to change your address

Changing your address is one of the most important things you'll do in your move. If you don't change your address properly, you risk losing contact with business associates, relatives, and friends. The Internet provides several sources for changing your address. Some are free and others are fee-based. Most of these companies notify magazines, utilities, catalogs, frequent-flyer programs, alumni associations, and book and record clubs, in addition to Internet service providers, cable companies, and other service providers.

> *Home To Home* (www.home-to-home.com) will assist you with an address or name change for a flat fee of about $15. Fill out the form and all your mail will go directly to your new home. It's a good way to avoid post office forwarding stickers and delays.

> *MoversNet.com* (www.moversnet.com) allows you to enter your change-of-address information, then print out the completed form. Sign the form and either give it to your letter carrier or mail it to your local post office. You can also print out change-of-address notification letters and mail them to your family, friends, and business associates. The service is free.

> *MaketheMove.com* (www.makethemove.com) is one of the most complete change-of-address services online. MaketheMove can assist you in setting up most or all of the services you require in your new hometown. Entering all the data may seem time-consuming, but it's a lot faster than notifying each utility and completing a change-of-address card for each magazine subscription.

Packing for your move

If you've chosen to do your own packing for the big move, it's a good idea to plan ahead and develop a game plan. For example, if there are things that you won't be using before moving day, pack and label them weeks in advance. Here are a few other helpful tips:

- Mark each carton with the name of the room in which the contents belong.

- Place your children's school records in a file and keep it with you. You'll need this documentation when registering at a new school.

- Pack the phone books from your old town. You may need to look up the telephone numbers of old friends and businesses after you move.

- Cushion the bottom and sides of boxes that will hold fragile items.

- Don't pack more than 30 pounds in any box. A box full of books, for example, can be too heavy to lift. For books, the boxes should be smaller than those used for lighter items.

- Pack room by room, and label each box with the contents, the room in which the box should be placed, and whether the contents are fragile.

- Make a "first night box" that includes essentials such as towels, sheets, blankets, soap, tissues, paper towels, toilet paper, plastic utensils, paper plates and cups, a flashlight, a screwdriver, a hammer, and a can opener.

You can get more information about packing for your move at the following sites, as well as from other moving company Web sites, many of which have already been mentioned in this chapter:

Virtualmoves.com (www.virtualmoves.com/ packing.html) provides online packing tips from the professionals.

Bright Idea
Before you move in, you'll likely want to change all the locks and, if you have time, paint, refinish floors, or make other changes that are difficult when a house is full of furniture and other belongings.

Moving.com (www.moving.com/packing/
howtopack.asp) gives you tips on packing and
loading your moving van like a pro.

Allied Van Lines (www.alliedvan.net/02guide/
032pack.html) shows how you can ensure a
smooth move by organizing your packing and
loading.

Deducting moving expenses from your income taxes

You can deduct allowable moving expenses if moving to your home is related to your job. Specifically,
you are eligible to deduct some of your moving
expenses if:

- Your new job or job transfer is at least 50 miles
  from your old home.

- You don't have a job and your new job is at
  least 50 miles from your old home.

- You are a member of the armed forces and
  have had a permanent change of station.

- You work full time. (Full-time work is defined
  as at least 39 weeks per year.)

If you meet these criteria and save all your
moving-related receipts, you can deduct certain
moving expenses from your adjusted gross income:

- Packing, crating, and transporting household
  goods and belongings for your personal
  household

- Mileage for use of your own automobile for
  moving your belongings, members of your
  family, or yourself

- Parking fees and tolls paid during the trip

- Storage and insurance of your personal possessions for up to 30 days

- Utility connection and disconnection fees

- The cost of shipping cars or pets

- Transportation and lodging (except meals) for you and your family while traveling to your new home

The Internet provides additional information on deducting moving expenses from your taxes. Some of my favorite sources are:

SmartMoney.com (www.smartmoney.com/ac/ tax/index.cfm?story=moving) explains in detail how you can deduct your moving expenses and what to do if your company pays for part of the move.

Times Online (timesonline.webpoint.com/ home/movetax.htm) discusses moving cost tax breaks and includes links to articles about how to handle moving delays, direct household moving costs, and employer reimbursements.

Internal Revenue Service (www.irs.ustreas.gov/ prod/forms_pubs/pubs/p52101.htm) explains who can deduct what moving expenses. The Web site also provides tips and explains exceptions.

Just the facts

- You can use online resources to develop a cost-effective moving plan.

- Use the Internet to find out if you should move yourself and what's involved in a do-it-yourself move.

- Guarantee yourself a smooth move by using the Internet to find the best ways to move your children, pets, and automobiles.

- Get practical, professional online advice on how to pack for your move.

- Save time and effort by using Internet-based services to change your address, disconnect utilities, and notify friends, relatives, and business associates of your new address.

- Get the whole story online from the IRS and other sources about which moving expenses you can deduct from your income taxes.

GET THE SCOOP ON...
Finding expert home improvement help online
■ Hiring a contractor or doing it yourself
■ Using the Internet to stretch your home
improvement buck ■ The best way to finance
your renovations

Online Help for Making Your House a Home

Chapter 15

In 1999, the National Association of Home Builders (NAHB) reported that about one-third of all homeowners are involved in some type of home improvement project. The trade organization continued by stating that about 25 million families spent around $120 billion on home improvements in 1999. For the second year in a row, this amount is higher than what's spent on new-home construction. One reason for this boom is that homeowners are staying in their homes longer than in the past. The median time is now 13 years, compared to 10 years a decade ago. The reasons why people are improving their homes have also changed. According to the NAHB, about two-thirds of all home improvements are for upgrades—not maintenance or repairs. Seven years ago, there was an even split between upgrades and repairs.

For many people, remodeling their homes is a better investment (even with little or no return) than selling and moving to another home. This chapter shows how the Internet can assist you with everything from painting your home to adding a new bedroom. You'll discover how to make your new house a home, plan and design your renovations, and use the Internet to get expert help. This chapter goes on to discuss the myths about home improvement contractors, how you can avoid home improvement scams, and what should be included in a construction contract.

This chapter also discusses how the Internet can assist you with do-it-yourself home improvements, restorations, and repairs. Find out which home improvements will give you the biggest bang for your buck, and how the Internet can help you find the right type of loan to finance your home improvements.

Remodeling your new home

Homeowners generally take one of two approaches to home improvements. The first is adding something that they always wanted—a swimming pool in the backyard, a marble surround in the bathroom, and so on. The second approach is adding something that is purely practical, such as an updated kitchen or wooden deck, to increase the value of the home.

Regardless of which approach applies to you, home improvements can make your house truly a home. Unless you live in a planned urban development or a historic neighborhood, you can usually do just about anything you want to your property. Some homes are located in areas that require home improvement approval from an architectural committee. However, even in the most regulated areas, you are usually free to do what you want with the interior of your home. This is one of the benefits of being a homeowner. However, if you plan a renovation, you can expect to encounter a few glitches. This chapter details how you and the Internet can whittle some of these hurdles down to a manageable size.

Planning what to do and how to do it

Each year, many consumer affairs groups receive complaints about home improvement problems. To make certain you don't become a member of this group, start by deciding exactly what you want to do. Write down what your primary home improvement objectives are and make tactical and strategic plans to implement your goals.

Having a clear idea of your home improvements goals will make you less susceptible to fast-talking salespeople and fraud. If you are planning a job that is likely to cost over $10,000, you would be wise to hire an architect to design and help monitor the tasks that need to be completed. If the job is less than $10,000, you may be able to use ready-made plans or those you can modify yourself, thus bypassing the need to hire an architect or general contractor. Make certain your plan meets your primary goal. To get started:

- **Develop a master plan.** Determine your current housing needs and wants, then prioritize the list. For example, you may want to build a backyard deck, then install a hot tub later on. It's often backward (and more costly) to install a hot tub, and then build a deck for it.

- **Define the scope of the project.** Decide exactly what you want. Develop a preliminary budget and add 20 percent to the total for cost overruns.

Bright Idea

If you're remodeling 50 percent of your home or key rooms such as the kitchen or the only bathroom, consider living somewhere else while the work is being done.

- **Create a project file.** Make a file for each home improvement project you plan to undertake. Use the file to organize building plans, budgets, contracts, and so on.

- **Begin a project journal.** Keep a separate notebook for design ideas, questions, and concerns.

- **Keep track of the changes you decide to make.** After all, each change will cost more money, and you want to make certain you have enough cash to finish the project. If you hired a contractor, make it clear that only written changes are allowable in your home improvement project. Know exactly how much each change will cost.

Dispelling myths about contractors

Almost everyone who has ever been involved in a home renovation or remodeling project has a horror story to tell. Many of these tall tales are based on urban legends and myths about contractors. Before you get started, you need to do away with these preconceived notions. The following list shows many of the myths about the home improvement industry:

- **Myth:** Excellent references mean you'll get an excellent job. **Reality:** Just because the contractor received great reviews from three friends doesn't mean that the company will do a great job with your particular project.

- **Myth:** Always go with the lowest bidder. **Reality:** Don't forget that you usually get what you pay for. If the lowest-bid contractor does shoddy work or is unresponsive to your requests, you may have to hire a second contractor. This will likely wipe out any cost savings you were expecting.

- **Myth:** Do the preparation work for the contractor and save money. **Reality:** If you don't know what you're doing, the preparation work you do may be costly. For example, you may accidentally remove a load-bearing wall and find that your kitchen starts to fall into your basement.

- **Myth:** All professionals know what needs to be done. **Reality:** Make certain to spell out exactly what you expect. Otherwise, you may get a surprise.

- **Myth:** The contractor didn't get permits, but he must know what he's doing. **Reality:** Municipal building departments often require permits even for changing a fuse box. Determine what you need permits for and what the current building code is. This can help you avoid discovering that your home is not built to code when you want to sell.

- **Myth:** If I pay for it, I should get exactly what I want. **Reality:** Make certain that someone else could live with the changes you make. Purple kitchen counters may appeal to you, but it's not something that everyone will appreciate.

  Myth: It's cheaper to bypass a contractor and do the work myself. **Reality:** It may be cheaper to do it yourself if you take the time to learn how to do it right, avoid making any mistakes, and have lots of spare time.

- **Myth:** Contractors pad their bills and take advantage of homeowners. **Reality:** Most contractors are reputable professionals. You can reduce the likelihood of hiring an unscrupulous contractor if you follow the guidelines in this chapter and use the Internet to assist in selecting prescreened candidates.

- **Myth:** A signed contract will protect you no matter what. **Reality:** A good contract is important, but you also need to learn how to effectively communicate with your contractor in order to resolve any misunderstandings.

- **Myth:** Hire a friend to do the work and get out of the way. **Reality:** This is probably the best way to lose a friend. No matter how well you know each other, your friend can't read your mind and know what you want without your airing your concerns and providing guidance.

Watch Out!
The home improvements you are planning may require a building permit, zoning changes, building inspections, or other types of licensing and approval. Check with your local building department to verify what's needed. You don't want to be prevented from selling your home in the future because you didn't follow the building department's rules today.

Defining your home improvement project online

Before you get started developing a budget, be sure you check out the local building code, because certain restrictions could immediately sink your project. You can start the creative process by collecting photos, ready-made plans, magazine articles, and Internet-based information about what you want.

Be honest with yourself. When you begin a renovation project, ask yourself if you can do the job or whether you need professional help. Larger or more complex projects may require the help of an architect and a contractor. Smaller projects, you may be able to do yourself.

For online resources to assist you in defining your project, see such Web sites as:

Builder Online: Spotlight Collection (www.builder. hw.net/special) provides a wealth of information about a variety of subjects, organized by topic.

HomePoint Advantage (www.homepoint.net/ products/products.html) provides helpful links to manufacturers who can help you find the product or solution you're looking for. Topics include construction, building materials, interior, exterior, finishing touches, restoration and remodeling, mechanical systems, plans, doors, windows, and more.

Remodeling Online (www.remodeling.hw.net) offers a virtual tour of remodeling an entire house and other home improvement resources.

Build.com (www.build.com) is a great place to research your ideas for home improvements. The Web site's home improvement directory is a helpful online resource.

Finding expert home improvement help

If you're planning a project that will change the design of your home, you'll likely need two types of professionals: an architect and a contractor. Major renovations sometimes require several subcontractors for electrical, plumbing, and drywall work. Your contractor is responsible for hiring and supervising the work of the subcontractors. If your home improvement project is limited in scope (say, replacing the kitchen counter or a bathroom vanity), the appropriate specialist, such as a plumber or carpenter, will be sufficient.

Architects generally cost 10 to 15 percent of your renovation costs or charge a flat fee of between $10,000 and $15,000. Set up appointments with at least three licensed architects. Explain what you want and how you expect the changes to mesh with your lifestyle. Most architects will not charge you for the first hour to discuss ideas. Make certain the architect has handled a project similar to the one you have in mind.

Finding a qualified contractor is easy when using the Internet. The NAHB lists certified graduate remodelers. Remodeling contractors generally cost about 20 percent of your renovation costs. These folks have at least five years of experience owning and managing remodeling companies and take continuing education courses to keep up with the changes in their discipline. Interview at least three contractors and ask them for rough estimates of their fees for your project. The following is a list of questions you should ask any contractor that you interview (adapted from "Home Sweet Home Improvement," www.pubelo.gsa.gov/cic_text/housing/homesweet_improve/homeimpv.htm):

- **How long have you been in business?** (If the company has been in business for less then three years, be wary. You want a contractor with a proven track record.)

- **Are you licensed and registered with the state (if applicable)?** (Discover what the licensing requirements are in your area. Telephone your state's consumer protection agency to verify the contractor's license.)

- **How many projects like mine have you completed in the past year?** (Ask for a typed list and compare the completed projects to your requirements. If possible, drive by the completed projects to inspect the materials and workmanship.)

- **Will my project require a permit?** (Be suspicious if the contractor you're interviewing asks *you* to get the permit. This could indicate previous problems.)

- **May I have a list of references?** (Get the names, addresses, and phone numbers of at least three clients.)

- **Will you be using subcontractors on this project?** (If the answer is yes, ask to meet them. Make certain they are licensed and have insurance coverage.)

- **What types and amounts of insurance do you carry?** (Most contractors are required to have workers' compensation and should carry personal liability and property damage coverage.)

After you've found a reliable, highly competent contractor you believe you can work with, you'll need to check out the contractor's financial stability. Find out if the contractor has filed for bankruptcy and if he or she pays bills in a timely manner. To help you in your research, ask for the names and telephone numbers of the contractor's subcontractors and suppliers. Visit completed projects that are similar to yours. Talk with the homeowners to discover if the project was completed within budget and on schedule. If there were problems, how did the contractor handle them? Could the problems have been solved in a better, more cost-efficient manner?

The Internet provides a wide variety of sources for online assistance in finding architects and contractors. Many Web sites divide contractors into categories in an effort to meet your special needs. The following are a few examples of what you'll find online:

> *101 Home Improvement Links* (www.sharewareplace.com/101/101house.shtml) provides a nationwide online listing of reliable sources for homeowners seeking contractors, architects, and designers.

Moneysaver
Many experts suggest that homeowners review their existing homeowners insurance policies to verify the type of coverage they have. Due to the increase in value of your home, you may want to increase your insurance coverage and take out special coverage to protect you while construction is in progress.

ImproveNet (www.improvenet.com) has a wonderful search engine called "Help me do a project," where you can choose the project type and select the project stage (for example, you have some ideas but are not ready to start, you've already begun the project, and so on). The search engine finds a list of prescreened architects and contractors from your geographic area who may suit your needs.

Avoiding home improvement scams

Your home is likely to be your most valuable asset. If you are planning a major design improvement, it's important to hire a competent contractor. However, not all contractors work within the law and some are less reputable than others. Each year homeowners complain to the Better Business Bureau (www.bbb.org) about home repair or remodeling fraud. The following are a few warning signs of home improvement frauds:

- Solicits door-to-door for business
- Only accepts cash payments
- Asks you to get the required building permits
- Doesn't have a listed telephone number
- Tells you that your job will be a "demonstration"
- Pressures you for an immediate decision
- Offers exceptionally long guarantees
- Asks you to pay for the entire job up front
- Suggests that you borrow money from a lender the contractor knows

If you're not careful, you can lose your home through a home improvement scam. The Internet provides a vast array of materials about how homeowners can avoid home improvement frauds, scams, and deceptions. Several examples are as follows:

American Association of Retired Persons (www.
aarp.org/consumer/homeimprovement.
html) provides a useful article titled, "What
Consumers Should Know About Home
Improvement Fraud."

New York City Consumer Affairs (www.ci.nyc.
ny.us/html/dca/html/homeimpv.html) has a
consumer guide for home improvements that
covers the basics of New York City's Home
Improvement Business Law, suggestions
for finding reliable home improvement
contractors, how to get a detailed estimate,
covering all the bases with your home
improvement contractor, and taking control
of the remodeling process.

Better Business Bureau Tips for Consumers (nsi.
org/tips/scams/tiphome.html) provides
hints about how to plan your project, hire a
contractor, finance your project, sign the
contract, and obtain a building permit.

*SmartMoney's Online Home Improvement Pricing
Estimator* (smartmoney.investing.lycos.com/
ac/home/living/index.cfm?story=price),

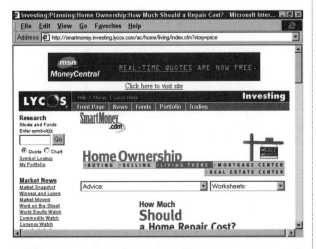

You can use SmartMoney's Home Improvement Pricing Estimator to get a good idea of what the components of your home repair will cost.

shown below, can help you determine the fair
market price for many household repairs.

Getting it in writing

If you hire an architect and a contractor, be sure to
get everything in writing and have all parties sign
the contract. Don't sign the contract until you
understand each and every clause. Waivers of liability, "hold harmless" clauses, lien waivers, and any
indication of clauses being waived or retentions
should be closely examined. There are two types of
contracts:

- **Fixed-price contract.** This type of contract guarantees your costs. If there are any changes to
  the project, you and the contractor negotiate
  the changes and sign a change order. This is
  the safest contract from the buyer's perspective.

- **Time-and-materials contract.** This type of contract gives you a rough estimate of the cost.
  The actual fee depends on the hours incurred.

It's important to have a well-thought-out
contract that covers all the things that might
happen in your home improvement project. The
following items are generally included in a good
contract (adapted from "Signing a Contract,"
www.improvenet.com/plan/expertadvice/
projectplanning/contract.htm):

- Contractor name, contact information, and
  license number.

- The scope of the work to be done (for example, demolition, construction, and cleanup).

- Materials and equipment to be used. Use
  descriptions of the quality, quantity, weight,
  size, color, or brand name to describe the
  materials you expect.

- Total contract price and schedule of payments by the homeowner to the contractor. (If the contractor has subcontractors, you may want to consider paying them directly.) If you pay the contractor and the contractor does not pay the subcontractors, you will still be liable for paying the subcontractors.

- Construction start and completion schedule (approximate dates when work begins and ends, timing of important milestones, retention of 10 percent until work is satisfactorily completed).

- Description of the change order process (signed change orders are used for any changes in the original design or completion date. Change orders spell out any additional costs or credits caused by the changes).

- Written warranties for all work, appliances, equipment, and materials that will be submitted to the homeowner.

- An arbitration clause that outlines how disputes will be settled.

- A mechanics lien clause that states the owners' rights under the law and lien release requirements.

When you're agreeing on a contract, make certain you check the contract's payment schedule, prices, and price calculations. Be sure each contract includes a general description of the work to be performed. State an expected completion date and include brand names and descriptions of the materials to be used. Keep a copy of the signed contract in your project file.

Bright Idea
If anything is missing from your contract, just write it in and get the contract signed and the changes initialed by the architect or contractor.

The Internet has many sources of information on home improvement contracts. The following are a few examples:

ImproveNet (www.improvenet.com/plan/ expertadvice/projectplanning/teamwork. htm) has an article titled "Teamwork and Conflict Resolution," which provides suggestions about what to do if things aren't progressing as planned. Also read "The Bare Bones About Construction Contracts" for a good understanding of the terms used in construction contracts.

B4UBuild.com (www.b4ubuild.com/links/ cadd.shtml) lets you download trial versions of home building programs, shareware, and demos.

Do-it-yourself home improvements

Do-it-yourself home improvements seem to be a part of American life. In fact, Home Depot, a nationwide do-it-yourself hardware store, recently became one of the few companies included in the calculation of the Dow Jones Industrial Average.

If you're thinking of doing the work yourself, keep in mind that some jobs, such as electrical, require professionals for safety reasons. (In some geographic locations, this is mandatory for all electrical work.) However, homeowners can easily complete many improvement projects in a weekend. For the do-it-yourselfer, the Internet is a wonderful resource. Examples of what you'll find online include:

Better Homes and Gardens (www.bhg.com/ homeimp), shown below, has a comprehensive guide for the do-it-yourselfer, with information on plumbing, carpentry, wiring,

Better Homes and Gardens' Home Improvement Encyclopedia provides a rich source of home repair and improvement advice.

decks, masonry, and concrete. The Web site includes helpful project cost calculators and an efficient search engine. If you're looking for easy-to-understand, step-by-step instructions, this is the place.

DoItYourself.com (www.doityourself.com) offers answers to the most frequently asked questions about do-it-yourself projects. Visit the help pages directory to find local suppliers and contractors, browse through the bookstore, or sign up for a free e-mail do-it-yourself newsletter.

Home Depot (www.homedepot.com) includes fixing, building, growing, decorating, and installation information for all your home repairs, as well as an online calculator for estimating costs of needed materials.

Home Repairs & Etc. (www.repair-home.com) provides home repair and routine maintenance information, along with simple repairs you can do yourself.

Lowe's (www.lowes.com) offers a site search feature, home safety tips, featured products, and a store locator. The handy reference library includes a how-to index, a paint problem solver, a how-to glossary, a lawn and garden glossary, and a house plan index.

Remodel Online (www.remodelonline.com) is an open directory of over 50,000 pages of home improvement, do-it-yourself, remodeling, and gardening information. The Web site is divided into four centers: homeowner, gardening, remodeling, and shopping.

Sound Home Resource Center (www.soundhome. com) includes home construction, remodeling, and maintenance solutions. This Web site gives you expert advice and includes a topic index, a glossary, a search engine, a bookstore, and other online resources.

Toiletology 101 (www.toiletology.com/index. shtml) lets you plunge in and flush out the facts about toilet repairs. This Web site includes almost everything you need to know (but never thought you would want to know) about toilet repairs.

True Value (www.truevalue.com) includes monthly deals, links to experts, featured projects (such as how to install a basement exhaust fan), a store locator, information on shopping online, and more.

Getting the most bang for your home improvement buck

Different home improvements add different amounts of value to your home. For example, you might be surprised to find that adding a tennis court or swimming pool might not add any value to your home when it's time to sell. Home improvements such as a new plumbing system, reinforced walls, or a new septic tank don't add anything to the sales price of your home. Therefore, if you're making home improvements to increase the value of your home, the rule of thumb is, *If it isn't broken, don't fix it.* The following is an overview of the costs you can and cannot expect to recoup if you make certain home improvements:

- **Landscaping.** You may want manicured gardens and love how your backyard looks in the spring. However, any money you spend will not add value to your home itself (although it will increase the "curb appeal" of your home).

- **Pools and spas.** You can spend up to $300,000 for a new pool, only to have it turn off prospective buyers. Pools require expensive upkeep. Additionally, swimming pools are often sources for liability since pool accidents can result in negligence suits.

- **Decks and porches.** Adding a redwood deck may be one of the least expensive but most surefire ways to increase the value of your home. This adds square footage to your home. A deck or porch will likely cost from $4,000 to $7,000. With your home improvement tax benefits and a higher sales value, you'll break even or profit if you build a deck. Other outside home improvements have a much lower cost-benefit trade-off. (For more on the tax benefits of home improvements, see "Paying for your home improvements" later in this chapter.)

■ **Bathrooms.** Adding a full bath pays for itself at
resale time, but the cost isn't low. Expect to pay
about $12,000 for that extra bathroom.

■ **Kitchens.** Kitchens have changed over the past
30 years. Now almost everyone in the family is
involved in food preparation. For most families, the kitchen sets the tone of the entire
house. Low-cost improvements (paint, wallpa-
per, re-flooring if necessary, and refinishing
cabinets) can provide a big payoff when you
sell your home. On the other hand, if you start
altering the floor plan, the costs may exceed
the payback. For example, if you pay $20,000
for a new kitchen, you won't recoup your
investment when you sell the house.

■ **Adding space.** If you can add space to your
home, you can usually increase its value. For
example, if you can convert the attic to a family
room, put a room over the garage, or finish
the basement for about $22,000, you'll recoup
about 84 percent of the costs when you sell the
home. By the way, waterproofing the basement
so that it's usable living space, which costs
about $3,000, will recoup more than 100 per-
cent of its cost when you sell.

In brief, some improvements are better investments than others. Changing floors, cabinetry, electrical, and plumbing fixtures will only add value to
your home if what's currently there is outdated.
Sometimes a $4,000 investment will return more
market value, for example, $14,000 in your home's
increased value. For example, painting is the least
expensive and most bankable home improvement
you can do. A new paint job can cover many problems and needed repairs. The National Association

of Realtors states that painting the exterior of a house costs about $3,250 and recoups about 81 percent of its cost when you sell your home. However, if your home is the most expensive one in the neighborhood, chances are additional home improvements won't increase its value.

Getting the most for your restoration money

Restoring an old home requires a lot of cash and renovation. The electrical system (if it exists) is usually too old to use; the plumbing system has to be restored, upgraded, or added; and many small repairs need to be completed. Generally, the cost of restoring an old home is equal to the cost of purchasing an inexpensive new home.

Even if you do a lot of the work yourself, you'll probably need to hire a contractor who specializes in restoration work. Also, you'll likely need an architect, even though the house is already built, to complete the planning and design phase of the restoration. The resulting blueprints are the only way you can discover what you truly want. The blueprints will also be the basis of your loan with the bank and contract with your general contractor.

For help with your restoration project (or just to explore the possibility of restoring an old house), the Internet provides lots of how-to information as well as journals of folks who have traveled down this road. The following is a sampling of what you'll find online:

> *Old-House Journal Online* (www.oldhousejournal. com) offers restoration and remodeling information, a bookstore, house plans, cost vs. value reports, and more.

> *Antique Hardware & Home Store* (www. antiquehardware.com) offers high quality

at reasonable prices. Check out its online catalog.

Balmer Studios (www.balmerstudios.com) manufactures architectural molding in gypsum plaster and formulated polyurethane, in addition to cornices, crown moldings, and fireplace mantels. Check out its products, services, and online literature.

SalvoWEB (www.salvo.co.uk), located in the United Kingdom, provides architectural antiques, antique garden ornaments, reclaimed building materials, architectural salvage, and a newsletter.

Paying for your home improvements

Many homeowners who are about to embark on their home improvement projects believe that they will do just a little bit at a time and not borrow any money. While noble, there are several limitations to doing a major home improvement project a bit at a time:

■ Often you can get price breaks on construction materials if your order is larger.

■ Doing all the work at one time often results in fewer errors or reduced costs when correcting errors.

■ The project only has value if it's completed. If you complete the project quickly, you get to realize the added value sooner.

Homeowners can usually finance their home improvements at lower than nonhomeowner rates, using their homes as collateral for the loan. Additionally, there are tax savings for the interest and points paid on the home improvement loan. According to Improvenet (www.improvenet.com), there are five ways to finance your home improvements:

- **Financing with a project-specific loan.** Use a project-specific home improvement loan to finance your new roof or room addition.

- **Financing with a line of credit.** Finance the project with a home equity line of credit. This allows homeowners to reborrow against the same loan from time to time for whatever reason.

- **Financing with a home equity loan.** Finance your existing loan and take out enough cash (from your acquired equity) to pay for your home improvements.

- **Financing by refinancing your current home loan.** Refinance your current loan and take out enough cash to pay off debts, buy a car, and pay college tuition, as well as your home improvements.

- **Financing using a combination of loan types.** Use a combination of these approaches.

Once again, the Internet can provide you with help 24 hours a day, 7 days a week for selecting the home improvement loan that's right for your personal financial situation. The following are just a few of the useful articles available online:

> *Money.com* (www.money.com) provides a free searchable archive, articles for financing home improvements, and an online refinancing calculator.

> *Financenter.com* (www.financenter.com) provides a helpful article. At the homepage, click

on Homes. In the ClickCalcs box, scroll down until you find "How Much Can I Borrow?"

SmartMoney (smartmoney.lycos.com/ac/home/living/index.cfm?story=refinancing) provides a valuable article about strategies for financing your home improvements entitled "Refinancing: Take the Low Road." This article shows how you can nail down the rate you want, have a hassle-free experience, use online alternatives, and more.

Just the facts

- Major or complex design changes may require hiring an architect and contractor.
- Not all home improvements will increase the value of your home.
- If you plan to restore a home, be prepared to spend lots of time and cash.
- It's not always wise to pay for large home improvements bit by bit.

Marketing and Selling Your Home Online

Chapter 16

According to the U.S. Census Bureau, in 1998, about 1.2 million homes were up for sale, and almost a million homes were sold or awaiting occupancy. For the first six months of 1998, home sales were 17 percent higher than those in the same time in the previous year. This increase might be attributed to low interest rates and lenders being more generous.

If you're considering selling your home, you can find plenty of information and advice on the Internet. Many online real estate services are free. With online assistance and this chapter to guide you to the best sites on the Internet, you'll master the basics in no time. You can start by discovering the best time to sell and where you can find real estate market information online. This chapter goes on to show you step-by-step how you can use the Internet to find out exactly how much your home is worth, then provides price listing strategies that can assist you in getting top dollar for your home.

In this chapter, you'll learn how you can make your home stand out from the crowd by providing prospective homebuyers Internet-based information about your neighborhood's demographics, economic trends, and crime statistics. Master how you can market your home online and offline. Find free online listings for your property and discover how the Multiple Listing Service (MLS) can give your home maximum exposure. Get online tips for making your home show better and find out how to hire an outstanding listing agent. The chapter concludes by showing what you can expect if you sell your home by yourself and how the Internet can help you.

Deciding when to sell

The best time to sell a house is right after you decide to sell. Waiting for a peak sales period does not guarantee that you'll sell quickly and get the price you want. If you wait to list your home for a high sales time, there will be more houses on the market and competition will be greater. Besides, peak selling times are different in different geographic locations.

Selling a home usually takes between 30 to 180 days, depending on the market conditions in your area. If you can take six months to sell your home, you'll likely get a greater return for your efforts. In other words, without time pressures you are less likely to accept a low offer.

If you have to sell in a hurry due to a corporate relocation or if you need to sell so you can close on your next home, there are some alternatives. First, you can rent for a short period of time, thus avoiding double mortgage payments. Second, you can go with a broker's guaranteed sales plan. This plan is a written promise to buy your home at a predetermined price if it doesn't sell by a certain date. The amount of the guaranteed price varies between brokers, so you may want to shop around for the best program. A good example of a guaranteed sales plan is the ERA Sellers Security Plan (www.era.com/aboutera/sellerssecurityplanbody.html).

As a general rule, people like to shop for a home when the weather is pleasant (usually between April and August). The exceptions to this rule are "snowbirds" who like to purchase homes in snowy areas of the country. These folks shop from January through March.

A "buyer's market" means there are more homes for sale than there are buyers. This market condition usually forces homeowners to lower their prices and homes take longer to sell. A "seller's market" means there are more buyers than home sellers. In this market, competition is stiff and some desperate homebuyers may offer more than the listing price for your home. In a seller's market, real estate agents work harder to get listings. A seller's or buyer's market can be limited to a city, a neighborhood, or even a street (say, Lombard Street in San Francisco, California). An average market favors neither the buyer nor the seller. Here's a sampling of what you'll find online:

> *U.S. Census Bureau* (www.census.gov/hhes/www/housing.html) provides an American Housing Survey, surveys of market absorption rates, and more.

> *Builder Online* (www.builderonline.com/store/usmarkt/ushmarkt.htx) provides information on what's happening in many

metropolitan markets, metropolitan market profiles, county activity, and more.

Chicago Title Company (www.ctt.com/hbs/default.htm) publishes demographic information, home price data, and information about the highs and lows for major U.S. metropolitan housing markets, in addition to Chicago Title Corporation's 23rd annual survey of recent homebuyers.

Using the Internet to set a price

After you decide to sell your home, the first step in the home selling process is to determine your home's value. The fair market price is the highest a buyer will pay for your home and the lowest price at which you are willing to sell. The Internet has many resources to assist you in determining the value of your home, including the following:

iOwn (rhs.iown.com/buy/rh_buy_index.htm) provides free sales information and can assist you in comparing sales prices so you can determine a realistic listing price. Select a neighborhood and get a list of recently sold homes (with price and date). You'll also find an overview of all sales activity in the area.

Home Price Check (www.homepricecheck.com), shown below, contains the purchase price records for over 20 million U.S. homes. The database is updated each week. Historical coverage varies by state, but where available, it includes the home prices for at least the past five years.

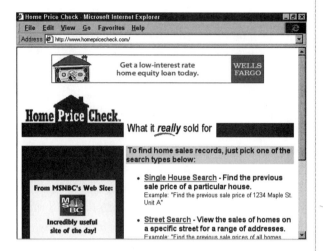

Home Price Check is constantly updated and usually posts home transaction prices six weeks after the close of a sale.

At *HomeGain* (www.homegain.com) you can find the same information that real estate professionals use to estimate the value of your current home or the home you're thinking of buying. Simply register and you'll receive free home valuation estimates instantly, including recent comparable home sales in your neighborhood and their sales prices. At the time of this writing, it covers 388 counties in 37 states. Click Coverage to see if it covers your area.

After reviewing comparable sales prices, you'll probably notice that there are no easy profits in real estate. Prices have leveled off since the 1980s, dropped slightly in the early 1990s in many areas, and appreciated somewhat in the late 1990s. House prices will vary over time. Consequently, over the years, many real estate agents have developed different approaches to selling real estate. Currently the two most popular approaches are as follows:

■ **List somewhat higher than the comparable rate.** The listing (or asking price) is usually set slightly higher than the fair market value. This way you can negotiate with a homebuyer. For example, in my neighborhood in Alexandria, Virginia, homes have recently sold for 5 to 10 percent less than the asking price.

■ **List slightly lower than the comparable rate.** The listing (or asking) price is set "below-market pricing." This can create interest in the home and multiple purchase offers within a few days after the new listing comes on the market for sale. This technique works well in a seller's market. If you receive several offers, the seller can counteroffer at a price higher than the asking price.

The Internet provides additional tips on pricing your home. The following are a few examples:

zipRealty.com (www.ziprealty.com/virtual_model/vm_5.jsp) offers information on preparing, showing, and pricing your home.

Consumer Information Center (www.pueblo.gsa.gov/cic_text/housing/sellhome/sellhome.htm) provides an introduction to selling your home, titled "Life Advice about Selling a Home."

Getting your house ready

Generally, the homes that sell the fastest are in near "model-home" condition. Therefore, unless you have a nearly new home, it's likely that your home will need a few repairs before you place it on the market. Be careful, though, because when you are planning to sell your home is not the time for major renovations like remodeling the kitchen or installing a swimming pool. However, you should try to make your house look its best by keeping it clean and making small repairs. You might even consider getting an inspection done so you're not surprised by anything a potential buyer's inspector turns up.

Making your house look its best

Curb appeal is a real estate term for anything prospective buyers can see from the street. A home that has curb appeal is neat and in good condition. It will usually attract potential homebuyers driving down the street. Often these folks make up their minds about buying your home before they enter the front door. To increase your curb appeal, you may want to consider a new exterior paint job (use light, neutral colors), mowing the lawn, putting children's toys or gardening tools out of sight, sealing the driveway, and adding potted plants at the front door.

Once inside your home, you need to make it easy for prospective homebuyers to imagine living there. To prepare your home for viewing, you'll need to make it as light, cheerful, and restful as possible.

The type and amount of work your home needs often depends on your asking price and the current condition of your home. Here are some fairly simple things you can do that will help you sell your home fast and for top dollar:

- **Clean up all the clutter and make your home look as clean and spacious as possible.** Clean as much from the walls, shelves, and counter tops as possible. Have a garage sale to get rid of extra furniture and knick-knacks or donate them to a local charity.

- **Clean the garage.** A dirty or messy garage or carport can quickly dampen a prospective homebuyer's enthusiasm.

- **Clean closets and crawl spaces in the bathrooms and bedrooms.** Turn on the light in your closets and put fresh towels in the bathrooms.

Bright Idea
Smells can turn off a prospective homebuyer. Opening all the windows and airing the house for a few hours in the middle of winter may not be possible. Try simmering a few drops of vanilla in a pan of water to freshen the air, or bake bread or cookies before a showing.

- **Install new light fixtures to give your home a fresh look.** Make certain you turn on all the lights when prospective buyers walk through the house. Open the drapes and light your dining room chandelier and living room lamps.

- **Clean or repair flooring.** If the carpets are worn, they should be replaced with neutral carpets with lots of padding. Refinish the hardwood floors if needed.

- **Fresh paint both inside and out increases curb appeal and hides a multitude of small problems.** Even if your home is fairly new, you may still need to paint stairways that have dirt on the walls or rooms that have seen a lot of use.

- **Re-grout sinks, bathtubs, walls, and floors where needed.** Replace any missing or broken doorknobs or drawer handles.

For more information on home repairs, including Internet sources, see Chapter 15, "Online Help for Making Your House a Home."

Getting your own inspection

It's often wise to order your own home inspection to catch any needed repairs or home improvements. If you wait, the homebuyer may use *his or her* home inspection report to negotiate a lower sales price.

Most buyers should hire their own inspector and termite and pest control inspector. Most individuals won't argue with an inspection completed by a member of the American Society of Home Inspectors (ASHI). For more on home inspections, see Chapter 9, "Online Help with Appraisals, Inspections, and Insurance."

If you have all the necessary and customary professional inspections completed before putting your home on the market, prospective buyers can see these reports and are likely to realize that you maintain your home well.

Ordering an inspection also protects you from claims that you did not disclose house defects (a room addition not built to code, lead-based paint, high radon levels, and so on). In this litigious age, the small inspection fee can prevent a major disclosure suit.

Marketing your home online and offline

Marketing your home is more than putting a "For Sale" sign in the front yard. You or your real estate agent should have a comprehensive marketing plan for your home that includes advertising, listing it on the MLS, and holding open houses.

Advertising

Advertising your home is one of the most important things you can do to find a buyer. Your Realtor can advertise using the Internet, newspapers, magazines, radio, TV, and direct mail. These approaches vary in terms of their cost and effectiveness.

MLS

The MLS includes more than one million homes for sale. (Keep in mind, though, that the MLS is a locally owned service of the Board of Realtors in each local area, not a national organization.) The MLS gives your home the widest possible coverage

Bright Idea
Some states have passed legislation about what a seller must disclose to a buyer. Therefore, before accepting a homebuyer's offer, you might want to get him or her to sign the state-required disclosure form (or, in states without seller disclosure legislation, a written acknowledgment of any major problems).

Bright Idea
To make your home stand out from the crowd, you can purchase a one-year home warranty that protects the homebuyer (and you) by covering repairs or replacement costs. One online example of a warranty plan is Blue Ribbon Home Warranty (www.brhw.com).

by making data about it available to thousands of real estate professionals. Participating brokerages agree to share commissions on the sales of homes and residential lots listed on the MLS by any one brokerage. For example, if you list your house with one Realtor and another actually sells the home, the two Realtors split the real estate commission.

Today, individuals can view your MLS-listed home via the Internet at Web sites such as Realtor.com (www.realtor.com) and MSN Home-Advisor (www.homeadvisor.msn.com). Your online MLS listing will often include a photo of your home, a brochure that can be printed out, the usual home statistics (number of bedrooms, bathrooms, etc.), and financing information.

If you hire a real estate agent to list your house, it can be listed at HomeSeekers.com (www.homeseekers.com), as well as at Realtor.com and MSN HomeAdvisor. If your local area is not covered, check the local Yellow Pages.

The Internet also provides many real estate listing Web sites that don't require Realtor participation. The following are a few examples:

> *Yahoo! Classifieds* (www.classifieds.yahoo.com) allows you to place a free ad in the extensive Yahoo! Classifieds.

> *The United States Real Estate Directory* (www.1realestate.com) is designed to simplify ways in which buyers and sellers locate United States real estate information on the Internet.

> *NewRealty.com* (www.newrealty.com), shown below, allows sellers to list their homes in the site database for free online exposure. One submission sends your information to three online real estate listing databases:

NewRealty.com (www.realty.com),
HomeScout (www.homescout.com), and
Yahoo! (www.classifieds.yahoo.com).

Get your home
listed in three
free online
databases at
NewRealty.com.

For an online guide to Internet real estate
listing database Web sites, see *The Real Estate
Library*'s article titled "On the Web for Buyers
and Sellers" (www.realtimes.com/rtnews/
rtcpages/19991015_web1.htm).

Holding open houses

There are two types of open houses: those for
Realtors and those for the public. During open
houses for Realtors, you allow top real estate agents
from the area to view your home firsthand. This
type of open house often leads to a quick sale.
Serious buyers work with real estate agents to find
homes. Consequently, the more agents who see your
home, the more exposure you'll have to qualified
buyers.

Public open houses are usually held on week-
ends. You (or your real estate agent) have to determine how often you need to have an open house to
stimulate activity. Although few homebuyers buy the
home they view at an open house, it's a good way to
keep the home before the public. Sometimes, these
public open houses are a good way to reach the
neighbors, who may have relatives or friends who
need to relocate to the area.

Working with a listing agent

Let's say you've evaluated all your options and
decided that now is the time to sell your home. The
next step is to decide if you want to hire a real estate
agent to sell the property for you. You'll have to pay
a commission, so what can a listing agent do for you?
Here are some benefits:

- **Provide information about the entire house
  selling process.** Your real estate agent will
  inform you of local customs and regulations
  that you might want to consider before putting
  your house on the market.

- **Determine the correct price for your property.**
  Your listing agent will show you comparable
  housing prices. He or she will also provide
  information about the selling prices of similar
  homes that have recently sold in your neighborhood, and make expert suggestions about
  market conditions in your neighborhood and
  in the region.

- **Develop a marketing plan for your property.**
  Your listing agent will provide you with a sales
  plan, arrange times of open houses, and list
  your home on the MLS. Your agent will pay for
  all advertising costs to market your home and
  provide "For Sale" signs and related materials.

■ **Pre-screen and accompany qualified buyers.**
Your real estate agent will field all telephone
calls about your home. He or she will "qualify"
potential buyers and verify that they can get
the financing to purchase your home.

You won't have to worry about being away
from your home when the right buyer comes
along. Your real estate agent will arrange
appointment times with potential buyers and
accompany them as they walk through your
home.

■ **Negotiate with potential buyers.** Any sales offer
will be presented to your real estate agent. He
or she will review the offer and point out its
strengths and weaknesses, as well as alert you
to any potential risks. For example, the offer
must be in writing and specific in its terms.
The obligations of each party must be clearly
stated.

■ **Monitor offers and suggest counteroffers.**
Your real estate agent will make certain that
you comply with the disclosures required by
law and monitor the response times of all
offers and counteroffers.

■ **Oversee the closing paperwork and accompany
you to the settlement meeting (if applicable).**
Your real estate agent will provide you with an
estimate of the closing costs you will have to
pay. He or she will also work with the buyer to
help pave the way to a smooth closing.

Outstanding agents make things happen. They
aggressively market their listings, use the MLS, run
weekly newspaper ads, put listings on the Internet,
and network with other agents by telephone or mail
to inform them of your listing. How can you tell a

winner from a loser? Start by considering only agents who are familiar with your neighborhood and recommended by friends or family.

Without any financial obligation, you can invite local real estate agents to your home and listen to their "listing presentations" about why they are the best agent to sell your property. Interview at least three agents and ask them to value your home. Ask your interviewees what they think of your other candidates and if they are well liked. They will usually tell you if the other agents are not honest, not well-liked, or have other unfavorable attributes. In other words, discover what the agent's reputation is with other real estate agents.

Don't sign a listing contract that lasts longer than three months. Remember, most homes sell within six months. If you sign a six-month contract, your agent doesn't have any incentive to sell your home quickly. Another option is to sign a six-month listing contract, with a three-month escape clause. This protects you from an agent who has forgotten about selling your house.

The Internet provides some additional information about hiring a listing agent. The following are a few examples:

Virtual Real Estate Store (www. virtualrealestatestore.com/selling-a-home-page.htm#what_happens_after_home_listed) provides consumer guides to the five keys to selling your home quickly and for top dollar. This is a good source for getting advice on how to select a listing agent.

SmartMoney (www.smartmoney.com/ac/ home/selling/index.cfm?story=choose) offers a beneficial article titled "Choosing a Broker

Wisely." There's also a helpful seller's checklist, an article on selling without a broker, and tax considerations when you sell your home.

eHome (www.ehome.com), shown below, hopes to combine the economic efficiency of the Internet with the personalized service of a real estate agent for a fixed fee. It provides an online alternative to traditional listing agents.

eHome provides a different approach for owners who want to sell their homes.

Selling your home without an agent

The primary reason owners sell their homes by themselves is to save money. The following two examples show how you can save money by not using an agent:

- If an owner has a $350,000 house and can sell it without a real estate agent, the cost savings can be almost the amount of a down payment on another home. For example, let's say real estate agent fees are 7 percent in your geographic area. Not paying any real estate commission results in a cost savings of $24,500.

■ FSBOs can be very beneficial to homeowners who don't have equity in their property. For example, if the real estate commission is 6 percent and the FSBO seller has only 4 percent equity position in the home, the seller pays the 2 percent difference out of pocket. On a $350,000 home, this cost is $7,000. Overall, $7,000 is not a lot of money, but for someone who doesn't have the cash, it can seem like a huge sum.

The problems of FSBOs

The cost savings and not having to pay commission out of pocket are very attractive to many homeowners. However, FSBO sellers can run into a number of problems with marketing their homes. Here are a few limitations that FSBO sellers may encounter:

■ There are more than 1.3 million homes for sale listed by Realtors in the MLS. If a property is a FSBO, it may or may not be included in this listing. This means that locating FSBOs can be difficult because they have limited publicity. After all, it's unlikely that a homebuyer will find a home for sale at the end of a residential cul-de-sac just by happening upon it.

■ FSBO sellers pay for newspaper classified ads, flyers, or postcards to advertise their homes. Newspaper ads often cost from $50 to $200 for three lines of text for a two-week ad. Flyers can cost from $100 to $200 dollars. If you buy a mailing list (about $200) and mail postcards, the total cost can be over $400. This type of marketing can make promoting a FSBO property very expensive.

- In some cases, it's not easy to make contact with the FSBO seller. If the owner is away from the home, there is no one to show the property to a potential buyer. Out-of-town buyers often don't have the time to contact the FSBO seller directly and make an appointment to visit the property. Additionally, prospective buyers tend to knock on the doors of FSBO sellers at odd times, instead of calling the telephone number on your yard sign.

FSBO help from discounted real estate brokerages

A new type of intermediary has appeared on the real estate scene. *Discounted real estate brokerages* now offer three types of service. First, a FSBO seller can pay a flat fee of 1 to 3 percent to get limited real estate agent services. Second, a FSBO seller can pay a fee for each type of real estate service selected by the FSBO seller. Third, a FSBO seller can pay a co-op fee for being successfully matched to a buyer. Let's take a closer look at these options.

Discounted listing services charge a flat fee of 1 to 3 percent for limited real estate services. This is a great option for FSBO homeowners who don't have the time or patience to sell their homes on their own.

There is a middle ground between full-service real estate agencies and independent FSBO sellers—menus of services. Services can be unbundled and sold piece by piece for a flat fee. The International Real Estate Directory (ired.com/buymyself/rioux/fsbo/) details what's often on the menu for fee-per-service discount brokerages.

According to the National Association of Realtors, about 51 percent of homebuyers find the homes they eventually purchase with the assistance of real estate agents. With "co-brokes," the buyer's real estate agent gets his or her half of the usual real estate commission (usually about $3^{1}/_{2}$ percent of the selling price) for bringing a buyer to the FSBO's seller's door.

Just the facts

- You can use online data to set a listing price.

- Consider having a pre-inspection done and completing needed repairs before you sell your home.

- Help the decision making of prospective buyers by providing Internet-based community reports.

- Give your home maximum exposure by listing it in the online version of the MLS and at free real estate listing databases.

- Use the Internet to find an outstanding listing agent or get online help if you sell your home without a real estate agent.

Appendixes

PART VII

Glossary

adjustable-rate mortgage (ARM) A type of mortgage in which the interest rate adjusts from time to time according to a pre-selected index that represents the current market rate. Monthly mortgage payments can increase or decrease over the life of the loan. Limits (called *caps*) can be set on the amount of interest changes or monthly payment changes.

agent An individual who is authorized to act as an intermediary in order to secure a sales contract to buy or sell a house. Also called a *real estate agent*.

aggregator An Internet intermediary that screens and forwards home loan applications to direct lenders. Lenders then render a decision about the loan application. Mortgage lenders use aggregators in an effort to reduce the cost of prospecting for customers and increasing the firm's approval rate. Consumers benefit because they receive faster approval times and lower loan costs.

amortization Where a certain amount of a payment is applied to principal and another amount is applied to interest.

annual percentage rate (APR)   The actual annual cost of credit. The APR represents the relationship of the total finance charge (interest, loan fees, points) to the amount of the loan.

application   A form used to record pertinent information about someone who is seeking a mortgage to finance real property.

appraisal   A written analysis by a certified appraiser used to determine the estimated value of a property.

appraised value   The opinion of the certified appraiser, usually based on three valuation methodologies.

appreciation   The increase in the value of property due to changes in market conditions or other causes. (The opposite of *depreciation*.)

assets   Anything of monetary value owned by an individual.

assumption   A homebuyer's commitment to take on the responsibilities of the seller's mortgage in exchange for ownership of the property.

bad credit   Late payments for financial obligations that appear on a credit report.

broker   The intermediary who, for a fee, brings two parties together and assists in the negotiation of a contract.

browser   A program that allows you to read information on the World Wide Web.

buyer's agent   A real estate agent who represents and protects the interests of the homebuyer.

cap   A limit of interest rate amount or the mortgage payment amount that can increase or decrease for an adjustable-rate mortgage.

clear title   Title to a property that is "clear" of any liens or other legal issues about ownership.

closing   The meeting where the transaction is "closed" and the transfer of the property is finalized by the buyer signing mortgage documents and paying closing costs. (Also called *settlement*.)

closing costs Expenses above the cost of the property incurred by buyers and sellers in the transaction. Closing costs vary from state to state.

collateral An asset (such as a car or home) owned by a borrower that guarantees the repayment of a loan. The borrower risks losing the asset if the conditions of the loan are not met and the loan is not repaid.

commission A fee charged by a broker or agent for negotiating a real property or loan transaction. Commissions are generally based on the purchase price of the real estate. Commissions are always negotiable, by law.

competitive market analysis (CMA) A way to determine a property's value by comparing it to similar, recently sold properties.

condominium A housing arrangement where the homeowner owns the interior walls of his or her personal living space and a percentage of the common areas.

contingencies Certain conditions included in a sales contract that must be met before the contract can be ratified or closed.

co-op A cooperative unit, in which the residents buy shares in order to occupy the unit.

counteroffer A written response to an offer that changes one or more of the conditions of the sales contract.

conventional mortgage Any mortgage that is not insured or guaranteed by the federal government.

credit history An individual's record of current and past payments to creditors. In general, this history shows a borrower's willingness to make credit payments in a timely manner.

credit rating agency   An organization that collects credit information from public records and credit providers and organizes the data into a credit report.

credit report   Usually generated by one of three credit rating agencies. This report uses public records and information provided by creditors to show an individual's credit history.

deed   A legal document that conveys ownership (title) of a property.

deed of trust   A legal document used in some states instead of a mortgage. In this situation, ownership (title) is conveyed to a trustee.

default   Failure to make mortgage payments as agreed or failure to comply with other requirements of a mortgage.

deposit   Sometimes called "earnest money," this is money offered by a prospective homebuyer to indicate his or her good faith in entering into a sales contract.

down payment   A portion of the purchase price of real property that a buyer pays in cash and does not finance with a mortgage.

dual agent   An agent who represents both the buyer and the seller in a real estate transaction in a limited capacity. A dual agent does not completely represent either party because of the potential conflict of interest inherent in dual agency.

earnest money   *See* deposit.

effective gross income   An individual's normal annual salary including overtime that is regular or guaranteed in some fashion. Income may be from more than one source.

equity   The homeowner's accrued money value in the property. The difference between the market value of the property and the outstanding balance owed on its mortgage.

escrow Money or documents deposited with a neutral third party to be delivered when a condition is fulfilled.

fair market value The highest price a willing and able buyer would pay and the lowest price a willing seller would accept.

Fannie Mae Formerly a government-sponsored enterprise, now a public company. Pursuant to a federal charter, purchases mortgages from lenders so they can make new loans.

Federal Housing Administration (FHA) An agency of the U.S. Department of Housing and Urban Development (HUD). The FHA insures residential loans made by private lenders. The FHA sets standards for construction and underwriting but does not lend money or construct houses.

federal truth-in-lending disclosure form A government-required form that discloses the annual percentage rate (APR), total principal of the loan, amount of interest that will be paid over the loan term, and the combined total of the principal and interest.

FHA mortgage An FHA-insured mortgage allows a low down payment mortgage for any borrower who meets certain guidelines established by the FHA.

fixed-rate mortgage A mortgage with a level interest rate that does not change during the life of the loan.

for sale by owner (FSBO) A home that's offered for sale without the services of a real estate agent.

foreclosure The legal process, under the terms of the mortgage, of seizing a property from the owner and selling the property so the proceeds can be applied to the payment of a defaulted mortgage debt.

Freddie Mac Formerly a government-sponsored enterprise, now a public company. Pursuant to a federal charter, purchases mortgages from lenders so they can make new loans.

gift letter A letter required by a lender to substantiate that a certain amount of funds applied to the down payment is a gift and not a loan.

government mortgage Any mortgage that is insured by the federal government. Examples of government mortgages are VA, FHA, and RHS mortgages.

hazard insurance Insurance to compensate for any physical damage from fire, wind, vandalism, or other hazards.

home equity loan A loan that allows a homeowner to borrow against a certain percentage of his or her equity in their property.

homeowners association An organization formed by homeowners in a subdivision or a condominium giving certain homeowners decision-making responsibilities for the welfare of the entire subdivision or condominium.

homeowners insurance A combination of hazard and personal liability insurance policies for a residence and its contents.

housing expense ratio Determined by dividing housing expenses by the gross monthly income. The higher the ratio, the heavier the debt load.

hypertext A system of writing and displaying text that is often used for the World Wide Web. Hypertext enables text to be linked in multiple ways, be available at several levels of detail, and contain links to related documents.

improvement Anything added or modified on real property to increase its value.

initial interest rate The original interest rate used for an ARM. Sometimes called a "start" rate.

inspection The evaluation of real property by a professional.

interest rate Rate of return on the principal amount. The rate is normally expressed as an annual percentage.

Internet A system by which computers in the world can communicate with each other through an external communications network.

liabilities An individual's financial obligations to others. Liabilities can be short-term (less than five years) or long-term (longer than five years).

lien A legally recognized hold or claim of one person on the property owned by another person as security for a debt, duty, or obligation.

link A hyperlink connection that can take you to another Web page or to another part of the same Web page.

listing Formally putting a piece of real property on the market. Putting the property on the MLS or advertising in a public notice, such as a newspaper, radio, or computer ad.

loan origination The process by which a lender brings into existence a mortgage for a borrower secured by real estate.

lock-in A written guarantee by a lender for a loan with a specific interest rate, contingent upon the mortgage being closed within a pre-set time period.

mortgage A legal agreement pledging a property to a lender as security for the payment of a debt.

mortgage banker A company that originates mortgages for resale in the secondary market.

mortgage broker An individual or company who, for a fee, brings borrowers and mortgage bankers together to originate a mortgage.

mortgage insurance A contract that insures the lender against the borrower's default. Mortgage insurance can cover a portion of the loan or all of the debt.

Multiple Listing Service (MLS) A network of local listings of Boards of Realtors covering over a million homes for sale across the country. The MLS is used by real estate agents both to sell and to locate properties to show their clients.

negative amortization When a monthly house payment is not enough to cover the entire principal and interest due, the amount of the shortfall is added to the remaining balance to create "negative" amortization. In other words, you can owe more than your original loan amount.

note The specific terms of a mortgage, including payment amount and schedule of repayment.

origination fee A fee paid to the mortgage lender for processing the application. The fees are based on "points." A point is 1 percent of the loan amount.

payoff The final payment of a mortgage loan. The payoff closes the mortgage loan.

PITI A shorter way of saying principal, interest, taxes, and insurance expenses. For some types of loans, borrowers need to have enough funds after a down payment and closing costs to cover the costs of PITI for a predetermined number of months.

point A point is 1 percent of the loan amount.

possession The day and time that a homebuyer formally takes over a property.

preapproval When a borrower submits a preapproval application to a lender and it is accepted.

This makes the borrower "credit-approved." Final loan approval is based on the property's certified appraisal and verification of the documentation submitted by the borrower.

prequalification The process of determining how much a homebuyer will be eligible to borrow before he or she applies for a loan.

principal The amount owed on a note or mortgage. When the loan is originated, it is the amount borrowed.

promissory note A document recording a pledge to repay a debt.

property tax The annual state, county, and local assessment against a certain piece of property.

purchase and sale agreement The contract between a borrower and a seller stating the conditions and terms of the property sale.

qualifying ratios Mathematical calculations used to determine if a borrower can qualify for a mortgage. Usually, lenders use two types of qualifying ratios. The first ratio is the borrower's current monthly debts divided by gross monthly income. The second ratio is the borrower's total debt (including the new house payment and related housing expenses) divided by the monthly gross income.

rate lock A written commitment from the lender to the borrower stating a specific interest rate for a set period of time.

real estate agent *See* agent.

Realtor A designation used for a real estate broker or associate who is affiliated with the National Association of Realtors.

recordation fees The charge for entering a mortgage loan or a deed into the public record.

relocation specialist An agent who exclusively deals with individuals who are moving from one area to another.

Rural Housing Service (RHS) An agency within the U.S. Department of Agriculture that provides financing to farmers and other qualified borrowers for buying property in rural areas of the U.S. The RHS sets eligibility guidelines but is not a lender.

second mortgage A mortgage that is subordinate to the first mortgage.

secondary market Where large quantities of loans are bought and sold to investors.

security The property that is pledged as collateral for a "secured" loan.

settlement Another term for closing.

single-family home A detached house where the owner owns the whole house and has rights to or owns the land on which the house sits.

survey A drawing of the boundaries that separate one piece of real estate from another.

termite inspection A specific inspection of the property for damage due to termite infestation.

title The legally recognized evidence of a person's right to possess a piece of property.

title insurance Protects the lender and buyer against losses due to disputes over ownership of the property.

title search A check of the public records to ensure that the seller is the legal owner of the property. Also verifies that there are no liens or other claims against the property.

townhouse An attached dwelling in which the owner owns the interior and exterior walls of the dwelling.

transfer of ownership   Any means by which the ownership of the real estate changes hands.

underwriting   The process of evaluating a borrower's loan application to determine the amount of lender risk. Underwriting includes the analysis of the borrower's creditworthiness and the appraised value of the property.

uniform resource locator (URL)   A standardized way of naming network resources, used for linking Web pages together on the World Wide Web.

unsecured loan   A loan that is not backed by collateral or secured by real property.

VA mortgage   A mortgage that is guaranteed by the Department of Veterans Administration (VA). Sometimes called a government mortgage. The VA is an agency of the federal government that guarantees residential mortgages of eligible veterans and reservists. The guarantee protects the lender against loss and encourages lenders to make no down payment loans to veterans.

zoning   The laws or policies of city or county authorities specifying how property may be used in specific areas.

Online Home Buying Resource Directory

Throughout the pages of *The Unofficial Guide to Buying a Home Online,* you've seen dozens of Internet resources that can assist you in buying a home without leaving your computer. This appendix is a compilation of the latest and greatest of the wide variety of resources available for online homebuyers. It's organized along the lines of the home buying process. It lists the Web sites you're most likely to use for preparing to buy a home, shopping for a home online, using the Internet for financing, and closing in on your new home in cyberspace.

This appendix is not comprehensive. With all the constant growth and change that characterizes the Internet, it's almost impossible for anyone to create a directory that lives up to such a claim. The Internet is a constantly changing resource. Some sites listed in this directory (and elsewhere in the book) may have changed or disappeared due to mergers with larger sites. Some Web sites just vanish for no reason. If a site has moved, you may find a link to the new location. If not, try a search engine, such as AltaVista (www.altavista.com) or Excite (www.excite.com), to locate the resource you need.

Discovering mortgage loan aggregators

You can go to the aggregator's Web sites and complete home loan application forms, which are then screened and sent to multiple lenders. These mortgage lenders then render a decision on the application. (For more information, see Chapter 1, "Preparing to Buy a Home.")

> *Quicken Loans* (www.quickenmortgage.com)
>
> *E-LOAN* (www.eloan.com)
>
> *iOwn,* formerly Homeshark (www.iown.com)
>
> *LendingTree.com* (www.lendingtree.com)

Determining your net worth

The first step in getting to your financial goal is to know your starting point. Determining your net worth is the place to start. There are many free online worksheets to assist you in the task. (For more information, see Chapter 2, "Creating a Financial Game Plan.")

> *MoneyWeb Net Worth Calculator* (www. moneyweb.com.au)
>
> *BYG Publishing* (www.bygpub.com/finance/ calculators.htm)
>
> *Iowa's News and Information Network* (www. fyiowa.webpoint.com/finance/calcnetw.htm)
>
> *SmartMoney* (www.smartmoney.com/ac/ estate/index.cfm?story=networth)

Learning how you spend your income

When you complete your net worth worksheet, you may discover a "shortfall." A shortfall means that you are living beyond your means. To help you change your spending habits, the Internet has many online sources to help you create a personal budget. (For more information, see Chapter 2, Creating a Financial Game Plan.")

MetLife's Budget Maker (www.metlife.com/ lifeadvice/money/docs/budget4.html)

ABC News (www.abcnews.go.com/sections/ business/dailynews/makeover0227/)

Personal Budgeting (www. personalbudgeting.com)

Right On the Money! (www. rightonthemoney.org/shows/104_budget)

Checking out credit reporting agencies

Credit bureaus keep records of when you pay on your loans, mortgages, rental agreements, and credit cards. (For more information, see Chapter 2, Creating a Financial Game Plan.")

Experian, formerly TRW (www.experian.com)

Equifax (www.equifax.com)

Trans Union (www.tuc.com)

Improving your credit score

Most home loans are underwritten using credit-scoring algorithms. Lenders won't tell how these formulas work, but there are several things you can do to immediately improve your credit score. (For more information, see Chapter 2, Creating a Financial Game Plan.")

ConsumerInfo.com (www.consumerinfo.com)

Mortgage.com (www.customlending.com/ learn_cl.asp)

What's a FICO Score? (www.smi-loan.com/
htdocs/faq/fico.htm)

Credit Repair Institute (www.legalresource.
com/credit4.htm)

Making the rent vs. buy decision

There are many advantages to buying a home (tax
benefits, appreciation, and so on). However, for
some people, renting may be smarter than buying.
Use these online resources to find out what's best
for you. (For more information, see Chapter 3, "Is
Now the Right Time to Buy a Home?")

Homefair (www.homefair.com/homefair/
sept95/frrent.htm)

Investor FAQs (invest-faq.com/articles/
real-es-rent-vs-buy.html)

LoanWorld (www.loanworld.com/calc/
rvb_cl.htm)

Calculating your maximum mortgage amount

The Internet provides many calculators to assist you
in determining the maximum amount a lending
institution will allow you for a mortgage loan under
normal conditions. (For more information, see
Chapter 3, "Is Now the Right Time to Buy a
Home?")

(Re)Finance Center Calculators and Advice
(www.reficenter.com/calculators.htm)

HomePath Calculators (www.homepath.
com/calcs.html)

Mortgagecalc.com (www.mortgagecalc.com)

Genus Credit Management (www.genus2.org)

Prequalifying for a mortgage

It's frustrating to find the perfect house, negotiate an offer, and then not be able to qualify for the needed financing. Avoid this situation by prequalifying online for a home loan before you start looking at houses. This way, you'll be confident about what you can afford. (For more information, see Chapter 3, "Is Now the Right Time to Buy a Home?")

> *Gateway Equity & Loan Network* (www.geloan.com/tools/prequal.html)

> *Accel Mortgage, Inc.* (www.interest.com/accel/pq-accel.html)

> *Lenox Financial Mortgage Corporation* (www.dreams.net/lxfm/rfp)

> *RE/MAX Gold* (www.remaxgold.com/prequal.htm)

Getting preapproved for a home loan

Preapproval goes a step further than prequalifying. With preapproval, your lender's underwriter has completed all the necessary checks on your financial background and guaranteed your loan. Many online mortgage lenders provide preapproval. (For more information, see Chapter 3, "Is Now the Right Time to Buy a Home?")

> *AppOnline* (www.apponline.com/frames/ap/preapp.htm)

> *Ameriwest* (www.ameriwest.com/applyonline.html)

> *Mortgage1.com* (www.mortgage1.com/preapp.html)

Countrywide (www.countrywide.com)

PNC Mortgage (www.pncmortgage.com/
pre_approval.html)

Looking into national house trends

Today, more Americans own homes than ever
before. A strong economy, low mortgage rates, and
affordable housing mean that now is the time to
start preparing to purchase or look for a home. (For
more information, see Chapter 4, "Finding a
Neighborhood Next Door or Across the Country.")

*Federal Reserve Bank of Boston—Regional
Economic Information Links* (www.bos.frb.
org/economic/reglink.htm)

Bureau of Economic Analysis (www.bea.doc.gov)

Economic Statistics Briefing Room (www.
whitehouse.gov/fsbr/employment.html)

USDA Economics and Statistics Search
(usda.mannlib.cornell.edu/usda)

American Community Network (www.acn.net)

Learning which state is right for you

The Internet has information about relocating to
each state. State governments, the Chamber of
Commerce, and corporations sponsor many Web
sites that provide information about employment
opportunities and housing data. (For more information, see Chapter 4, "Finding a Neighborhood
Next Door or Across the Country.")

Washington Homefinders Inc. Real Estate
(www.nwdir.com/relo.htm)

Alaska Employment & Unemployment (www.
labor.state.ak.us/research/research.htm)

Iowa Economy (www.state.ia.us/trends)

Nebraska Databook & Economic Trends (info.ded.state.ne.us)

Relocate America (www.relocateamerica.com)

Relocating to the right city

Careful online research will allow you to discover which cities have the strongest job growth and most reasonable house prices. (For more information, see Chapter 4, "Finding a Neighborhood Next Door or Across the Country.")

RPS Relocation (www.rpsrelocation.com/ community.htm)

Regional Financial Association (www.rfa. com/free.stm)

U.S. Census Bureau (www.census.gov)

Fedstats (www.fedstats.gov)

Finding neighborhood reports

Whether you're moving across town or across the nation, you'll need an online neighborhood report to evaluate your new neighborhood. Reports vary in quality and price. (For more information, see Chapter 4, "Finding a Neighborhood Next Door or Across the Country.")

Realtor.com (www.realtor.com)

DataQuick (www.dataquick.com)

Monster Daata.com (www.monsterdaata.com)

American Demographics (www. demographics.com)

CrimeCheck (www.crimecheck.com)

Using calculators to compare the cost of living

Online cost-of-living calculators can assist you in determining if relocating offers the financial benefits you believe it will. (For more information, see Chapter 4, "Finding a Neighborhood Next Door or Across the Country.")

> *Homefair* (www.homefair.com/homefair/cmr/salcalc.html)

> *Fortune* (www.pathfinder.com/money/bestplaces/col/compare.html)

> *DataMasters* (www.datamasters.com)

> *Cost of Living Calculator* (204.203.220.1/ERIRA.htm)

Finding a real estate agent

The Internet has made real estate agents more important than ever. Agents can advertise their access codes in newspaper ads so potential customers can see their listings and contact them by e-mail, telephone, or pager. (For more information, see Chapter 5, "Using a Real Estate Agent.")

> *The Chicago Sun-Times* (www.suntimes.com/realestate/homebuyingfaq1.html)

> *Open House America* (www.openhouse.net/realtors.html)

> *Homeowners.com* (www.homeowners.com/new35.html)

> *Realtor.com* (www.realtor.com)

> *MSN HomeAdvisor* (www.homeadvisor.msn.com)

Looking into buyer's agents

Recent legislation protects homebuyers more than ever before by allowing exclusive buyer's agents. Buyer's agents can be easily located and contacted online. (For more information, see Chapter 5, "Using a Real Estate Agent.")

> *HomeBuyer Agents* (www.homebuyeragents. com/presentation/slide7txt.html)
>
> *HomeWEB* (www.homeweb.com)
>
> *The Buyer's Agent* (www.forbuyers.com)
>
> *ExclusiveBuyersAgents.com* (www. exclusivebuyersagents.com)
>
> *National Association of Exclusive Buyer Agents* (www.naeba.org)

Finding help for selecting the best real estate agent

The Internet provides a vast array of recommendations and checklists to assist first-time and experienced homebuyers in selecting a real estate agent. (For more information, see Chapter 5, "Using a Real Estate Agent.")

> *The Motley Fool* (www.fool.com/house/find/ find3.htm)
>
> *Memphis Area Association of Realtors* (www.maar.org)
>
> *The* Chicago Tribune *Real Estate Essentials* (chicagotribune.com/marketplaces/homes/ ws/0,1246,16622,00.html)
>
> *Better Business Bureau: Tips for Consumers Selecting a Real Estate Agent* (www.bbb.org/ library/selectagent.html)

Evaluating real estate agents

Find out how to select and evaluate the performance of your real estate agent. If you decide to fire your real estate agent (before your contract term expires), discover what your options are using the Internet and hundreds of online real estate resources. (For more information, see Chapter 5, "Using a Real Estate Agent.")

> *1Agent* (www.1agent.com)
>
> *Minnesota Attorney General's Office* (www. ag.stat.mn.us/home/consumer/housing/ homebuyers/default.html)
>
> *Oregon Directory Real Estate Guide* (www. presys.com/shopper/cities/realestate/ rightagent.html)
>
> *The Home Spot* (www.homespot.com/ r3real2.htm)

Selecting an out-of-state-real estate agent

If you're moving out-of-state, you may discover that you need two real estate agents: one to sell the house you currently live in, and one who is a market expert in the area you plan to move to. (For more information, see Chapter 5, "Using a Real Estate Agent.")

> *Residential Referral Network* (www. galaxymall.com/realestate/referrals/ works.html)
>
> *Relocationscout* (www.relocationscout.com)
>
> *American Relocation Center* (www. buyingrealestate.com)

Better Homes and Gardens (www.
bhg-real-estate.com/consumer/realserv/
relocate/relocate.html)

U.S. Relocation (www.usa-relocation.
com/index_main.htm)

Resources for special housing requirements

If you have special housing requirements, the Internet is your best research resource. With the help of this guide, you can easily locate government agencies, religious organizations, and not-for-profit groups that can assist you in renting or purchasing a home that meets your special needs. (For more information, see Chapter 6, "Finding Your Dream Home Online.")

California Department of Developmental Services (www.dds.cahwnet.gov/OW/ah03.htm)

American Association of Homes and Services for the Aging (www.aahsa.org)

HUD for People with Disabilities (www.hud/gov/disabled.html)

Alliance for National Renewal (www.ncl.org/anr)

Using scorecards to evaluate homes

Use a scorecard to compare and contrast the homes that may be of interest to you. It's easy to get confused after viewing three or four homes in one day. The Internet provides several types of scorecards that you can print out and use when you visit a house. (For more information, see Chapter 6, "Finding Your Dream Home Online.")

Our Family Place (www.ourfamilyplace.com/ homebuyer/scorecard.html)

HomeAdvisor What You Want Checklist (homeadvisor.msn.com/ns/homes/ whatyouwant.asp)

Realtor.com Worksheet (www.realtor.com/ aspcontent/compare.asp)

House Hunter's Helper (www. hypervigilance.com/househunt.html)

The advantages and limitations of a new house

New houses have hidden additional costs but are low on maintenance. Additionally, new homes appreciate faster than resale homes for the first eight years. (For more information, see Chapter 6, "Finding Your Dream Home Online.")

NewHomeNetwork.com (www. newhomenetwork.com)

Homebuilder.com (www.homebuilder.com)

InterNest (www.internest.com/xyz/ newhomesstart.asp)

The advantages and limitations of an established house

Established houses are often less expensive, charming, and have mature landscaping. However, they may be a maintenance nightmare due to sagging walls, cracked floor supports, and the lack of a sufficient number of electrical outlets. (For more information, see Chapter 6, "Finding Your Dream Home Online.")

Washington Post *Home Hunter* (www. washingtonpost.com)

Realtor.com (www.realtor.com)

CyberHomes (www.cyberhomes.com)

MLS Listings (www.mlslistings.com)

OpenHouse.com (www.openhouse.com)

Should you buy a fixer-upper?

Usually a fixer-upper is the least desirable home in a most desirable neighborhood. The fixer-upper includes the costs needed to bring the property up to its market potential. Therefore the cost of a fixer-upper is the price of the house plus the required renovations. (For more information, see Chapter 6, "Finding Your Dream Home Online.")

Old-Houses.com (www.old-houses.com)

BuildingOnline (www.buildingonline.com)

BuildNet (www.buildnet.com)

FixerUpper: The Home Improvement Community (www.fixerupper.com/xi/places/home/index.rage?loc=fixerupper)

Using comparable market analysis tools

The Internet can assist you in spotting overpriced homes. You may pay less than you expect by using online comparable market analysis tools. (For more information, see Chapter 6, "Finding Your Dream Home Online.")

House Clicks (www.houseclicks.com/selling/cma.html)

Coldwell Banker (www.coldwellbanker.com)

Transamerica (www.taintellitech.com/products/reap/index_reap_content.htm)

Yahoo! Real Estate (www.realestate.yahoo.com/realestate/homevalues)

Getting the right mortgage

The Internet can help you with what may be the biggest financial decision of your life—purchasing a home. The World Wide Web provides vast amounts of information on selecting and financing your dream home. (For more information, see Chapter 7, "Online Mortgage Advice and Lending.")

> *FHA* (www.hud.gov/mortprog.html)
>
> *VA* (www.va.gov)
>
> *Money Maze Loan Advisor* (www.maze. com/rates/advisorq.htm)
>
> *BankSITE* (www.banksite.com/ccontent.htm)

Learning about the mortgage process

Knowing what paperwork you'll need and what kinds of costs to expect can save you time and reduce your anxiety or frustration. (For more information, see Chapter 7, "Online Mortgage Advice and Lending.")

> *Mortgage Mart* (www.mortgagemart.com)
>
> *Mortgage-X* (www.mortgage-x.com)
>
> *Quicken Loans* (mortgage.quicken.com)
>
> *Complete Mortgage Guide* (www. homemortgageguide.com)

What lenders look for in your credit report

Knowing what lenders look for in your credit report and how you can improve your credit score can assist you in working with a mortgage lender. (For more information, see Chapter 7, "Online Mortgage Advice and Lending.")

Credit Infocenter (www.creditinfocenter.com)

Nolo Encyclopedia (www.nolo.com/
encyclopedia/dc_ency.html)

Keystroke (www.keystroke.com/mortgage/
homefinance/buying/fico_score.html)

First Team (www.firsteam.com/buysell/
buy4.htm)

Credit Quality Estimator (www.snws.com/
loan-bin/credit)

Shopping for the lowest mortgage rates

You don't need to leave your computer to find
the right type of home financing at the lowest rate.
(For more information, see Chapter 7, "Online
Mortgage Advice and Lending.")

MortgageQuotes.com (www.
mortgagequotes.com)

RateNet (www.rate.net/index.htm)

Bankrate.com (www.bankrate.com)

National Mortgage Loan Directory (www.
mortgageloan.com)

All about private mortgage insurance

If your down payment is less than 20 percent, most
lenders require you to carry private mortgage insurance (PMI). PMI provides assurance that if you
default on your payments, the lender will be able to
recoup some of the money that was borrowed. (For
more information, see Chapter 7, "Online
Mortgage Advice and Lending.")

Private Mortgage Insurance Companies (www.
privatemi.com/main.html)

Understanding Private Mortgage Insurance
(www.hsh.com/pamphlets/mgicpmi.html)

Homebuyer Questions and Answers (www.
pmigroup.com/homebuyer/qanda.html)

Finding a no or low down payment home loan

The Internet can introduce you to a variety of loan programs that require no down payment, a low down payment, or home loans with below-market interest rates. (For more information, see Chapter 8, "Avoiding the Down Payment Cash Crunch.")

Mortgage University (www.amo-mortgage.
com/library/index.html)

FamilyHaven (www.familyhaven.com/
money/lowdownpayment.html)

*Fannie Mae's Community Home Buyer's Program
(CHBP)* (www.homepath.com/hsp5.html)

Freddie Mac Affordable Gold 100 no down
payment program (www.mortgage-x.com/
library/affordable_gold_100.htm)

Information Center (www.pueblo.gsa.gov/
cic_text/housing/low_down/low_down.txt)

Avoiding the paperwork with no- and low-document loans

Don't want to hassle with the paperwork of getting a home loan? Want to avoid lenders snooping into your financial affairs? You can prevent a lot of lender scrutiny with no-document or low-document home loans. These loans can often get you to the closing quicker and with fewer headaches. (For more information, see Chapter 8, "Avoiding the Down Payment Cash Crunch.")

National Mortgage Directory (www.
mortgageloan.com)

National Mortgage News (www.nmnews.
fgray.com)

RealEstateWeb (www.real-estate-web.com/links)

Interest.com (www.interest.com/editorial/
Mortgage_column/mtg_story_970624.htm)

Bankrate.com (www.bankrate.com/brm/
news/mtg/19990624.asp)

Creative financing

Real estate listings don't advertise no down payment
or low down payment homes. However, you can
often fashion no and low down payment offers that
are advantageous to the seller and the buyer. (For
more information, see Chapter 8, "Avoiding the
Down Payment Cash Crunch.")

The Mortgage Money Guide (www.
remax-of-boulder.com/set1/finance/
money9.htm)

RealEstateWeb Library (www.real-estate-web.
com/library/money9.htm)

Homeowners.com (www.homeowners.com/
new89.html)

Spotting special first-time homebuyer deals

The Internet lists many cities, local, and state entities that offer first-time homebuyers special programs that pay for the homebuyer's down payment
or that offer lower-than-usual interest rates. (For
more information, see Chapter 8, "Avoiding the
Down Payment Cash Crunch.")

Homeward Bound in Texas (www.amcity.com/
austin/stories/1997/10/27/focus5.html)

*Affordable Home Ownership in Washington's King
County* (www.metrokc.gov/exec/news/
7698nr1.htm)

First-Time Homebuyer Mortgage Programs for Iowa
(www.ifahome.com/partner_sf.htm)

The California Housing Financing Authority
(www.chfa.ca.gov)

Getting an appraisal

Virtually all government-related loans require certified appraisals. Since most mortgage lenders are
tied into the government in one way or another, this
means that all mortgage loans need a certified
appraisal. (For more information, see Chapter 9,
"Online Help with Appraisals, Inspections, and
Insurance.")

DataQuick (www.dataquick.com)

The Home Purchasing Guide (www.
homeowners.com/new135.html)

Bankrate.com (www.bankrate.com/brm/
news/moving_on/edit/appraisals.asp)

Appraisal FAQ List (www.hom.net/~owas/
faqlist.html)

Finding a property appraiser

Certified property appraisals are usually required if
you're going to use a mortgage to purchase your
new home. Use the Internet to find a qualified
appraiser and to check his or her background. (For
more information, see Chapter 9, "Online Help
with Appraisals, Inspections, and Insurance.")

National Association of Real Estate Appraisers
(www.iami.org/narea.html)

*Federal Financial Institutions Examination
Council Appraisal Subcommittee* (www.asc.gov)

Appraisal Institute (www.appraisalinstitute.org)

Appraisal Network (www.appraisal-network.com)

Getting a home inspection

Home inspections are necessary to point out the patent (easily recognizable) and the latent (hidden) defects in a property. (For more information, see Chapter 9, "Online Help with Appraisals, Inspections, and Insurance.")

Home Inspection Kit (www.freddiemac.com/
homebuyers/index.html)

Home Inspection and You (www.pueblo.gsa/
gov/cic_text/housing/inspect/inspect.txt)

American Society of Home Inspectors
(www.ashi.com)

Insight Professional Home Inspection (www.
inspectit.com/insight/questions.html)

How to Hire a Home Inspector (www.
realtimes.com/rtnews/rtcpages/
19990820_inspector.htm)

Shopping for homeowners insurance

Mortgage lenders require homeowners insurance. The Internet is the perfect place to shop for home insurance quotes and to discover what type of policy is best for your financial situation. (For more information, see Chapter 9, "Online Help with Appraisals, Inspections, and Insurance.")

InsWeb (www.insweb.com)

4FreeQuotes.com (www.4freequotes.com)

4instantquotes (www.4instantquotes.com/ insurance/index.html)

QuoteShopper (www.quoteshopper.com/ shop_ann.htm)

Understanding title insurance

Your lender will require a title search and title insurance to protect its investment. Some title companies send the results of their title searches via e-mail, or your lender can view the report using an Internet browser. (For more information, see Chapter 9, "Online Help with Appraisals, Inspections, and Insurance.")

Stewart Title (www.stewart.com)

Lender's Service, Inc. (www.lenderservice.com)

Insure.com The Basics of Title Insurance (www. insure.com/home/title.html)

FreeAdvice.com (www.freeadvice.com/ gov_material/hud-title-insurance-6-97.htm)

Paying the right price for a home

You can determine the value of a home by using Internet automated valuation models. Some automated valuation reports are free and others are fee-based. (In some cases, lenders accept these online reports as certified appraisals.) (For more information, see Chapter 10, "Negotiating and Closing the Deal.")

Appraisal Network (www.appraisal-network. com/avm.htm)

CSWOnline (www.cswonline.com/ index.shtml)

HomeValueCheck (www.homevaluecheck.com)

RealEstate.com (www.realestate.com)

Yahoo! By Address (realestate.yahoo.com/realestate/homevalues/)

Acxiom/DataQuick (products.dataquick.com)

Getting help negotiating your offer

When making an offer for your dream home, expect to negotiate with the seller. However, don't think that the purpose of all negotiations is to lower the purchase price. In some hot markets, you may have to negotiate how much you're willing to pay above the asking price. (For more information, see Chapter 10, "Negotiating and Closing the Deal.")

Real Estate—FAQs Home Buying (www.suntimes.com/realestate/homebuyingfaq3.html)

MSN HomeAdvisor Guide to "Negotiating the Deal" (homeadvisor.msn.com/ns/offerclosing/finalsteps.asp)

The Eight Rules of Negotiating (www.homespot.com/r4main3a.htm)

Paragon Decision Resources (www.pdr.com/beforeoffer.htm)

Preparing a great offer

The Internet can assist you in preparing an offer the seller can't refuse, but do your homework first. If the seller accepts your offer, it immediately becomes a legally binding sales contract. (For more information, see Chapter 10, "Negotiating and Closing the Deal.")

Real Estate Offers and Contracts (www.nolo.com/encyclopedia/articles/re/re17.html)

Homebuyer's E-Guide (recenter.tamu.edu/ hguide/hboffer.html)

Inman News Features (www.inman.com/ inmanstories.asp?ID=10005&cattype=)

Making an Offer (www.homespot.com/ homespot/r4main3e.htm)

Understanding the closing

When the seller accepts your offer, you'll usually go to a closing meeting to finalize the transaction and take possession of your new home. Become familiar with what happens at these meetings and get a copy of everything you sign. (For more information, see Chapter 10, "Negotiating and Closing the Deal.")

Fannie Mae's HomePath (www.homepath. com/hpp51.html)

Realtor.com (www.realtor.com/closing/ closing.asp)

Owners.com (www.owners.com/tools/ library/showarticle.asp?id=17)

Our Family Place (www.ourfamilyplace.com/ homebuyer/closing.html)

iRichmond (irichmond.com)

Getting a grip on closing documents

What you don't know about closing costs can cost you thousands of dollars. Become an educated consumer to avoid overpaying or making a mistake at the closing table. Check out these important closing documents. (For more information, see Chapter 11, "Costs and Tax Benefits Associated with Buying a Home.")

Settlement statement (records what goes on at the closing): *HUD Web site* (www.hud. gov:80/fha/sfh/res/resappa.html)

Truth-in-lending disclosure (shows the major financial terms of the loan): *Lenders Trust* (www.lenderstrust.com/forms.html)

Promissory note (the borrower's promise to repay the loan): Refer to *HUD's "Buying Your Home Guide"* (www.hud.gov/fha/sfh/res/ sfhrestc.html)

Deed or deed of trust (conveys title of the property): *Lenders Trust* (www.lenderstrust. com/forms.html)

Looking for errors in closing documents

Most homebuyers are surprised by high closing costs. Use an online calculator or worksheet to determine your costs in advance. Next, compare your settlement statement with the average costs listed online. You can even compare your good faith estimate (which you received from your lender) to your settlement statement. If a fee doesn't seem right, you may have discovered an error. (For more information, see Chapter 11, "Costs and Tax Benefits Associated with Buying a Home.")

Financenter.com (www.financenter.com)

Realtor.com Closing Cost Worksheet (www.realtor. com/aspcontent/closingcostsworksheet.asp)

MSN HomeAdvisor Estimate of closing costs (www.homeadvisor.msn.com/ns/ offerclosing/settlement.asp)

Government's Consumer Information Center (www.pueblo.gsa.gov/cic_text/housing/ settlement/sfhrestc.html)

Pitt Miller Example of a Good Faith Estimate
(www.pitt-miller.com/good.htm)

Deducting closing costs from your taxes

Many of your closing costs are tax-deductible. Find out which ones you can write off by using information provided by online IRS publications and other expert sources. (For more information, see Chapter 11, "Costs and Tax Benefits Associated with Buying a Home.")

Department of the Treasury IRS (www.irs.ustreas.gov/prod/forms_pubs/pubs/p530toc.htm)

IRS Publication 936 (www.irs.ustreas.gov/prod/forms_pubs/pubs/p936toc.htm)

Lycos Real Estate Guide (www.lycos.com/realestate)

The IRS Problem Solver (www.taxhelponline.com/solp5.htm)

Finding FSBO properties

In the past, for sale by owner (FSBO) properties were expensive to advertise and received little exposure. Today, there are well over a hundred FSBO Web sites. These sites can be regional, national, or global. Many have search engines to assist online homebuyers in finding homes. (For more information, see Chapter 12, "The Internet and Do-It-Yourself Real Estate.")

4SaleByOwner (www.4salebyowner.com)

Advanced Real Estate Listing Service (www.homeportfoliojunction.com/home/index.htm)

BuyOwner.com (www.buyowner.com)

RealScout.com (www.realscout.com)

Virtual For Sale By Owner (www. virtualfsbo.com)

Private For Sale.com (www.privateforsale.com)

Locating assistance for owner-builders

The Internet can assist you in building your own home in three different ways: by providing online resources designed for the do-it-yourself owner-builder, by providing data about contractor-assisted home programs, and by offering information about pre-cut and partially assembled home kits. (For more information, see Chapter 13, "Getting Online Help with Becoming an Owner-Builder.")

The Owner Builder School of Oregon (www. ownerbuilderschool.com)

YouBuild Owner Builder Center (www. youbuild.com/home.htm)

Equity Builders (www. degeorgehomealliance.com)

Landvest Owner-Involved Building Program (www.landvesthomes.com/ownerin.html)

All American Homes (www.allamerhomes.com)

Endeavor Homes (www.endeavorhomes.com)

Uncovering ready-made house plans

Deciding what type of home you want to build can be difficult after viewing the thousands of house plans that are available on the Internet. (For more information, see Chapter 13, "Getting Online Help with Becoming an Owner-Builder.")

Alternative Home Plans (www. alternativehomeplans.com)

Homes for Today (www.homes4today.com)

Stephen Fuller (www.stephenfuller.com)

Planhouse.com (www.planhouse.com)

Discovering estimating and budgeting software

If you're wondering how to prepare your materials and cost estimates for building a home, the Internet can assist you with free downloadable trial copies of job-costing software. (For more information, see Chapter 13, "Getting Online Help with Becoming an Owner-Builder.")

Craftsman Book Company (www.craftsman-book.com/downloads/index.htm)

ConstructSoftware (www.constructsoftware.com/demos/demos.html)

National Cost Estimator (www.nwbuildnet.com/nwbn/esti_books.html)

UDA Construction Office 99 (www.uniteddesign.com/home_building_guides.html)

Spotting pre-screened contractors

The Web has free directories of pre-screened contractors and subcontractors so you don't have to wonder if the company you hired is truly qualified for the job. (For more information, see Chapter 13, "Getting Online Help with Becoming an Owner-Builder.")

Contractor.com (www.contractor.com)

American Builders Network (www.americanbuilders.com)

ContractorNet (www.contractornet.com)

NorthWest BuilderNet (www.nwbuildnet. com/nwbn/barnsoutbuildings.html

Planning a smooth move

Discover how you can use online resources to develop a cost-effective moving plan. (For more information, see Chapter 14, "Getting Moving Help Online.")

SmartMoney.com (smartmoney.com/ac/home/ buying/index.cfm?story=moving)

RELO.com (www.relo.com/relo/ publicgoodies/faq.cfm)

Windham International (www. windhamworld.com)

Homefair (www.homefair.com/wizard/ wizard.html)

Atlas Van Lines (www.atlasvanlines.com)

Looking into do-it-yourself moving

Use the Internet to find out what's involved in a do-it-yourself move. (For more information, see Chapter 14, "Getting Moving Help Online.")

Probe Consultants Economical Do-it-Yourself Residential Moving Guide (www.go-probe. com/beforeumove.shtml)

Moving.com Do-It-Yourself Moving (www. moving.com/gmoving/diy.asp)

MoveCentral (new.movecentral.com/ planyourmove/)

U-Haul (www.uhaul.com)

AAA Move (www.aaamove.com)

Finding a full-service mover

Partner with the Internet to discover if you received a good moving estimate from a full-service mover. (For more information, see Chapter 14, "Getting Moving Help Online.")

Realtor.com (www.realtor.com)

Avatar Moving (www.avatar-moving.com/kb/doc_apples.html)

Allied Van Lines (www.alliedvan.net/02guide/04charg.html)

Bekins (www.bekins.com)

Effortlessly changing your address

Save time and effort by using free Internet-based services to change your address. Use free or fee-based online services to disconnect utilities and notify friends, relatives, and business associates of your new address. (For more information, see Chapter 14, "Getting Moving Help Online.")

Home to Home (www.home-to-home.com)

MoversNet (www.moversnet.com)

StartSmart.com (www.startsmart.com)

Realty Times (www.realtimes.com/rtnews/rtcpages/19981020_utilityconect.htm)

Identifying tax-deductible moving expenses

Get the whole story from online IRS resources and other providers about which moving expenses you can deduct from your income taxes. (For more information, see Chapter 14, "Getting Moving Help Online.")

SmartMoney.com (www.smartmoney.com/ac/tax/index.cfm?story=moving)

Times Online (timesonline.webpoint.com/home/movetax.htm)

Internal Revenue Service (www.irs.ustreas.gov/prod/forms_pubs/pubs/p52101.htm)

IRS Tax Info For You (www.irs.ustreas.gov/prod/ind_info)

Making home improvements

Home improvements can make your house a home. If your home improvements are complex or involve major design changes, you may need an architect and general contractor. However, don't let this stop you; the Internet has many Web sites that specialize in helping homeowners find qualified help. (For more information, see Chapter 15, "Online Help for Making Your House a Home.")

Remodeling Online (www.remodeling.hw.net)

Build.com's Home Improvement Web Site Directory (www.build.com)

Builder Online: Spotlight Collection (www.remodeling.hw.net/spotlight)

HomePoint Advantage (www.homepoint.net/)

ImproveNet (www.improvenet.com)

Getting help for home repairs

Unfortunately, owning a home means you are now responsible for all the home's fix-ups and maintenance. Don't despair—the Internet is a great source for help in this area. (For more information, see Chapter 15, "Online Help for Making Your House a Home.")

Toiletology 101 (www.toiletology.com)

Remodel Online (www.remodelonline.com)

Home Repairs & Etc. (www.repair-home.com)

Home Depot (www.homedepot.com)

Lowe's (www.lowes.com)

Restoring an old house

If you plan to restore a home built before 1930, be prepared to spend lots of time and cash. Find out online what works and get tips from e-mail newsletters, online journals of restorers, and restoration supply Web sites. (For more information, see Chapter 15, "Online Help for Making Your House a Home.")

Old-House Journal (www.oldhousejournal.com)

Antique Hardware & Home Store (www.antiquehardware.com)

Balmer Studios (www.balmerstudios.com)

SalvoWeb (www.salvo.co.uk)

Paying for home improvements

It's not always wise to pay for large home improvements bit by bit. Homeowners often get below-market interest rates on home improvement loans, in addition to the tax benefits of deducting loan points and interest paid from income taxes. (For more information, see Chapter 15, "Online Help for Making Your House a Home.")

Money.com (www.money.com)

Financenter.com (www.financenter.com)

HUD Home Investment Partnership Program (www.hud.gov)

Owners.com (guides.iown.com/scripts/refinance.dll/start?source=owners2)

Selling your home faster

Give your home maximum exposure by listing your property in the online version of the Multiple Listing Service (MLS) and at free real estate listing databases. (For more information, see Chapter 16, "Marketing and Selling Your Home Online.")

> *Yahoo! Classifieds* (www.classifieds.yahoo. com)
>
> *The United States Real Estate Directory* (www.1realestate.com)
>
> *NewRealty.com* (www.newrealty.com)
>
> *HomeScout* (www.homescout.com)
>
> *Realty.com* (www.realty.com)

Note: If you hire a real estate agent to list your house, your home can be listed at the HomeSeekers (www.homeseekers.com) and MSN HomeAdvisor (homeadvisor.msn.com) Web sites.

Choosing a listing agent

Use the Internet to find an outstanding listing agent or get online help if you sell your home without a real estate agent. (For more information, see Chapter 16, "Marketing and Selling Your Home Online.")

> *The Virtual Real Estate Store* (www. virtualrealestatestore.com/ selling-a-home-main-page. htm#what_happens_after_home_listed)
>
> *SmartMoney.com* (www.smartmoney.com/ac/ home/selling/index.cfm?story=choose)
>
> *eHome* (www.ehome.com)

Home Buying Bibliography

Albrecht, Donna G. *Buying a Home When You're Single.* Chicago, IL: John Wiley & Sons, April 1994.

American Bar Association. *The American Bar Association Guide to Home Ownership: The Complete and Easy Guide to All the Law Every Home Owner Should Know.* New York, NY: Times Books, April 1995.

Becker, Norman. *Complete Book of Home Inspection.* New York, NY: Tab Books, June 1993.

Bradley, Beth (contributor), and Alan D. Perlis. *The Unofficial Guide to Buying a Home.* Indianapolis, IN: IDG Books Worldwide, January 1999.

Burgess, Russell W. *Real Estate Home Inspection: Mastering the Profession.* Chicago, IL: Real Estate Education Company, December 1998.

Burnside, Kevin. *Buying a Manufactured Home: How to Get the Most Bang for Your Buck in Today's Housing Market.* Chicago, IL: Van Der Plas Publications, July 1999.

Carlisle, Ellen. *Smooth Moves.* New York, NY: Teacup Press, March 1999.

Cross, Carla. *Buyer Beware: Insider Secrets You Need to Know Before Buying Your Home—From Choosing an Agent to Closing the Deal.* Chicago, IL: Real Estate Education Company, April 1998.

Dworin, Lawrence. *Profits in Buying and Renovating Homes.* New York, NY: Craftsman Book Company, December 1990.

Eldred, Gary W. *The 106 Common Mistakes Homebuyers Make (& How to Avoid Them)* (2nd Edition). Chicago, IL: John Wiley & Sons, February 1998.

Eliers, Terry. *How to Buy the Home You Want, for the Best Price, in Any Market: From a Real Estate Insider Who Knows All the Tricks.* New York, NY: Hyperion, April 1997.

Evans, Blanche. *Homesurfing.Net: The Insider's Guide to Buying and Selling Your Home Using the Internet.* Chicago, IL: Dearborn Trade, September 1999.

Ferguson, Myron E., and Linda West. *Build it Right!: What to Look for in Your New Home.* New York, NY: Home User's Press, Revised edition June 1997.

Fields, Alan, and Denise Fields. *Your New House: The Alert Consumer's Guide to Buying and Building a Quality Home* (3rd Edition). New York, NY: Windsor Peak Press, November 1999.

Glink, Ilyce R. *10 Steps to Home Ownership: A Workbook for First-Time Homebuyers.* New York, NY: Times Books, December 1996.

———. *100 Questions Every First-time Home Buyer Should Ask: With Answers from Top Brokers from Around the Country.* New York, NY: Times Books, February 1994.

Glossbrenner, Alfred, and Emily Glossbrenner. *Smart Guide to Buying a Home*. Chicago, IL: John Wiley & Sons, March 1999.

Good-Garton, Julie. *The Frugal Homeowner's Guide: To Buying, Selling & Improving Your Home*. Chicago, IL: Real Estate Education Company, March 1999.

Harlan, Don, et al. *Buyer Agency: Your Competitive Edge in Real Estate* (3rd Edition). Chicago, IL: Real Estate Education Company, September 1997.

Harris, Jack, and Jack P. Friedman. *Keys to Purchasing a Condo or a Co-op*. New York, NY: Barrons Educational Series, May 1990.

Hymer, Diane Davis. *Starting Out: The Complete Home Buyer's Guide*. New York, NY: Chronicle Books, February 1997.

Irwin, Robert. *Buy Your First Home! Finding the Right House, Surviving the Mortgage Process, Avoiding the Pitfalls*. Chicago, IL: Real Estate Education Company, April 1995.

____. *Buying a Home on the Internet: The Only Home-Buying Guide You'll Ever Need*. New York, NY: McGraw-Hill, January 1999.

____. *Find It, Buy It, Fix It: The Insider's Guide to Fixer-Uppers*. Chicago, IL: Real Estate Education Company, March 1996.

____. *For Sale By Owner Kit* (3rd Edition). Chicago, IL: Real Estate Education Company, October 1998.

____. *Robert Irwin's Pocket Guide for Home Buyers: 101 Questions and Answers for Every Home Buyer*. New York, NY: McGraw-Hill, March 1998.

____. *Tips and Traps When Buying a Home* (2nd Edition). New York, NY: McGraw-Hill, January 1997.

_____. *Tips and Traps When Selling a Home* (2nd Edition). New York, NY: McGraw-Hill, February 1997.

Kiplingers Personal Finance Staff, Knight A. Kiplinger (Introduction). *Buying & Selling a Home* (6th Edition). New York, NY: Kiplinger Books, March 1999.

Lank, Edith. *The 201 Questions Every Homebuyer and Homeseller Must Ask!* Chicago, IL: Real Estate Education Company, September 1995.

_____. *The Home Buyers Kit: Finding Your Dream Home, Financing Your Purchase, Making the Best Deal, Gaining Tax Benefits.* Chicago, IL: Real Estate Education Company, September 1997.

Leiter, Irwin E. *How to Buy a Condominium or Townhome: With Simple Forms and Worksheets.* New York, NY: Galt Press, October 1997.

Levine, Leslie. *Will This Place Ever Feel Like Home? Simple Advice for Settling In After You Move.* Chicago, IL: Real Estate Education Company, December 1998.

Masters, Thomas K. *How to Buy a Home with No or Poor Credit.* Chicago, IL: John Wiley & Sons, April 1996.

Molloy, William J. *The Complete Home Buyer's Bible.* Chicago, IL: John Wiley & Sons, March 1996.

Mungo, Ray, and Robert H. Yamaguchi (contributor). *No Credit Required: How to Buy a House When You Don't Qualify for a Mortgage.* New York, NY: Signet, April 1993.

Myers, David W. *If You're Clueless Abut Buying a Home and Want to Know More.* Chicago, IL: Real Estate Education Company, April 1999.

O'Hara, Shelley. *The Complete Idiot's Guide to Buying and Selling a Home* (2nd Edition). New York, NY: Alpha Books, December 1997.

Page, Stanley. *10 Minute Guide to Buying and Selling Your Home.* Indianapolis, IN: IDG Books Worldwide, December 1996.

Preston, Edward. *How to Buy Land Cheap* (5th Edition). New York, NY: Breakout Productions, Inc., December 1998.

Rejnis, Ruth (editor). *Century 21 Guide to Buying a Second Home: For Vacation, Retirement, Investment and More!* Chicago, IL: Dearborn Trade, February 1998.

Rejnis, Ruth, and Claire Walter (contributor). *Buying Your Vacation Home for Fun & Profit.* Chicago, IL: Dearborn Trade, October 1996.

Robinson, Marc, and Mare Robinson. *Financing a Home (Time Life Books, Your Money Matters).* New York, NY: Time Life, August 1996.

Ross, John. *Lease-Purchase America!: Acquiring Real Estate in the 90's and Beyond.* New York, NY: Starburst Publishers, August 1993.

Scher, Les, and Carol Scher (editor). *Finding & Buying Your Place in the Country.* Chicago, IL: Real Estate Education Company, June 1996.

Shenkman, Martin M., and Warren Boroson (contributor). *How to Buy a House with No (or Little Money Down).* Chicago, IL: John Wiley & Sons, May 1995.

Smith, Marguerite. *Your Dream Home: A Comprehensive Guide to Buying a House, Condo or Co-op.* New York, NY: Warner Books, May 1997.

Tyson, Eric. *Home Buying for Dummies*. Indianapolis, IN: IDG Books Worldwide, May 1996.

Vila, Bob, and Carl Oglesby. *Bob Vila's Guide to Buying Your Dream House*. New York, NY: Little, Brown & Company, February 1990.

Watkins, A.M., and Patrick Hogan. *How to Avoid the 10 Biggest Home Buying Traps*. Chicago, IL: Real Estate Education Company, May 1996.

Webb, Martha. *Finding Home: Buying the House That's Right for You*. New York, NY: Three Rivers Press, August 1998.

Widemer, James I. *The Smart Money Guide to Bargain Homes; How to Find and Buy Foreclosures*. Chicago, IL: Dearborn Trade, February 1994.

Woodson, R. Dodge. *100 Surefire Improvements to Sell Your House Faster*. Chicago, IL: John Wiley & Sons, September 1993.

____. *The Condo and Co-op Handbook: A Comprehensive Guide to Buying and Owning a Condo or Co-op*. Indianapolis, IN: IDG Books Worldwide, September 1998

AAA Move, 312, 407
ABF U-Pack Moving, 312
About.com, 122–23
Accel Mortgage, 168, 385
Accredited Buyers Representative
    (ABR), 107
Address changes, 321–22, 408
Adjustable-rate mortgages
    (ARMs), 160, 369
Advanced Real Estate Listing
    Service, 267, 404
Advertising your home, 357
Affordable Home Ownership,
    191, 398
Aggregators, 8–9, 147–48, 369,
    382
All American Homes, 405
Allen Auto Transport, 321
Alliance for National Renewal,
    391
Allied Van Lines, 310, 319, 324,
    408
Alternative Home Plans, 290, 405
American Association of Homes
    and Services for the Aging,
    66, 391
American Association of Retired
    Persons (AARP), 337
American Builders Network, 294,
    406
American Community Network,
    386
American Demographics, 387
American Mortgage Listings, 164
American Moving and Storage
    Association, 306
American Relocation Center,
    115, 390
American Society of Home
    Inspectors, 206, 207, 399

Ameriwest, 385
Amortization, 369, 376
Amortization calculators, 156
Annual percentage rate (APR),
    153, 156–58, 173, 370
Annuities, 26
Antique Hardware & Home
    Store, 345–46, 410
AppOnline, 38, 162, 385
Appraisal Institute, 198–200, 399
Appraisal Network, 199, 201, 399,
    400
Appraisals, 196–203, 370
    certified, 196, 197, 398
    comparable sales reports,
        201–3
    fees, 154, 196, 249
    methodologies used, 200–201
    reports, 200–203
    in rural areas, 197–98
Appraisal Standards Board of the
    Appraisal Foundation, 196
Appraisers, 196–97, 199–201,
    398–99
Appreciation, 125, 370
APR (annual percentage rate),
    153, 156–58, 370
Architects, 289–90, 333, 338–40
Archway Home Plans, 291–92
"As is" clauses, 230, 232, 273
Assets, 29, 37, 148, 370
Assumption, 249, 370
Atlas Van Lines, 308, 407
Automated valuation models,
    201–3
Avatar Moving, 310, 408

Balmer Studios, 346, 410
Bank of America Economic
    Analysis and Research, 82

Bankrate, 16, 176, 395, 397, 398

Bankruptcies, 44–45, 47, 49

BankSITE, 394

Basic Form (HO-1), 210, 211

Bekins, 304, 408

Better Business Bureau, 55–56, 337, 389

Better Homes and Gardens, 116, 340–41, 391

B4UBuild.com, 279, 297, 299, 340

Black Homes Online, 8

Bringing You Home, 270

Broad Form (HO-2), 210, 211

Budgets (budgeting), 30–34, 60, 382–83

Build.com, 333, 409

Builder Online, 332, 351, 409

Builder's agents, 105

"Builder's risk" insurance, 299–300

Building codes, 298–99

Building.com, 135–36, 393

Building inspections, 299

Building lots, 285–89

Building Online, 135, 393

Building regulations, 297–99

BuildNET, 135, 284, 294, 393

Bureau of Economic Analysis, 81, 158, 386

Bureau of Labor Statistics, 84–86

Buyer's agents, 103, 112–14, 370, 389

Buyers' market, 60

Buying a home, 59–67

   determining price range, 36–39, 71–74

   established homes, 124, 131–36, 392–93

   housing options, 63–67, 120

   needs and wants and, 62–63

   new, 124–31

   online, 3–24

      benefits of, 5–7, 9–10

      disadvantages of, 10–11

      first-time homebuyer checklist, 22–23

      getting started, 11–21

      insider tips to, 21–22

      process of, 16–19

      "rules of the game," 21

   reasons for, 4–5, 59–67

   renting versus, 67–71, 384

   time crunch and, 74–76

BuyOwner, 267, 268, 404

BYG Publishing, 30, 382

Calculators, online, 15–16, 30, 71, 73–74, 174, 384

   cost-of-living, 87–88, 388

   interest rates, 156

   mortgage rates, 156–58

   rent versus buy, 17, 70–71, 384

California Department of Developmental Services, 66, 391

California Housing Financing Authority, 191–92, 398

Census Bureau, U.S., 82, 95, 351, 387

Century 21, 19, 110, 138, 256, 287–88

Certified Residential Specialist (CRS), 107

Chase Mortgage, 166

Chicago Sun-Times, 104, 388

Chicago Title Company, 352

Chicago Tribune, 65, 110, 122, 389

Cities

   cost of living for different, 85–88, 388

   finding right, 84–88, 387

Closing, 193–257, 370–71

   after the, 236

   appraisals, 196–203, 370

   counteroffers, 228–31

   final walk-through, 232–33

   FSBO offers, 272–75

   home inspections, 203–9, 375, 399

   homeowners insurance, 75–76, 154, 209–16, 399–400

   negotiations, 217–31, 401

   offers, 23, 222–28, 401–2

   online resources for, 236–37, 402

   title insurance, 214–16, 378, 400

Closing agent fees, 154
Closing costs, 152–55, 239–54, 371
  actual versus estimates, 245
  average, 247–48
  documents related to, 242–44
  online sources for, 241–42
  reducing, 252–54, 404
  seller paying, 229, 241
  tax-deductible, 255, 404
  types of, 246–52
  understanding, 240–45
Closing dates, 233, 240
Closing documents, 149–50, 402–4
Closing meeting, 233–36
Coldwell Banker, 19, 138, 141, 393
Colorado Real Estate, 115
Commissions, 104–6, 112, 273, 371
Comparable market analysis (CMA), 140–42, 224, 371, 393
Comparable sales reports, 201–3
Complete Mortgage Guide, 394
Computitle Limited, 214, 378
Condominiums, 64, 65, 122, 185–87, 252, 371
Construction-estimating software, 283–85, 406
Construction loans, 294–96
ConstructSoftware, 284, 406
Consumer Info, 43, 383
Consumer Information Center, 12–13, 241, 245, 354, 403
Contingencies, 226–27, 230, 371
Contractor-assisted programs, 281–83
Contractor.com, 293, 406
ContractorNet, 294, 406
Contractors, 279, 406–7
  contracts with, 338–40
  evaluating, 292–94
  finding, 334–35
  myths about, 330–32
Contract reviews, 227
Contracts, 151, 222–23, 226–31
  counteroffers, 23, 228–31, 371

  finalizing, 231
  information in, 223
  offers, 222–28
Co-ops, 64–65, 371
Copelan Insurance Agency, Inc., 299–300
Cost approach, 200
Cost of living, for different cities, 85–88, 388
Cost-of-living calculators, 87–88, 388
Counteroffers, 23, 228–31, 371
Countrywide Credit Industries, 155, 163, 164, 254, 386
Creative financing, 184–89
Creative Homes, 282, 286
Credit bureaus, 41–42, 383
Credit cards, 45, 50, 54, 55–56, 152
CreditCheck Monitoring Service, 43
Credit Infocenter, 49–50, 395
CreditMedic, 43
Credit problems, 53–56
Credit Quality Estimator, 395
Credit repair, 48, 54, 383–84
Credit Repair Institute, 384
CreditReport-Net.com, 42–43
Credit reports, 39–53, 74–75, 120, 372, 394–95
  checking out your, 42–44
  contents of, 40–41
  correcting errors, 49–51
  deleting credit inquiries, 51–53
  fees, 154, 249
  FICO scores, 44–47
  online sources for, 42–43, 383
  types of, 39–40
Credit scores, 40, 44–45, 383–84
Credit Union Land, 36
Crime, 92–94
CrimeCheck, 93, 387
Cross Country Relocation, 316, 317
CSWOnline, 202, 400
Cyberhomes, 18, 137–38, 393

DataMasters, 87–88, 388
Dataquick, 94, 387, 398, 401
Debt
  over 36 percent, 36, 72,
    183–84
  qualifying ratios and, 36–39,
    71–74, 183, 377
Debt Counselors of America, 54
Deeds, 372, 403
Default, 372
Delivery fees, 154–55
Delta Funding, 39
Deposits, 225–26, 231, 372
Direct Marketing Association, 53
Disclosure forms, 149–50
Disclosures, 227, 273–74
Discounted real estate broker-
    ages, 365–66
Discounting brokers, 105
Discount points. *See* Points
Documentation stamps, 251
Document fees, 153
Doing Business in Rhode Island,
    83
DoItYourself.com, 341
Down payments, 17, 146, 173–92,
    372
  assistance programs, 189–90
  coming up with, 174–80
  creative financing, 184–89
  for first-time homebuyers,
    189–92
  government-sponsored,
    180–84
  how much to put down,
    176–77
  no and low, 19, 177, 180–84,
    396
  small, 178–80
  20 percent or greater, 158–59,
    173, 174, 177
Dual agents, 103, 372

Earnest money. *See* Deposits
Eastern Mortgage, 39
Economic Information Links, 82,
    386
Economic Statistics Briefing
    Room, 81–82, 386

Effective gross income, 372
eHome, 363, 411
eHow, 204, 271
Eight Rules of Negotiating, 222,
    401
E-LOAN, 8, 9, 155, 170, 382
eMortgages, 171
Employee Relocation Council,
    74
Endeavor Homes, 405
Environmental issues, 218
Equifax, 41–42, 383
Equity, 188–89, 372–73
Equity Analytics, 27
Equity Builders, 405
Equity Direct Mortgage
    Corporation, 156
Escrow, 254, 373
Escrow fees, 154
Escrow reserves, 250
Established houses, 124, 131–36,
    392–93
  advantages of, 131–32
  fixer-uppers, 134–36, 393
  limitations of, 132
  options in, 133
Estimating software, 283–85,
    406
Exclusive Buyers Agents, 113,
    389
Existing houses. *See* Established
    houses
Expendable income, 33–34
Experian, 41, 52, 218, 383
Express Auto Transport, 321

Fair housing laws, 265
Fair Issac & Company (FICO),
    40, 44–47, 383–84
Fair market value, 373
FamilyHaven, 396
Fannie Mae, 111, 160, 237, 373,
    402
  Community Home Buyer's
    Program, 183, 396
Federal Financial Institutions
    Examination Council
    Appraisal Subcommittee,
    199, 399

Federal Housing Administration (FHA), 146–47, 373, 394
   loans, 37, 63–64, 72–73, 160–61, 181–82, 185, 373
Federal Reserve Bank of Boston Regional Economic Information Links, 82, 386
Federal Trade Commission (FTC), 51
Fedstats, 95–96, 387
FICO scores, 40, 44–47, 383–84
Final walk-through, 232–33
Financenter, 15, 70, 73, 241, 347–48, 403, 410
Financial help, 53–56
Financial planning, 25–56
   credit reports and, 39–53
   debt ratio and, 36–39
   goals, 33–34
   myths about, 26–27
   online assistance with, 53–56
   process, 27–35
Financial profiles, of homeowners, 58–59
Financing, 143–92, 226, 229
   FSBO, 265–66
   owner-builders, 294–96
Find-a-Mover, 305
Fire-resistant material discounts, 213
First Indemnity of America Insurance Company, 300
First Team, 395
First-time homebuyers, special programs for, 189–92, 397–98
Fixed-rate mortgages, 159, 185, 373
Fixer-uppers, 134–36, 393
Flood insurance, 133
Foreclosures, 44–45, 47, 49, 373–74
For sale by owner (FSBO) sales, 261–76, 373
   agents and, 100, 263–64
   benefits of, 264
   closing the deal, 272–75
   discounted real estate brokerages and, 365–66

fair housing and, 265
financing options, 265–66
listings of, 138
notification services, 271
online listings, 261–62, 266–70, 404–5
problems of, 264–65, 364–65
For Sale By Owner Network, 268
401(k) retirement plans, 26, 176
4SaleByOwner, 267, 404
Freddie Mac, 183, 374, 396
FSBOs. See For sale by owner (FSBO) sales
Full residential mortgage credit reports, 39–40
Full-service brokers, 106

Gateway Equity & Loan Network, 385
General Services Administration, 164, 212
Gift letters, 36, 152, 374
Good faith estimate, 403
Government-based closing costs, 250–51
Government-sponsored down payment plans, 180–84, 374
Graduated-payment mortgages, 160
Graduate of the Realtors Institute (GRI), 107

HandiLinks.com, 315
Hanover Mortgage Company, 39
Harvest Mortgage, 46, 48
Hazard insurance, 154, 250, 299–300, 374
Hertz Truck & Van Rental, 312
HomeBuilder, 129–30, 392
HomeBuyer Agents, 97, 114, 389
HomeBuyerPower, 123, 127, 129, 298, 392
Homebuyer's E-Guide, 228, 402
Home Buyer's Information Center, 235, 279–80
Home Depot, 340, 341, 410
Home equity loan, 374
Homefair, 19, 38, 71, 88, 164–65, 308, 310, 384, 388, 407

Homefinders, Inc. Real Estate,
    82–83, 386
HomeGain, 353
Home improvements, 327–48,
    409, 410
  do-it-yourself, 340–42
  financing, 346–48
  finding expert help, 333–40
  scams, 336–38
  value added by, 342–46
Home inspections, 203–9, 226,
    229, 375
  defect finder checklist, 204
  fees and costs, 203, 252
  online resources for, 205–6,
    399
  on your own, 204–5
  professional, 205–6
  reports, 207–9
  selecting an inspector, 206–7
  specialized, 203–4
Home-Links, 20
Home loans. See Down payments;
    Loans; Mortgages
Homeowners associations, 93,
    252, 374
Homeowners.com, 388, 397
Home ownership
  financial profiles of owners,
    58–59
  rewards of, 9–10
Homeowners insurance, 75–76,
    154, 209–16, 227, 250,
    399–400
  basics of policies, 210–12
  discounts, 213–14
Homeowners Online, 112
HomePath, 157, 160, 165, 237,
    384, 402
HomePoint Advantage, 332–33,
    409
Home Price Check, 352
Home Purchasing Guide, 198,
    398
Home repairs, 409–10
Home Repairs & Etc., 341, 410
HomeScout, 359, 411
Homes for Today, 290, 406
Home Spot, 288, 390

Home to Home, 322, 408
HomeValueCheck, 202, 401
Homeward Bound, 191, 398
HomeWEB, 98, 389
House Clicks, 141, 393
House Hunter's Helper, 121,
    392
House plans, 289–92, 405–6
Housing and Urban
    Development, Department
    of (HUD), 58, 66–67, 150,
    160, 391
  HUD-1 settlement statement,
    242–43, 245
  loans, 160–61, 181–82
Housing expense ratios, 374
Housing options, 63–67, 120,
    122–23
Housing prices, 60–61, 218–20,
    229
  comparable market analysis,
    140–42, 393
  determining price range,
    36–39, 71–74
  finding best online, 136–42
  overpriced, 139–40, 273
  from region to region, 80–81
  trends in, 80–82
Housing trends, 80–82, 386
HSH Associates, 157, 165

iCreditReport, 43
Impounds, 250
ImproveNet, 289–90, 336, 340,
    347, 409
Incidental recording fees,
    154–55
Income, 30–34, 148
Income capitalization approach,
    201
Income taxes, deducting moving
    expenses from, 324–25
"In-file" credit reports, 39
Information Links, 82, 386
Initial interest rate, 375
Inman Real Estate News, 228,
    252, 402
Insight Professional Home
    Inspection, 206, 399

Inspections. *See also* Home
    inspections
    building, 299
Insurance, 33, 374
    hazard, 154, 250, 299–300, 374
    mortgage, 153, 245, 250, 376
    moving and, 317–19, 321
Insurance Information Institute,
    212
Insurance News Network, 212
Insurance Resource, 300
InsWeb, 212, 399
Interest, 146, 147
Interest rates, 18, 27, 61–62, 149,
    155–58, 375, 395
    by APR, 156–58
    finding best, 155–56
    trends, 61–62
Internal Revenue Service (IRS),
    190, 255–56, 325, 409
    Problem Solver, 257, 404
InterNest, 392
Internet service providers (ISPs),
    7–8
iOwn, 9, 17, 162, 268, 352, 382
IRAs (individual retirement
    accounts), 176
iRichmond, 237, 402

Keystroke, 46, 170, 395
Kit homes, 279

Land for sale by owner, 288–89
Landscaping, 132, 343
Leases, 253
Lender-based fees, 246, 248–49
Lenders
    qualifying ratios and, 36–38,
        71–72, 183, 377
    sub-prime, 38–39
Lenders Interactive Online
    Network, 162
Lender's Service, Inc., 215–16,
    400
LendingTree, 9, 148, 382
Lenox Financial Mortgage
    Corporation, 385
Liabilities, 29, 31, 148, 375
Liens, 375

Limited-service brokers, 105
Listing agents, 102, 360–63, 411
Listings, 75, 119–42, 375
    established houses, 124,
        131–36
    of homes for sale by owner,
        138
    Multiple Listing Service, 100,
        108, 139, 184, 350, 357–58,
        376, 393, 411
    national, 137–38
    new houses, 124–31, 392
    online newspaper ads, 137
    organizing your search,
        120–23
    state, 138
    updates bots for, 18
Loan documents, 75
Loan origination, 146, 375
    fees, 153, 245, 248–49, 376
Loans
    construction, 294–96
    conventional, 72–74, 147,
        158–60, 371
    FHA, 37, 63–64, 72–73,
        160–61, 181–82, 185, 373
    home improvement, 347–48
    HUD, 160–61, 181–82
    low-document, 396–97
    no-document, 396–97
    no-points, 252–53
    Veterans Administration (VA),
        161–62, 180–81, 379
Lock-in, 375
"Low-ball" offers, 225
Lowe's, 342, 410
Lycos Real Estate Guide, 257, 404

Market approach, 200
Marketing your home, 349,
    357–60
Mature homeowner discounts,
    214
Mediators, 103
Medical services, 92
Memphis Area Association of
    Realtors, 110, 389
MetLife's Budget Maker, 32, 383
Model homes, 126, 130–31

Money.com, 32, 86, 88, 347, 410
Money Maze Loan Advisor, 394
MoneyWeb Net Worth Calculator,
    30, 382
Monster Daata, 94–95, 387
Mortgage bankers, 375
Mortgage brokers, 376
Mortgage.com, 38, 61–62, 155,
    162, 383
Mortgage101.com, 162, 177, 198,
    385
Mortgage Company Search
    Engine, 165
Mortgage credit certificates
    (MCCs), 190–91
Mortgage insurance, 153, 245,
    250, 376
Mortgage Insurance Companies
    of America, 178
Mortgage Link, 157
Mortgage Mag, 165
Mortgage Mart, 14, 156, 165,
    170–71, 394
Mortgage-net, 158
Mortgage promissory notes,
    244
Mortgage Qualifier, 38
MortgageQuotes, 157, 395
Mortgages, 13–15, 18–19, 145–71,
    244, 375, 394
    aggregators, 8–9, 147–48, 382
    assuming someone else's,
        184–85
    credit reports, 39–40, 146
    defined, 146–47
    documentation for, 149–52
    fees associated with, 152–55
    FHA, 37, 63–64, 72–73,
        146–47, 152, 160–61,
        181–82, 373
    finding online, 162–66
    FSBO, 265–66
    interest rates, 149, 155–58, 395
    lenders requirements, 148
    "no documentation," 38
    preapproval for, 166–71,
        385–86
    prequalification, 149, 166–71,
        385–86

    process, 149–58, 394
    types of, 158–62
Mortgage University, 175, 396
Mortgage-X, 181, 182, 394
Motley Fool, 110, 389
MoveCentral, 313, 407
MoverQuotes.com, 309
MoversNet, 322, 408
Moving, 19, 303–26
    do-it-yourself, 311–14, 407
    expenses, 408–9
    full-service, 408
    packing for, 322–24
    planning, 304–10
    resources, 407–8
Moving.com, 310, 313, 314, 324,
    407
Moving companies, 314
Moving expenses, deducting,
    324–25
Moving-Guide, 314
MSN HomeAdvisor, 20, 74, 102,
    121, 122, 164, 219, 221,
    237, 287, 358, 388, 392,
    401, 403, 411
MSN Sidewalk Real Estate Buyer's
    Guide, 20–21
Multi-family homes, 63–64
Multiple Listing Service (MLS),
    100, 108, 139, 184, 350,
    357–58, 376, 393, 411
Multiple-policy discounts, 213
Municipal services, 133

National Association of Exclusive
    Buyer Agents, 104, 113, 389
National Association of Real
    Estate Appraisers, 199, 399
National Association of Realtors
    (NAR), 80, 102
National Cost Estimator, 406
National Council of State
    Housing Agencies, 21
National Foundation for
    Consumer Credit, 54–55
National Housing Fair Housing
    Advocate Online, 265
National Mortgage Directory,
    397

National Mortgage Enterprises, Inc., 296
National Mortgage Loan Directory, 395
National Mortgage News, 397
National Multi Housing Council, 67
Nationwide housing trends, 80–82, 386
Negotiations, 217–31, 253, 401
    being realistic, 221
    closing the deal, 233–37
    counteroffers, 23, 228–31, 371
    final walk-through, 232–33
    FSBO, 272–75
    information gathering for, 218–20
    offers, 23, 222–28, 401–2
    preparation for, 220
    using the Internet for, 221–22
Neighborhood reports, 89, 90–96, 387
    online resources for, 93–96, 387
Neighborhoods, 17–18, 75, 79–96, 120
    finding right, 84–96, 387
    housing trends, 80–82, 386
    relocating to different states, 82–83, 386–87
Net cash flow, 30, 31
Net worth, 28–30, 69, 168, 382
NewHomeNetwork, 122–23
New houses, 124–31, 392
    advantages of, 125–26
    Internet searches for, 129–30
    limitations of, 126–27
    model homes, 126, 130–31
    options in, 128–29
    trends in, 127–28, 386
NewRealty.com, 358–59, 411
Newspaper ads, online, 8, 137
"No documentation" mortgages, 38
No down payments, 19, 177, 180–84, 396
Nolo Press, 14–15, 395
Non-recurring closing costs, 246–50

Nonsmoker's discounts, 213
NorthWest BuilderNet, 284, 294, 407
Norwest Mortgage, 163–64

Occupancy, 229
Occupational Outlook Handbook, 101
Offers, 23, 222–28, 401–2
    contingencies to, 226–27
    deposits, 225–26, 372
    determining your price, 224–25
    FSBO, 272–75
    "low-ball," 225
    online help with making, 228
Old-House Journal, 345, 410
Old Houses.com, 135, 393
1Agent, 114, 390
101 Home Improvement Links, 335
Open House America, 111–12, 388, 393
Open houses, 359–60
Origination fees, 153, 245, 248–49, 376
Our Family Place, 121, 233, 392, 402
Overpriced homes, 139–40
Owner Builder Construction Loans, 282
Owner-builders, 277–300, 405
    building regulations, 297–99
    contractor-assisted programs, 281–83
    deciding to build your own home, 278–85
    estimating software, 283–85, 406
    evaluating contractors, 292–94
    financing, 294–96
    hazard insurance, 299–300
    house plans, 289–92, 405–6
    location and, 285–89
    overview of construction process, 279–80
    seminars and classes, 279, 280–81, 405

Owner-builders *(cont.)*
staying on schedule and within
your budget, 296–97
Owner Builder School of
Oregon, 280–83, 405
Owners.com, 237, 262, 268–69,
402, 410

Pacific Rim Finance, 296
Pack-and-stack services, 305
Packing, for moving, 322–24
Paragon Decision Resources, 223,
401
Payoffs, 376
Personal finance software, 35
Pest inspections, 203, 204
Physical inspection reports, 75
PITI (principal, interest, taxes,
and insurance expenses),
146–47, 376
Planhouse Home Plan Studio,
290–91
Plans, house, 289–92, 405–6
PNC Mortgage, 167, 386
Points, 153, 248–49, 255, 376
no-points loans, 252–53
Pools and spas, 343
Possessions, 376
Preapproval, 166–71, 376–77,
385–86
Prepaid interest, 154, 246, 249–50
Prequalification, 149, 166–68,
377, 385–86
Price-level-adjusted mortgages
(PLAMs), 160
Price range, 36–39, 71–74
Principal, 146, 147, 377
Private For Sale, 271, 272, 405
Private mortgage insurance
(PMI), 154, 159, 177–78,
245, 395–96
Probe Consultants, 313
Processing fees, 153
Promissory notes, 377, 403
Property Profile Reports, 218–19
Property taxes, 93, 95, 133, 251,
255, 377
Prudential Geisinger Realty,
288

Purchase and sale agreement,
377
Purchase contracts. *See* Contracts

Qualifying ratios, 36–38, 71–74,
183, 377
Quicken, 9, 35, 42, 71, 74, 147,
166, 382, 394

Radon inspections, 203, 204
Rate lock, 377
RateNet, 395
Real Direct, 18
Real estate agents, 97–118, 136,
369, 388–90
benefits and disadvantages of
using, 98–101
changing, 117–18
commissions and, 104–6
credentials, 107–8
evaluating, 390
finding best, 111–17, 389
out-of-state, 114–17, 390–91
responsibilities of, 102–4
types of, 101–4
what to look for in, 106–11
Real Estate Book Online, 139
Real estate brokers, 103–4, 370
Real Estate Center, 222
RealEstate.com, 203, 401
Real Estate Digest Credit, 43
Real Estate Home Buying FAQ,
221, 401
Real Estate Library, 14, 198,
207
Real estate market, 17, 60–61,
140
Real Estate Offers and Contracts,
228, 401
RealEstateWeb, 397
RealScout, 269, 405
Realtor.com, 16–18, 21, 65, 89,
121, 137, 139, 234, 237,
310, 358, 387, 388, 392,
393, 402, 403, 408
Realty Times, 61, 80–81, 319, 320,
408
Recent Homes Sales Report,
218–19

Recordation fees (recording fees), 247, 251, 377
Recurring closing costs, 246–50
Reference guides, 12
Referral fees, 105
Regional Financial Association, 85, 387
Regional housing trends, 80–82, 386
Regulations, for building, 297–99
Relocations, 5, 74, 79–96
  cost of living for different cities, 85–88, 387
  to different cities, 84–88, 387
  to different states, 82–83, 386–87
  finding out-of-state agents, 114–17, 390–91
  to foreign countries, 80
Relocation Scout, 115, 390
Relocation services, 304, 315–17
RELO.com, 305, 407
RE/MAX, 110, 138, 385
Remodeling, 328–33, 409
Renegotiable mortgages, 160
Renovation costs, 134–35
Renting a home, 67–71, 384
  with option to buy, 187–88
Research sites, 11–12
Residential lots, 285–89
Residential mortgage credit reports, 39–40
Residential Referral Network, 115, 390
Resources, 11–16, 381–418
Restoration, 345–46, 410
RHS (Department of Agriculture, Rural Housing Services), 181, 378
RPS Relocation, 85, 387

Safety-device discounts, 213
Sales contracts. See Contracts
Sales prices. See Housing prices
SalvoWEB, 346, 410
Savings, 30, 148
Schools, 17–18, 91, 95
Scorecards, 120–22, 391–92

Searching online, 119–42
  comparable market analysis, 140–42, 393
  established houses, 124, 131–36
  finding best prices, 136–42
  focusing your, 122–23
  new houses, 124–31, 392
  scorecards, 120–22, 391–92
Secondary markets, 378
Second mortgages, 378
Security, 378
Sellers' market, 61
Seller-take-back, 185–87
Selling a house
  current home, 227
  getting your house ready, 354–57
  listing agents, 360–63
  setting a price, 352–54
  time for, 350
  without an agent, 363–66
Settlement, 371, 378
Settlement costs. See Closing costs
Settlement meetings, 151, 233–36
Settlement statements, 150, 242–43, 403
Shared appreciation mortgage (SAM), 188–89
Shirmery Report, 61, 158
Shortfalls, 32–33, 382–83
Sidewalk Real Estate Buyer's Guide, 20–21
Single-family residences, 63, 65, 66, 378
SmartMoney, 305, 325, 337, 348, 362, 382, 407, 408, 411
Sound Home Resource Center, 342
Special Form (HO-3), 210, 211
Special housing requirements, 66–67, 391
Star Home Inspection Group, 232, 233
StartSmart, 408
State loan programs, 182
Statement of income, 38, 42
Stephen Fuller, 291, 406
Stewart Title, 215, 400

Street maintenance, 133
Style of homes, 63–67, 120,
    122–23
Subagents, 103
Sub-prime lenders, 38–39
Subsidized interest rate loans,
    191–92
SunChase Financial Corporation,
    296
Surveys, 252, 378

Tax benefits and savings, 5, 59,
    70, 255–57
  closing costs, 255, 404
  online help, 256–57
  what can you write off, 255–56
Taxes
  income, deducting moving
    expenses from, 324–25
  property. *See* Property taxes
  transfer, 251
Tax reports, 152, 167
Termite inspections, 203, 252,
    378
Texas Help-U-Build, 283
Time limits, 227
Times Online, 325, 409
Title fees, 154
Title insurance, 214–16, 245, 378,
    400
Titles, 214, 227, 378
  clear, 370
Title searches, 214–16, 245, 378
Townhouses, 65, 378
Transamerica, 393
Transfer of ownership, 379
Transfer taxes, 251
Trans Union Corporation, 42,
    383
Trends in housing, 80–82, 386
Trucking services, 305
Truth-in-lending statements, 150,
    243–44, 373, 403
203K rehab loan, 134–35
2001 Beyond, 95

U-Haul, 313–14, 407
Underwriting, 379

Underwriting fees, 153
Uniform resource locators
    (URLs), 379
Uniform Standards of
    Professional Appraisal
    Practices, 196
United States Real Estate
    Directory, 358
Unsecured loans, 379
Update bots, 18
USDA Economics and Statistics
    Search, 96, 386
U.S. Relocation, 116–17, 391
Utilities, 133

Valuation reports, 400–401
Verification, for mortgages,
    149–50
Veterans Administration (VA),
    63–64, 162
  loans, 161–62, 180–81, 379
Virtual For Sale By Owner, 269,
    405
Virtual Real Estate Store, 362,
    411

Walk-throughs, 232–33
Washington Post HomeHunter,
    137, 392
Westcliffe Land & Investment
    Company, 287
Windham International, 304,
    407
Wire fees, 154–55

Yahoo!, 38, 82
Yahoo! Auctions, 269, 288
Yahoo! By Address, 401
Yahoo! Classifieds, 358, 359, 411
Yahoo! Real Estate, 17, 141–42,
    393
Yestermorrow Design Build
    School, 281
YouBuild Owner Builder Center,
    281, 405

ZipRealty.com, 354
Zoning, 133, 297–98, 379

The *Unofficial Guide*™ Reader Questionnaire

If you would like to express your opinion about achieving financial freedom or this guide, please complete this questionnaire and mail it to:

The *Unofficial Guide*™ Reader Questionnaire
IDG Lifestyle Group
1633 Broadway, floor 7
New York, NY 10019-6785

Gender: ___ M ___ F

Age: ___ Under 30 ___ 31–40 ___ 41–50 ___ Over 50

Education: ___ High school ___ College ___ Graduate/Professional

What is your occupation?

_____

How did you hear about this guide?
___ Friend or relative
___ Newspaper, magazine, or Internet
___ Radio or TV
___ Recommended at bookstore
___ Recommended by librarian
___ Picked it up on my own
___ Familiar with the *Unofficial Guide*™ travel series

Did you go to the bookstore specifically for a book on buying a home online? Yes ___ No ___

Have you used any other Unofficial Guides™?
Yes ___ No ___

If Yes, which ones?

_____
_____
_____

What other book(s) on buying a home online have you purchased? _____
_____
_____

Was this book:
___ more helpful than other(s)
___ less helpful than other(s)

Do you think this book was worth its price?
Yes ___ No ___

Did this book cover all topics related to achieving financial freedom adequately?
Yes ___ No ___

Please explain your answer:
_____
_____
_____

Were there any specific sections in this book that were of particular help to you?   Yes ___   No ___

Please explain your answer:
_____
_____
_____

On a scale of 1 to 10, with 10 being the best rating, how would you rate this guide? ___

What other titles would you like to see published in the _Unofficial Guide_™ **series?**
_____
_____

Are Unofficial Guides™ **readily available in your area?**   Yes ___   No ___

Other comments:
_____
_____
_____
_____

Get the inside scoop...with the *Unofficial Guides*™!

Health and Fitness

The Unofficial Guide to Alternative Medicine
ISBN: 0-02-862526-9 Price: $15.95

The Unofficial Guide to Conquering Impotence
ISBN: 0-02-862870-5 Price: $15.95

The Unofficial Guide to Coping with Menopause
ISBN: 0-02-862694-x Price: $15.95

The Unofficial Guide to Cosmetic Surgery
ISBN: 0-02-862522-6 Price: $15.95

The Unofficial Guide to Dieting Safely
ISBN: 0-02-862521-8 Price: $15.95

The Unofficial Guide to Having a Baby
ISBN: 0-02-862695-8 Price: $15.95

The Unofficial Guide to Living with Diabetes
ISBN: 0-02-862919-1 Price: $15.95

The Unofficial Guide to Overcoming Arthritis
ISBN: 0-02-862714-8 Price: $15.95

The Unofficial Guide to Overcoming Infertility
ISBN: 0-02-862916-7 Price: $15.95

Career Planning

The Unofficial Guide to Acing the Interview
ISBN: 0-02-862924-8 Price: $15.95

The Unofficial Guide to Earning What You Deserve
ISBN: 0-02-862523-4 Price: $15.95

The Unofficial Guide to Hiring and Firing People
ISBN: 0-02-862523-4 Price: $15.95

Business and Personal Finance

The Unofficial Guide to Investing
ISBN: 0-02-862458-0 Price: $15.95

The Unofficial Guide to Investing in Mutual Funds
ISBN: 0-02-862920-5 Price: $15.95

The Unofficial Guide to Managing Your Personal Finances
ISBN: 0-02-862921-3 Price: $15.95

The Unofficial Guide to Starting a Small Business
ISBN: 0-02-862525-0 Price: $15.95

Home and Automotive

The Unofficial Guide to Buying a Home
ISBN: 0-02-862461-0 Price: $15.95

The Unofficial Guide to Buying or Leasing a Car
ISBN: 0-02-862524-2 Price: $15.95

The Unofficial Guide to Hiring Contractors
ISBN: 0-02-862460-2 Price: $15.95

Family and Relationships

The Unofficial Guide to Childcare
ISBN: 0-02-862457-2 Price: $15.95

The Unofficial Guide to Dating Again
ISBN: 0-02-862454-8 Price: $15.95

The Unofficial Guide to Divorce
ISBN: 0-02-862455-6 Price: $15.95

The Unofficial Guide to Eldercare
ISBN: 0-02-862456-4 Price: $15.95

The Unofficial Guide to Planning Your Wedding
ISBN: 0-02-862459-9 Price: $15.95

Hobbies and Recreation

The Unofficial Guide to Finding Rare Antiques
ISBN: 0-02-862922-1 Price: $15.95

The Unofficial Guide to Casino Gambling
ISBN: 0-02-862917-5 Price: $15.95

All books in the *Unofficial Guide*™ series are available at your local bookseller, or by calling 1-800-428-5331.